MY BATTLE
OF ALGIERS

BOOKS BY SANCHE DE GRAMONT

NONFICTION

*The Secret War: The Story of International Espionage
Since World War II*

The Age of Magnificence: Memoirs of the Court of Louis XIV
by the Duc de Saint-Simon (selected, edited, and translated by)

*Epitaph for Kings: The Long and Splendid Decline of the
French Monarchy and the Coming of the Revolution*

The French: Portrait of a People

The Strong Brown God: The Story of the Niger River

FICTION

Lives to Give

This Way Up: The Memoirs of Count Gramont

BOOKS BY TED MORGAN

*On Becoming American: A Celebration of What It Means
and How It Feels*

Rowing Toward Eden

Maugham: A Biography

Churchill: Young Man in a Hurry (1874–1915)

FDR: A Biography

Literary Outlaw: The Life and Times of William S. Burroughs

*An Uncertain Hour: The French, the Germans, the Jews,
the Klaus Barbie Trial, and the City of Lyon, 1940–1945*

Wilderness at Dawn: The Settling of the North American Continent

*A Shovel of Stars: The Making of the American West—1800
to the Present*

*A Covert Life: Jay Lovestone, Communist, Anti-Communist,
and Spymaster*

Reds: McCarthyism in Twentieth-Century America

MY BATTLE OF ALGIERS

A Memoir

Ted Morgan

Smithsonian Books

Collins
An Imprint of HarperCollinsPublishers

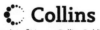

HarperCollins books may be purchased for educational, business, or sales promotional use. For information please write: Special Markets Department, HarperCollins Publishers, 10 East 53rd Street, New York, NY 10022.

First Smithsonian Books edition published 2005.

BOOK DESIGN BY NICOLA FERGUSON
MAPS BY EVE STECCATI

The Library of Congress Cataloging-In-Publication Data has been applied for.
ISBN-10: 0-06-085224-0
ISBN-13: 978-0-06-085224-5

05 06 07 08 09 WBC/RRD 10 9 8 7 6 5 4 3 2 1

This book is dedicated to two old friends:

Tom Wallace, my excellent agent, a friend of 50 years, who in 1960, when he was an editor at Putnam, commissioned my first book for a thousand-dollar advance upon signing.

Rob Cowley, my brilliant editor, a friend of 40 years, and a distinguished military historian.

Acknowledgments

Special thanks:

To Don Fehr, who saw the merit in this book.

To my wife, Eileen, for her superb and indispensable editorial help.

To Alain Seznec, Jean Aslanian, and André Bayens, for their recollections.

To Roger Rives, for his photographic memory of Algiers.

To Paul Lochak, for our extended discussions on the war.

And to those who refreshed my memory but did not want their names used.

SPAIN

BALEARIC ISLANDS

Mediterranean

Algiers
Boufarik
Blida
Miliana
Médéa
Orléansville
Champlain

Oran

Montagnes des Beni Chougrane

Massif de l'Ouarsenis

ALGERIA

Montagnes des Oulad Naïl

MOROCCO

Montagnes des Ksour

Gardhaia

SARDINIA

S e a

Bougie

Philippeville ● Bône

● Ouelma

● Constantine

Sétif

Montagnes de la Medjerda

Montagnes du Hodna

● Batna

● Cherchela

Djebel Aurès

● Biskra

TUNISIA

● El Oued

● Touggourt

NORTH

TRIPOLI

rue Rovigo

rue d'Isly

rue Rovigo

Place Bugeaud

Marché de la Lyre____

rue Michelet

rue d'Isly

Square Bresson____

Boulevard Carnot

Boulevard Carnot

Port

rue Victoire

Boulevard Valée

rue Randon

rue Marengo

CASBAH

rue de la Lyre

Mediterranean Sea

NORTH

Each war tells us something about
The way the next war will be fought.

—HERODOTUS

Contents

Preface

The battle of Algiers was a relatively brief chapter in the history of an eight-year war. Its importance derives from the innovative tactics employed by the insurgents to turn the Algerian capital into a battlefield. The systematic use of urban terrorism as we see it today originated in Algiers in 1957.

With its population of 600,000 French and 300,000 Arabs, and with one third of the latter living in the Casbah's cramped alleyways, Algiers was vulnerable to the violent destabilization of its civilian population. The insurgents' methods were targeted assassinations and the placement of bombs. In order to strike at the "golden youth" of Algiers, the bombs went off in the cafés where they gathered and the casinos where they danced. Bombs were also placed at soccer stadiums and downtown bus stops, killing Arabs as well as French. The killing of women and children was a deliberate tactic to create a climate of insecurity in the heart of the carefree capital of a colonized Arab country. It was a way of saying: "Algiers is no longer yours." It was also a way of summoning reprisals from French forces, which would bring the city's Moslem population more firmly into the rebel camp. The cordoning off of the Casbah, the patrols, the searches, the raids, the arrests of thousands of suspects turned moderate Arabs into rebels.

Although effective, urban terrorism in Algiers was as primitive, when compared with Iraq, as a harquebus is to a rocket-propelled grenade. The key weapon of the suicide bomber had not yet been used in colonial wars. The Algerian Arabs were Moslems, but even the militant ones, while hating French oppression, had been exposed to the values of the Enlightenment in French schools, and did not have the required religious fervor to blow themselves up.

The insurgents of Algiers did not have the technology to make roadside bombs, nor were there any car bombs, for they were not as well funded as the Iraqi insurgents and could not afford to buy cars for demolition. They were, however, able to make bombs by hand in their jury-rigged Casbah labs, and to recruit young Arab girls who could pass for French to carry them by hand to downtown cafés, where they left the bombs in beach bags under a seat until a timer exploded them.

The Battle of Algiers can be seen as a somewhat dissimilar and miniature model for the Battle of Baghdad and other Iraqi cities. In Iraq there is nothing comparable to the French *colon* minority of one million that ruled Algeria. The rebels were nationalists who wanted independence. There were only two sides, the French against the FLN (National Liberation Front), with small numbers of rebels who were turned by the French, and a passel of French Communists who collaborated with the rebels. Iraq more closely resembles a five-sided civil war, with the Sunnis, the Shiites, the Kurds, and the foreign fighters, all fighting each other, and the Americans trying to shore up the government and maintain security.

Iraq is turning out to be the worst foreign dilemma America has faced since Vietnam, just as Algeria was the worst for France since Indochina.

The damage done to the city in the Battle of Algiers was minimal, thanks in part to the use of small arms by the paratroopers who fought there. Just as the rebels had no suicide bombers, the paratroopers had no attack helicopters, no tanks or artillery, and no rockets. More to the point, there was no significant combat in the Battle of Algiers. The rebels used hit-and-run terrorism and the paras (paratroopers) dismantled the bomb networks by tracking down the leaders. A few who refused to surrender were killed in gunfights.

It took only the 6,000 paras of General Jacques Massu's 10th Division to win the Battle of Algiers, thanks to the systematic use

of torture. Each of the four para regiments involved had its own interrogation center, and there was another center under a parallel
chain of command where it was well known that those who went in
alive came out dead. The conventional wisdom today regarding torture is that it is ineffective, since someone being tortured will tell
you anything you want to hear to avoid the pain. In the Battle of
Algiers, however, torture was effective. The paras built up their information incrementally, one fact at a time, sometimes no more than
a name or an address. They had interrogators who had been taught
by the Vietminh in the prison camps of Indochina. The trick was to
convince the suspect that the interrogator knew more than he did,
and to ask questions that did not compromise the suspect. When the
Arab telephone (word of mouth) spread the details of the torture
centers, some captured rebels talked from fear of being tortured.
Others died without having talked. In Iraq and at Guantanamo, torture was used in sensationalized but ineffective ways. The presence
of untrained women reservists at Abu Ghraib prison contributed to
the circus atmosphere. In other holding centers, multiple incidents
of torture have been documented on the part of ignorant but brutal
young soldiers. At Guantanamo the interrogators were equally
clumsy and often did not know the identity of the suspects. The real
problem with torture, however, is not its effectiveness, but its morality. Torture dehumanizes the victim and corrupts the tormenter. A
para may say that he is using torture to obtain information to save
lives, but he will carry the stain with him for the rest of his life. In
the case of Indochina veterans, their experiences may have turned
some of them into sociopaths with little regard for human life. There
is also in every army a small number of brutes and sadists who like
their work.

The paras won the Battle of Algiers in 1957, but the French lost
the war. After General Charles de Gaulle came to power in 1958, he
realized Algeria was a lost cause and gave the Algerians independence in 1962. When the news came out that torture was being used,
public opinion in metropolitan France turned against the war. The
French never again fought another major colonial war, but the urban

terrorism practiced by the rebels has found disciples in Iraq. De Gaulle realized that the Algerian war was unwinnable in that the rebels could never be extinguished. No matter how many battles were won, there would always be more. For the same reason, the war in Iraq, with its porous borders, is unwinnable.

PART I

Introduction: A Child's History of Algeria

I T'S NO TROUBLE for a child to understand colonialism. Children are told to be good, and if they're not, they're punished. Children are colonized by their parents, whether overbearing or permissive. Children are under the discipline of their parents, as the natives of a colony are under the discipline of the occupier, and children rebel as do the occupied. Even a child can understand that the feigning of virtues one does not possess is called hypocrisy.

North Africa, separated from Europe by the lakelike Mediterranean and inhabited by Berber tribesmen, was successively occupied by the Phoenicians, the Romans, the Vandals, and the Arabs, who converted the tribes to Islam in the ninth century. Then came the rise of the great jigsaw, the Ottoman Empire, which at various times included Hungary to the north, Arabia to the east, and Algeria to the west. Spanning five centuries, Ottoman rule devised a system of theoretical vassalage. The sultan in Constantinople was the head of the Moslem community centered in Mecca, the city toward which praying Moslems turned and to which they journeyed on pilgrimage. But in terms of temporal rule, Algeria was like the branch office of a conglomerate. The *dey*, or governor, made his own decisions and signed his own treaties with Christian powers but paid tribute to the sultan.

From the time they fell under Turkish rule in the sixteenth century, Algeria, Tunisia, and Tripoli were known as the Barbary states. The Turks pioneered piracy, a naval form of terrorism, in the Mediterranean. Algeria without piracy, which made up a large part of the national product, could not have existed. The *dey* of Algiers had a government department in charge of piracy, which employed thousands, from the carpenters who built the ships to the sailors who manned them, from agencies in charge of supplies and weaponry to teams of accountants and auditors who kept the books, from prison guards who mistreated captured passengers in ankle chains to the auctioneers who sold them as slaves.

The *deys* were elected by their fellow soldiers from the ranks of the 4,000 Janissaries who ran things in Algiers. This privileged caste kept the natives quiet through tribal alliances and payoffs to tribal leaders. The normal method of succession was strangulation. Between 1801 and 1812, three *deys* were replaced that way. One of the French consuls described the system as "despotism tempered by assassination."

It was no picnic being a consul, who had to contend not only with the *dey's* whims but also with the animosity of the local population toward non-Moslems. In 1798, the French consul, Dominique Moltedo, presented a formal complaint to the *dey* that while he was relaxing on the terrace of his home near the mosque, a Turk standing in front of the mosque had shouted, "Down with the faithless. Down with the Christians, whose faith is dung."

As every French schoolchild knows, on April 29, 1827, the consul in Algiers, Pierre Duval, came to pay his repects to the *dey*, Hussein, at the end of Ramadan. Perhaps made irascible by his month-long fast, the *dey* slapped the consul with a fly whisk and called him a rascal, which created a diplomatic incident. The *dey* exported large quantities of wheat to France and believed that he was owed 8 million francs.

The fly-whisk incident led to the French invasion of Algeria in

1830. But why did the French wait three years to avenge their honor? The answer had to do with the king, for after Napoleon's abdication in 1815, France had restored the monarchy. In 1830, 73-year-old Charles X, the younger brother of the decapitated Louis XVI, had been on the throne since 1824. By reason of temperament (embittered by long years of exile after the 1789 revolution), age (too old to change), and the vicissitudes of life (having seen his brother sentenced to death), he was a pious promoter of the old order. He had himself crowned in the Rheims cathedral, to emphasize the compact between the king and the pope.

His reactionary regime dramatized the failure of the last Bourbon to reconcile the spirit of the monarchy with the expectations of the people after the revolution. Charles X pushed through unpopular laws, such as giving the returned émigrés a billion francs for the loss of their property. He declared the death penalty for sacrilegious acts committed in churches, as a favor to the religious right. The rumor spread that he had secretly become a Jesuit and that he spoke directly to God.

As Charles the fervent horseman cantered on the road to disaster, surrounding himself with fanatical reactionaries, a powerful opposition arose in the polarized nation. When the Chamber of Deputies met in March 1830, a majority denounced the king's ultraconservative ministers. The king struck back by dissolving the chamber and ordering new elections in July. This was where the invasion of Algeria came in, as a diversion, a good way to deflect public opinion away from the troubles at home. Charles needed to touch up his coat of arms with a headline-grabbing pocket war.

On July 5, 1830, 300 French ships sailed from Toulon and landed 37,000 men on the beaches of Sidi Ferruch, 20 miles west of Algiers. Charles got the headlines he wanted: "Our gallant troops are crushing the barbaric Turks." To reassure the international community, France announced that it was making war on the rulers in order to put an end to a tyrannical regime and bring freedom to a backward people. The French convinced themselves that they would be greeted as liberators of a people long oppressed by the despotic Turks.

On July 14 the *Times* of London said: "France upbraids us with the misgovernment and oppression of India. We should be curious to know how she will govern Algeria." The French themselves did not know; they were improvising as they went along. But they had the firepower, and the French artillery dispersed the Turkish troops. It took three weeks for the *dey* to capitulate, and he sailed for Constantinople with his harem of 60 women, his officials, and his soldiers.

Just as Algeria fell to the French, there was a crisis at home, for in the July election, the opposition won a decisive majority. The king responded with a set of arbitrary decrees, on July 26, dissolving the newly elected Chamber of Deputies, restricting the already limited number of voters, and cracking down on the press.

The next day, Paris exploded, with barricades in the streets, students and workers behind them, and army units fraternizing with the insurgents. In three days, known as the *Trois Glorieuses,* Paris was in the hands of the rebels, and on August 2, 1830, Charles X abdicated in favor of Louis-Philippe of the Orléans royal branch, who became known as "the citizen king."

King Louis-Philippe had no plans for Algeria, that "sandy waste," and left matters to the military, who favored settlement. One thing was certain: The occupation of Algeria was not temporary. The obstacle to settlement, however, was the lack of security. Despite the departure of the Turks, fierce Arab resistance persisted to preserve *Dar el Islam* (the home of Islam) against the people of "the cross, the bell, and the pig."

At first, Algeria tended to be a repository for the unwanted. Socially conscious priests sent the unemployed; orphanages, their orphans; jails, their convicts; police, their anarchists; and do-gooders, their beggars. Settlements tended to stay close to garrisons, for the war raged against Arab tribes, who murdered isolated settlers. The settler plowed with a rifle over his shoulder and went to town for supplies in armed convoys. Fortified villages were locked at night, and sentries were posted.

In 1832, a charismatic Arab leader led the tribes to victories that forced the overextended French to sign a treaty giving him control over much of western Algeria. Abd-el-Kader rallied the tribes and for 12 years ruled a region where the French could not venture. He created the rough draft of a true state with courts, schools, taxes, officials on fixed salaries, and the abolition of tribal rank. Religious faith was the single force that brought the quarrelsome tribes together under a leader known for his piety, who preached hatred of the infidel. He set an example of austerity, living in a tent like his men.

Thomas-Robert Bugeaud, who was named governor-general of Algeria in 1841, in order to prosecute the war with a free hand, decided on a scorched earth policy. He invented the *razzia*, which consisted of destroying the villages and the crops of Arabs loyal to Abd-el-Kader. In his opus on strategy, Bugeaud advocated "burning the villages, cutting down the fruit trees, setting fire to the crops, emptying the silos, seizing the women, the children, and the old people, the livestock and the furniture. Only then will the rebels capitulate."

Protests in France to these overzealous tactics brought Bugeaud before the Chamber of Deputies on January 15, 1846. When several deputies upbraided him, he replied: "These murmurs seem to indicate that the Chamber finds our methods barbaric. Gentlemen, you can't fight a war with humanitarian instincts.... I prefer French interests to the interest of those who decapitate our wounded and imprison our soldiers."

Eventually, the *razzias* paid off and Abd-el-Kader fled to Morocco. In 1846, realizing that further resistance was useless, he returned to Algeria and surrendered. Imprisoned in the French city of Pau, the rebel leader died in 1883. Having broken the back of Arab resistance, Bugeaud drove the rebels into the mountains and began colonizing the rich coastal plain. As governor-general from 1841 to 1847, he ruled that "wherever there is fresh water and fertile land, there one must locate *colons*, without concerning oneself to whom these lands belong." The settlers were in the plain, protected by the army. The Arabs were in the mountains, looking up at heaven and its promise of an afterlife. By 1847, when Bugeaud left, 250,000 acres had been handed out to 36,000 settlers.

To organize the new pattern of land use, based on the displacement of Moslems, a Domain of the State agency was created, which drafted the regulations to force them off their land. In a tribal society, there were few written records; disputes were settled within the family or the tribe. The Domain of the State ruled that if a Moslem could not produce a written title, the land went to the state by default, while another ruling authorized the state to give vacant land to the settlers. This of course produced a cottage industry of fictitious titles. But thousands of acres were taken by the Domain of the State from Moslems unable to prove ownership.

Meanwhile, in France, another regime change was about to occur. Under the reign of the sluggish Louis-Philippe, an economic crisis in 1846 led to bankruptcies and high unemployment. Riots erupted in Paris in February 1848, and 40 rioters were killed in a fusillade on February 23. Louis-Philippe abdicated and fled to England. A republic, the second since 1792, emerged from the chaos and lasted for four years. The leaders of the Second Republic, who included romantic poet Lamartine, thirsted for justice for the enslaved peoples of Poland, Hungary, Italy, and Germany, where the 1848 revolution had spread. But on the matter of Algeria, they were more ardently colonialist than the monarchy. Lamartine, whose *Méditations* were said to have brought a new music to French poetry, explained to the Chamber of Deputies that "Bedouins . . . are a race apart . . . predatory men who cannot be tamed by any civilization."

The constitution of the Second Republic made Algeria an integral part of France, divided into three *départements*, with the same layered bureaucracy of prefects, judges, and police commissioners, and each *département* sent two deputies and one senator to the parliament in Paris. Local government passed from the military to the *colons* (settlers), and every town and village could elect its mayor.

The one discrepancy from France proper was that 90% of the population, the Moslem majority, were not French citizens but French subjects. A Moslem could not be a citizen unless he repudiated the law of Islam, the Sharia, and accepted the French civil code, which the vast majority refused to do. The Moslem religion was deemed incompatible with French citizenship, mainly because of polygamy. No French citizen kept four wives or divorced his wife by saying "I repudiate thee" three times.

The post-1848 status of Algeria was a boon to settlement. The *colons*, who were now in the saddle, floated various plans to marginalize the Moslems. One, called the American Solution, was their wholesale removal to reservations in the Sahara, which was not adopted. Instead, the *colon* plan was to increase settlement by 12,000 a year. In Paris, the National Assembly voted 50 million francs to promote that project. In the first year, 42 settlements were founded on 150,000 acres by 13,700 settlers, many of whom were Parisians who knew nothing about farming.

At that time, the train went only as far as Lyon, and from there the settlers proceeded by horse-drawn barges down the canals, as the townspeople stood on the banks cheering them on. From Marseilles, they crossed the Mediterranean to the port of Bône in eastern Algeria and were escorted to their farms by the army, the men walking and the women and children riding on the gun carriages with their mattresses and kitchen utensils, into the mountain-ringed valleys where the army had pitched tents with a little straw on the ground to sleep on, and there was not yet an acre of cultivated land. And so they built their cabins and they plowed their land, and they died of cholera and malaria. Close to their settlements stood the first headstones of an improvised cemetery, and on Sundays in the town of Bône, a military band gave a concert.

The fever of emigration spread every time there was a revolution or a war, but also in normal times, for in France there was no primogeniture; land was parceled out equally among the heirs, and many families had less than an acre. Prior to 1830, the migrants had gone to America, the land of promise, but after 1830 they went to Algeria, the land of promises, where they were given free land and could remain French. From Le Havre to New York, it was a 6-week trip on a sailing vessel, until after 1860, when steamships made the trip in 12 days. From Marseilles to Algeria, it took 2 days.

In their hunt for settlers, American recruiting companies put out anti-Algerian propaganda: "Don't go there! You'll die in the desert! You'll be killed by Bedouins! Your children will be eaten alive!" One Texas recruiter paid the *Rhine Observer* in Cologne to print lurid stories to frighten would-be settlers. And yet by 1850, the *colons* numbered more than 100,000, half of whom weren't French but European exiles from the revolution of 1848 and the castoffs of Spain and Malta.

In December 1849, Napoleon III, the nephew of the great Napoleon, was elected president of the Second Republic for a four-year term, largely owing to his name recognition. The constitution barred a second term, so in December 1851 he carried out a coup d'état, and a year later he had himself crowned emperor. The Second Empire, as it became known, lasted almost 20 years.

Napoleon III was the first head of state to become actively involved in Algeria and to visit his French domain, in 1860. He was an Arabophile who tried to navigate a skillful policy of tolerant paternalism.

He wrote his governor-general, Pélissier, on February 7, 1863: "We must convince the Arabs that we have not come to Algeria in order to oppress them or rob them of their property." If the French continued to confiscate land, he said, "it would be necessary to drive the Arab population back into the desert and inflict upon it the fate of the Indians of North America."

At that time, the senate in Paris drafted a law to clarify land tenure by returning land confiscated by the Domain of the State to the tribes and converting it into private property. Napoleon III realized that unless you had stable land laws, colonialism was doomed. Under Islamic law, the true owner of tribal land was God. But since God was not a real estate broker, tribal land had to be converted into property with deeds and titles, so that the Arabs could obtain mortgages, sell or rent their land, or buy more. With the introduction of European real estate practices, Algeria made the change from a tribal to a capitalist economy, which favored the most efficient farmers. Tribal land was broken up into *douars* (communes), and nomadic tribesmen became landlords. The grip of tribal custom was loosened, and the Arabs were funneled into a system not their own.

By 1870, land had been returned to 533 tribes and divided into *douars*, the smallest of which had a population of 240 and covered 900 acres, while the largest, near Sétif, in the eastern mountains of Kabylie, had a population of 90,432 and spread over about 20,000 acres. What the Domain of the State had taken away, Napoleon III returned. The reclassification reduced state lands by more than one third, from 3,500,000 acres to 2,100,000.

The *colons* chafed at the reduction of state land, which they warned would stall settlement. Extremists such as Eugène Bodichon, a doctor with a private practice in Algiers, said the Arabs were "the enemy" and had to be "exterminated." Such dire solutions went against the grain of Napoleon's reformist regime. His reign, however, came to a disastrous end when he led his troops into battle against the Prussians and was captured at Sedan. He was deposed in a bloodless revolution on September 4, 1870, ushering in the Third Republic.

Alsace and Lorraine became German provinces, and some of its 5 million inhabitants decided to leave rather than raise sons who would serve in the German army. France saw the exodus as an opportunity to revive its stagnant colonial policy and pacify a land still in a state of rebellion. Hundreds, then thousands, left their homes and their lands for the Algerian adventure. A drumbeat of propaganda told them that they were not going into exile but to a new France. What was Algeria but Alsace with a sunnier climate?

In June, 1871, the National Assembly adopted a plan to set aside 250,000 acres to resettle the refugees from Alsace and Lorraine. But with state lands depleted, where were these lands to be found? Fortunately, just in time, there was a major Kabyle uprising. Between January 1871 and January 1872, French troops fought 200,000 Kabyle guerrillas in the rugged mountains of eastern Algeria. Author Louis Bertrand called it a "formidable insurrection that nearly flung us back across the Mediterranean."

It was triggered by the growing Kabyle resentment over the law of 1867, which ruled that all forest lands belonged to the state unless claimants could produce deeds. Deprived of their forests, a major source of income, the Kabyles erupted into full-scale revolt. Once brought to heel, they were harshly punished. The government confiscated 1,250,000 acres of their arable land and levied a fine of 31,500,000 francs, paid in gold.

Thus the Alsatians made their homes in Algeria, thanks to two military defeats, that of the French by the Prussians and that of the Kabyles by the French. Massive arrivals in 1872 created bottlenecks, for it took time to survey the newly acquired Kabyle acres. Between 1871 and 1895, the apogee of settlement, the government handed out 1,600,000 acres to newcomers. There was said to be a "patriotic bias" toward those who had left their homes to remain French, but in fact it was a transaction that benefited the government as well as the settlers.

The Alsatians served the political and military needs of colonialism, for they were spread across the country to populate rebellious areas. The army helped them build fortified villages on the sides of hills, with crenelated bastions where the men could fire at attackers. The soldiers also built roads, dug irrigation canals, and planted eucalyptus trees. But the harsh conditions of life, the droughts, the locusts, the sparrows devouring ripening grain, the fevers and epidemics, the dysentery from bad water, the city folk who didn't know enough to wear a wide-brimmed hat under the scorching sun, discouraged the first wave of Alsatians. Hundreds sold their land and fled to America or back to Alsace. The principal reason was that the military had led them to poor locations for tactical reasons, in the hills rather than the fertile valleys. When a second wave of Alsatians arrived in a pacified Algeria, the government duplicated conditions in Alsace by building villages in the valleys grouped around church and school.

THE LAND grab and the disenfranchisement of the Arabs were accomplished under the cover of a republican ideology of progress and "civilizing influence." The maintenance of French superiority required the systematic disparagement of the polygamous and nomadic Arab majority: The Arab was not a Cartesian; he could not think rationally. His laziness and immorality were inbred. How could citizenship be granted to men who kept their women in bondage and had no notion of land ownership? The *colons* had to establish this degraded image to validate their exploitation of the natives. But when they stigmatized the Arabs for laziness and opposition to progress, they failed to discern that in many instances these were signs of passive resistance to French rule.

Emile Larcher, a law professor at the University of Algiers, did not even bother to envelop his thoughts in the ideology of progress when he wrote in 1903: "The French are a victorious people imposing their might on a defeated race. There are masters and there are subjects, the privileged and the underclass. There is no equality." Here was the true *colon* ideology, without trimmings.

Dozens of books celebrated the vitality of the *colons*, while Islam was described as stagnant and decrepit. Emile Gautier, another professor at the University of Algiers, expressed this position in the 1930s when he said the Arab was "an anarchist, a nihilist, a destroyer, a negator." Racism entered the language with a colorful variety of derogatory terms for the Arabs, such as *bicot, bougnoul, melon, tronc de figuier, raton,* all the approximate equivalent of *nigger*. With these displays of racism, the *colons* could remind themselves that they had earned the right to rule an inferior people.

Another element of contempt was to neglect the education of Arab children and then say: "They can't even read or write." As late as 1955, only one of eight went to school. Those who did were taught not only that their ancestors were Gauls but also that the French revolution had given the world universal suffrage and equality before the law. In addition, France had brought civilization to a nation of backward nomads and had made the desert fertile through irrigation. After school, the children went home, where there was no electricity or running water.

Algeria was France only in the sense that 10% of the population voted, served on juries, was elected to political office, and was subject to French law. Moslems came under the *Code de l'Indigénat* (the latter a word that meant both "native" and "indigent"), consisting of a list of treasonable acts for which Moslems could be punished, enacted in 1874. The sentence for these crimes included a fine of 15 francs and five days in prison for "remarks against France and against the government," or for "refusal to work," or for "unauthorized meetings of more than 20." The alternative for the Moslems, renouncing their religion to obtain French citizenship, amounted to apostasy.

WHEN the twentieth century dawned in Algeria, the *colons* seemed to be in full control of a country four times the size of France. Only one fifth of its surface was cultivated, and of that fifth, the *colons* owned more than half after 70 years of confiscation. They owned most of the well-watered land in the narrow coastal plain, with its vineyards, orchards, and citrus groves. They owned the fields of winter wheat and barley, and the armada of harvesters to bring in the crops. They owned the cotton and tobacco plantations, the cigarette factories, the shipping lines, the construction companies, the iron mines of Ouenza, the zinc mines near Tlemcen, and the phosphate deposits in Tebessa. The Arabs provided cheap labor and domestic help. The *colons* provided elected officials, from the mayors of small towns to the six deputies and three senators who sat in Paris and lobbied for high tariffs on Spanish and Italian fruits and vegetables to protect imports from Algeria. Algeria could export its wine and oranges to France duty-free, and this was how the great *colon* fortunes were made.

The insurrections of the previous century had for the most part petered out, though occasional uprisings still erupted among tribes that the French listed as *insoumis* (unsubdued). Thousands of French troops continued to be garrisoned in Algeria 70 years after the invasion, to maintain security and extend France's grip southward into the Sahara. During World War I, the French recruited thousands of Algerian Moslems to fight in their army. Graves with Arab names throng the cemeteries of Verdun.

*   *   *

With the coming of World War II and the defeat of France in June 1940, a collaborationist regime under octogenarian Marshal Philippe Pétain governed France from Vichy, known for its curative baths.

Algeria became a Vichyite bastion, for the *colons* loved Pétain and quickly named dozens of avenues and boulevards after him. They were devoted to a regime that was quick to adopt anti-Semitic legislation. The 1870 decree granting Algeria's Jews citizenship was voided. Jewish civil servants were dismissed and Jewish students were expelled from the lycées. The *Dépêche d'Alger* was scandalously pro-Vichy, praising Nazi victories in Russia and the sinking of British warships, particularly after the British sank most of the French fleet at Mers el-Kebir to thwart a German takeover. Many *colons* approved when Pierre Laval, the head of the Vichy government, said in June 1942: "I hope for a German victory." In the cafés of Algiers, the *colons* told each other: "The Old One [Pétain] is getting the best of Adolf."

In 1942, American envoy Robert Murphy arrived in Algiers to prepare for the Allied landing with the help of French resistance groups. He had with him a posse of a dozen vice-consuls, none of whom spoke Arabic. The German consul described them in a confidential report to Berlin as "a perfect picture of the mixture of races and characteristics in that wild conglomeration called the United States of America."

The French didn't want Americans meddling with the Moslem population. In his memoirs, Murphy observed that "Algeria's miscellaneous tribes ... had been illogically incorporated in European France. ... The one bond that held most of them together was Islam, a religion foreign to the French administration."

One of Murphy's many visitors was the nationalist leader Ferhat Abbas, who offered the support of the Algerian Moslems against Nazi forces in exchange for an American-backed election of a native

Algerian assembly. On November 7, Murphy recalled, he saw Abbas, "the most ardent Algerian Arab nationalist. He had approached me once or twice to discuss Algerian independence . . . and he wanted to know what was the American government's latest attitude toward an autonomous Algeria. . . . I told him that Americans were generally sympathetic to all desires for independence, but that our present purposes . . . were concentrated on defeating the Nazis."

The next morning, November 8, 1942, the citizens of Algiers awoke to see hundreds of iron gray warships bobbing on the waters of the Mediterranean. Allied troops stormed the beaches of Sidi Ferruch, where the French had landed in 1830, and marched on Algiers. The deployment of American forces made a lasting impression on the Arabs. France's collaborationist regime was now vanquished, as France had been previously defeated by the Germans, and was no longer a major power. The *colons* who had backed Vichy now had to join the Americans and the hated British in a half-hearted alliance.

The GIs handed out cigarettes and chewing gum and set up canteens where Arab children could get powdered milk. They conveyed a contagious impression of democratic expansiveness and served as the unwitting agents of emancipation. A *colon* woman I later met, who had been in her early twenties in 1942, told me she had a "fling" with a GI. "It was amazing," she said. "I felt that I was not sleeping with a man, but with a continent."

De Gaulle took over in Algeria, after a six-month interlude during which he overcame the obstacles placed in his way by Roosevelt and Churchill. By the spring of 1944, he had an army of 230,000 men in the field, with five divisions that fought in the Italian and Normandy campaigns and reclaimed Paris. Thousands of young Arabs fought in de Gaulle's army, and from their ranks would come the core of the rebel army. Army service taught them armament and tactics. It also taught them anti-French extremism, for they were often assigned to segregated regiments and denied entry in the officer corps. Three of the historic leaders of the National Liberation Front (FLN) served in de Gaulle's army. Ahmed Ben Bella fought at Monte Cassino in General Alphonse-Pierre Juin's division. De Gaulle himself pinned the *Médaille Militaire*, the highest Free French decoration, on Ben Bella's chest, for exceptional courage in saving the life of an officer under fire. Belkacem Krim, the Kabyle leader of the rebellion, and Mohammed Boudiaf, the leader in eastern Algeria, were also non-coms in de Gaulle's divisions.

World War II put an end to the global colonial status quo and awakened nationalist aspirations in the Third World. In 1945, France was a shaky victor, the sick man of Europe after five years of German occupation, and gave up two of its protectorates, Syria and Lebanon. In Algeria, hopes of independence were revived. On May 8, the celebration of Victory in Europe Day became a springboard for anti-French demonstrations in 11 Algerian cities.

In Sétif, a bustling market town on the high plains of eastern Algeria, and the home of Ferhat Abbas, it was market day as well as V-E Day. The Moslem multitudes filled the streets. A procession of perhaps 5,000 formed outside the mosque. Its stated aim was to lay the wreath for those who had fallen in the war. But the marchers also carried banners saying "Down with colonialism," and "Long live a free Algeria."

The police were ordered to seize the banners and arrest those who carried them. In the ensuing scuffle, shots rang out, and the crowd went wild, attacking *colons* and vandalizing property. At least 21 *colons* were killed in Sétif that day; in towns like Guelma, near the Tunisian border, and Blida, south of Algiers, similar scenes took place. More shocking than the Arab riots, however, were the French reprisals, which seemed to be proclaiming, "We're going to show you, once and for all." In the jails of Constantine, Arab inmates were shot through the bars of their cells. Other suspects were taken up in planes and thrown in the sea. French warships fired their big guns on coastal villages. The toll for what became known as "the hour of the gendarme" was an estimated 6,000 dead. For many Algerian Arabs, it was the point of no return, the point where they decided that they were better off fighting back than being massacred. Hopelessness leads to militancy, and the rebellion of a few becomes the revolution of the many.

*   *   *

T HAT OCTOBER 1945, at its founding meeting in San Francisco, the United Nations charter included a paragraph on the
right of subject peoples to self-determination. But Algeria was still
governed as it had been in 1900, with a governor-general named by
the French president. Under the postwar Fourth Republic, temporiz-
ing politicians tried to square the circle—that is, to reconcile *colon*
demands for maintaining the status quo with the Moslem majority's
pressing need for change.

Under the government of Socialist Premier Paul Ramadier, a
scholar of ancient Greece, the National Assembly passed a statute in
1947 creating an Algerian assembly of 120 deputies, divided in two
electoral colleges of 60, one representing the 370,000 *colons* and the
60,000 assimilated Moslems and the other representing the 8,000,000
other Moslems. Important measures in this assembly required a two-
thirds vote, effectively giving the *colons* a veto. The heavy *colon* thumb
was on the scales. Such an obvious contrivance for thwarting majority rule, at a time when the First Indochina War served as an example for the Arabs, was doomed. A friend of mine said at the time,
"What if in Normandy they had two electoral colleges, one for the
peasants and one for the bankers?" The two colleges made nonsense
of the idea that Algeria was a part of France.

In 1947, a cluster of young men broke away from the reformist
party of Messali Hadj and formed a paramilitary group called the
Organisation Secrète, which began training guerrillas in the mountains. They started with 300 desert war surplus Italian rifles, which
they paid for by selling their homes. The OS was a forerunner of the
FLN.

On April 9, 1949, Ahmed Ben Bella, the OS leader, carried out an
armed robbery of the Oran post office. The take was 3,170,000 francs
($9,000). In May 1950, he was arrested in Algiers and sentenced to
forced labor for life. On March 16, 1952, he escaped from his prison
in Blida, south of Algiers, and fled to Cairo, where a band of young
officers led by Gamal Abdel Nasser had deposed King Farouk. This

was a striking example of a corrupt regime overthrown by Arab nationalists.

In May 1954, the month of the fall of Dien Bien Phu, 22 leaders of the OS met in the Algiers suburb of Clos Salembier. These were men in their twenties and thirties, not university graduates like Ferhat Abbas but the sons of humble families who had experienced French oppression on farms, in factories, and in the army. Many were defectors from the Messali Hadj movement. They were not ideologues, and they modeled their movement on the French resistance against the Nazis. It was at this May meeting that they adopted the name National Liberation Front (FLN) and formally endorsed the armed struggle. At a later meeting, they decided on November 1, All Saints' Day, for an insurrection in the craggy Aurès Mountains of eastern Algeria, long a refuge for outlaws, where shepherds tended their meager flocks and peasants lived in abject misery. In the heart of this neglected and desolate region, the "forces of order" consisted of seven gendarmes.

On All Saints' Day, there were 70 more or less coordinated attacks, supposedly synchronized to start at 3 AM. In Biskra, a winter resort on the edge of the Sahara, several bombs exploded. In Batna, a garrison town in the Aurès Mountains, at 3,000 feet, about 50 miles north of Biskra, Colonel Lucien Blanche, commander of the garrison, was shot and killed in his staff car. At Kenchela, a town of 4,000 with 800 *colons*, 64 miles east of Batna, one of the rebel leaders, Salem Boubakeur, was in charge of the distribution of weapons, which were hidden in a thermal bath outside town called Fontaine Chaude. On Sunday, there was a soccer game attended by police, which gave Salem the chance to distribute weapons.* The local team won, and the *colons* repaired to cafés in a festive mood. The armed FLN groups gathered that night in the forest, wearing World War II U.S. Army surplus uniforms.

---

*The role of soccer in molding Algerian nationalism has been neglected. It was only when Arabs were allowed to play on French teams and became stars that the Algerian masses had nonreligious heroes to admire.

Salem described the weapons as he handed them out: "The MAS 56 is an excellent rifle, and it's a pleasure to use the weapons of the French against them." Someone asked him the difference between a Beretta and a Thompson submachine gun. "The same difference as between America and Italy," he said. On Monday the rebels attacked the gendarmerie barracks, but the gendarmes unleashed their wolf-hounds, and the attackers fled. They attacked a police barracks, killed the lieutenant commanding the detachment, and recovered four hand-guns. They exploded a couple of bombs in a *spahi* barracks and set fire to the stables.

A sweep the next day arrested 100 Arabs, including Salem. The gendarmes let a dog loose in his cell that bit his arm. The next morn-ing, when the dog refused to bite him, one of the gendarmes said, "The dog's a friend of the *fels*" (*fellaghas*, or FLN). Then they threw dog food on the floor of the cell and told Salem to eat the dog food, and when he got down on his hands and knees, the dog bit his hand and the gendarmes stood behind him, laughing.

A bus from Biskra was chugging up the road that Monday morn-ing to the mountain town of Arris, south of Batna, at 4,000 feet, when it was ambushed in the Tighanimine gorges by 15 rebels in uni-form. The rebels looked over the passengers and spotted a French couple, rural schoolteacher Guy Monnerot and Janine, his bride of two months. When they told Monnerot and his wife to get off the bus, a distinguished-looking, gray-bearded Arab with the Legion of Honor ribbon pinned to his immaculate white djellaba, tried to stop them. He was the *caïd* (Moslem judge) Ben Hadj Saddok, a tribal chief and one of the rare Arabs who had reached the rank of captain in the French army. "These two young people are here to teach our children," he said. "Leave them alone." The reply was a burst from a Sten gun, and the *caïd* fell, mortally wounded. The rebels stood the Monnerots by the side of the road, shot them, and left them to die. But Janine Monnerot survived. And so the cycle of violence and re-prisal began.

Abane Ramdane, one of the most obdurate FLN leaders, argued that the laws of war had changed since the World War II bombings, from the London blitz to Dresden and Hiroshima, and that the killing of civilians was no longer off limits. "We need blood in the headlines," he said, "to make the world aware."

The Algerian rebels can be credited with launching modern terrorism. As they saw it, terrorism was the use of guerrilla tactics in cities to obtain political ends. After the All Saints' Day attacks, the FLN sought to alert the world that they were a force to reckon with. Providentially, 29 African and Asian nations opposed to colonialism held a conference in April 1955 in the hilltop town of Bandung, Indonesia, and invited two FLN "observers," Ait-Ahmed Hocine and Mohammed Yazid. Ait-Ahmed had taken part in the robbery of the Oran post office. Yazid, a one-time law student and follower of Messali Hadj, was a born diplomat, debonair and reasonable. In its report, the conference expressed its sympathy "for the people of North Africa," which gave the FLN its first glimmer of international recognition. Even though the CIA men attending the conference mocked it as "the darktown strutter's ball," the two Algerians obtained promises of aid. Nehru, the prime minister of India, told them: "We would like to intervene, but first, do something."

Another attention-getting action was required to put the FLN on the map. Terrorism and political gains were intertwined. That August in Philippeville, a pretty oceanside city of 21,000 in eastern Algeria, where the rebels were strongest, the FLN struck. On August 18, guerrilla teams slipped in by night and hid in cellars. On Saturday, August 20, when half the city-dwellers were at the beach, the bells of St. Lucie Church rang out the noon hour and hundreds of armed rebels emerged from cellars and were joined by Arab peasants carrying scythes and axes. They marched down the main street toward the Place de Marque, as if on parade, killing as they went and setting fire to houses. The deputy prefect, Dupuch, cabled Algiers in a panic that the city had fallen and locked himself in a basement. But a foreign legion unit was brought in, took up positions with machine guns, and mowed down 134 rebels.

Ten miles east of Philippeville there was a sulphur mine where French engineers and their families, 130 in all, lived on site with

2,000 Algerian miners. The FLN leader at the El Halia mine, Zig-houd Youssef, ordered the miners to massacre the French civilians and their families and to show no pity. At noon on August 18, the miners attacked those who had stayed home on a broiling summer day. In a collective frenzy, they hacked up children and disemboweled women. Fourteen adults and 23 children were killed. One of the sur-vivors, an engineer who had to be hospitalized for shock-induced dementia, later recalled that he was hiding under a bed in the shad-owy light of his prefab when something rolled across the floor against his leg. He felt it, and it felt at first like a ball of wool. Then he real-ized it was hair. It was his wife's head. Troops arrived too late, but 60 prisoners were taken and executed on the spot.

El Halia became the emblematic FLN atrocity, reinforcing the French conviction that they were dealing with savages. "That was when the insurrection became a war," said Jacques Chevallier, the liberal mayor of Algiers. The French had been slow to react after the All Saints' Day attacks, insisting that the FLN consisted of "just a few groups scattered in the mountains," and that French troops were involved not in a war but in "maintenance of order." Under the Fourth Republic, political power in France was fragmented among ineffec-tive parties that formed unstable coalitions, incapable of leadership and in the thrall of lobbies. The French intelligentsia was blind to events. André Siegfried, the French Walter Lippmann, wrote in a 1954 column: "The French presence on the other side of the Mediter-ranean is identical to the Roman presence of antiquity."

In January 1955, Jacques Soustelle arrived in Algeria as governor-general. Trained as an ethnologist, he had done fieldwork on the Ma-yans and the Aztecs. Soustelle had joined de Gaulle in London during the war and became the head of his intelligence service at the age of 31. He combined the ethnologist's professional interest in precolonial people with the conspiratorial bent of a secret service agent.

Soustelle at first had a plan to accomplish the genuine integra-tion of Algeria into France, by blending the two electoral colleges into one and extending the vote to all Arabs, including women. True integration would make the Arabs a minority in a greater France.

But in August, Soustelle visited El Halia and saw the mangled and decapitated bodies of women and children. A visceral reaction of utter revulsion led him to say: "I won't negotiate with cutthroats." Soustelle was the first to call the FLN methods terrorism, "this previously unknown and undefined scourge, which the state must learn to oppose."

When he asked for more troops, the French desperately juggled divisions, moving them from their adjacent protectorates, Morocco and Tunisia, then from Germany, which angered France's NATO allies, since those armed divisions had been trained to fight the Soviets in Europe, not the Algerians in the mountains of Kabylie. In August 1955, the army had to call up 60,000 reserves and maintain 180,000 conscripts with a stop-loss order preventing them from retiring on schedule. Never before had a conscript army, nearly 3 million over eight years of war, gone overseas when the mainland was at peace.

In 1956, when the French granted independence to Tunisia and Morocco in order to concentrate on Algeria, the FLN was blessed with two friendly border states. Tunisian guerrillas who had been fighting the French from Libya turned their camps over to Ben Bella. Both countries provided the FLN with logistical bases, and commandos moved easily across the porous borders. FLN agents such as Yazid, who in 1956 was an observer at the United Nations, used Moroccan and Tunisian passports.

French elections that January of 1956, which became known as the crucial year of the war, brought to power a Socialist government under Prime Minister Guy Mollet. A colorless former lycée English teacher who looked as if he were at the blackboard even when he wasn't, Mollet presided over the longest-lasting government of the Fourth Republic (January 1956 through May 1957). Like others, he started out wanting a negotiated solution to the war, naming as governor-general 79-year-old five-star general Georges Catroux. Despite his age, Catroux brought to the post his considerable experience in the Arab world, as de Gaulle's man in Egypt, Algeria, and

Syria during World War II, and as Minister for Moslem Affairs in the de Gaulle provisional government of 1944.

But when Catroux said he wanted "an honorable solution" to the war, the *colons* translated that as "sellout." To prepare the ground for his arrival, Mollet decided to fly to Algiers right after being invested as prime minister in early February. He was warned that there was unrest among the ultras and that agitators had threatened to assassinate Catroux. Mollet took the precaution of sending 12 companies of riot police (the CRS) to Algiers ahead of him, and he landed on February 6. The ultras were ready with a boisterous welcome.

Mollet went directly from the airport at Maison Blanche to the Monument to the Dead on the Plateau des Glières, on a rise in the center of town, to lay the customary wreath. Thousands of ultras were already there, milling around the statue of Joan of Arc and screaming "Mollet *au Poteau*" (the firing squad), "Resign," and "Throw him out to sea." When he got out of his car with the wreath, he was pelted with tomatoes, eggs, dried horse dung, and clumps of sod. As Mollet laid the wreath, the crowd surged and the CRS fired tear gas. He made it back to his car thanks only to the CRS, who charged the crowd, swinging their clubs and heavy capes, which were lined with lead pellets. Once Mollet was gone, the demonstrators stomped on the wreath he had just placed.

Mollet drove to the governor-general building, abashed by the fierce rancor of the demonstrators. The first thing he did was call Catroux in Paris and ask for his resignation. He caved in to an organized show of force directed by teams of ultras. His authority as prime minister had been flouted. It was the worst humiliation of his life, worse even than two years of German captivity.

The riot had the desired effect. The traumatized Mollet changed course. He was now determined to fight an all-out war against the FLN. With a single street demonstration, the ultras engineered the resignation of a governor-general named by the prime minister and overturned the government's Algerian policy. Once again, as with Soustelle, they showed they could wag the dog. It was as if there were no Arabs in Algeria.

To replace Catroux, Mollet chose his crony from the Resistance and the Socialist Party, Robert Lacoste, who was the minister of finance in his government. Short, with a large head on a squat and muscular body, Lacoste looked like one of those stumpy, thick-backed Camargue steers, on two legs and without the horns. He knew nothing about Algeria, but he had a blustering, bullying manner that passed for decisiveness.

Lacoste arrived in Algiers on February 10, 1956. His friends told him he was crazy, it was a real shithouse over there, but he replied, "We all know politics is no bed of roses. I'm like a good soccer player. I know when to push straight ahead and when to feint." He got on well with the *colons*, and was soon co-opted by them, for like them, he was jovial, quick-tempered, and garrulous, and he didn't mind doing business over a bottle of *gros rouge* and a five-course meal.

Soon after his arrival, he said in a directive to civil servants and French troops: "From a terrorized and suffering Moslem population we must demand only one thing: recognition of the French fatherland and our flag, and that is all."

Just as the French determined to fight an all-out war with 400,000 men, the FLN leaders held a summit conference in the summer of 1956, for they were too dispersed. The "internals" who did the fighting inside Algeria resented the "externals" based in Cairo and their luxurious life. Communications were primitive, and there was too much improvisation and too little cohesion among the six *wilayas*, or military regions, in which Algeria had been divided. In their correspondence, the leaders denounced each other with colorful jargon. One was a "Berbero-materialist," another a "decaying bourgeois," and a third "a westernized parasite."

Abane Ramdane, a doctrinaire "internal" leader, organized the summit in August 1956, and found a quiet cabin far from French troops on the Soummam River in a forest in Kabylie. The summit opened on August 20, presided over by the leader from Oran, Ben M'Hidi. About 20 leaders and their aides were on hand, though one of the "externals," Ben Bella, still in Cairo, was conspicuous by his absence.

The Soummam summit called for an independent Algeria and made it clear that the FLN was now a national movement able to field a guerrilla army, and representing a wide spectrum of the Moslem population, from clerics and elites to illiterate peasants. A 34-member national council (CNRA) was set up, and at the top, a five-member executive committee.

The FLN was gaining international acceptance, not only from Nasser but also from its newly independent allies, Tunisia and Morocco. In October 1956, a conference was planned in Tunis to discuss some form of North African union. The sultan of Morocco, Mohammed V, and the Tunisian president, Habib Bourguiba, would preside, and a number of FLN leaders would attend. The sultan invited an FLN delegation of four to meet him in Rabat prior to flying to Tunis—Ben Bella, Ait-Ahmed, Mohammed Khider, and Mohammed Boudiaf, all historic leaders.

In Paris, Prime Minister Mollet viewed these meetings with alarm. In Algiers, the French special services monitored the movements of Ben Bella and his friends. They knew that on October 22 the four Algerians were flying from Rabat to Tunis aboard a chartered DC-3 with a French pilot named Grelier, a major in the air force reserves. General Frandon, commander of the French air force in Algeria, thought it would be feasible to intercept Ben Bella's plane. Max Lejeune, the minister of defense, agreed. Guy Mollet was kept in the dark. The DC-3 left Rabat in the late afternoon, flying over the Balearic Islands to avoid Algerian air space, while the sultan took his own plane to Tunis. From Algiers, Major Grelier received the order to land at the Maison Blanche airport instead of proceeding to Tunis. The French air hostess told the passengers: "Please fasten your seat belts. We are about to land in Tunis." At 9 PM, the plane landed at Maison Blanche, and the passengers, thinking they were in Tunis, sauntered down the gangplank into the arms of the French police. They were arrested, handcuffed, and flown to Santé prison in Paris.

International opinion called the hijacking an act of piracy, but the *colons* applauded, describing the jailed leaders as "traitors with three passports who fly all over the map to incite anti-French hatred." The sultan of Morocco was so furious that his guests had been hijacked that he gave the FLN $500,000 to buy weapons. Predictions that the French had decapitated the FLN proved to be wishful thinking, for the advantage of collegial leadership was that empty chairs could quickly be filled. But a negotiated solution was now out of the question.

It was at this point, in the fall of 1956, that Algeria entered my life.

How I Went to War

I SHOULD EXPLAIN THAT I got into Yale thanks to affirmative action, then known as a little help from a wealthy alumnus. In 1952, I was wasting away at the Sorbonne, at a time when France was still hung over from the Second World War. Professors advised students not to attend their overcrowded classes but to pick up mimeographed copies of their lectures. A friend of mine who was attending law school told me that on the first day of class, the dean announced to the assembled students: "Half of you will flunk out. What France needs are good carpenters, not bad lawyers."

My mother had promised my father that she would send me to a French university, but I had spent most of my life in the States and I wanted to get into a good Ivy League college. She gave in to my entreaties and contacted her friend Hamilton Colket, who was a philanthropic Yale alumnus. I think he had a swimming pool named after him. We met in Paris, and over dinner at the Tour d'Argent, at a table with a view of Notre Dame (where, for $75, he had the cathedral illuminated, which was a form of philanthropy for the other diners), Ham Colket quizzed me on my plans as he dug into his *canard au sang*. He was a kind but canny man and took the precaution of giving me a biography of Lenin to read, in case I showed signs of latent subversive instincts. I told him the system would never work if the doctors were paid the same as the nurses. Also they did not believe in beauty pageants or competitive eating, the bedrock of a free society. He saw that I had a capitalistic bent, based on wage differentials and competition at all levels.

That summer I went to New Haven and had a chat with Whitney Griswold, the president of Yale. I was admitted into junior year, with credit from my year at the Sorbonne, on the condition that I take a course in American history. I majored in poli sci and learned that there was no such thing. But in my American history seminar, I had my eyes opened through the case system. To understand the Supreme Court, we studied the opinions of Chief Justice John Marshall. Compared with the homilies in the history books of the French lycées, the case system was a quantum leap.

I ambled through my two years at Yale, then a preppy enclave where it seemed mandatory to have several middle names and Roman numerals after your last name. The fraternity subculture and its determined drinking was something I saw only as a guest. Once I went to the Fence Club with a friend who was so drunk that he threw a glass at his reflection on the mirror behind the bar. Since I was also drunk, I did the same, to be companionable. "You can't do that," the bartender said. "You're not a member."

To overcome my outsider status, I became a joiner. I played intramural squash and tennis. I sang in the second-string glee club, the Adelphi, which had the fringe benefit of invitations to perform at the Seven Sisters. I helped arrange exhibits of rare books for the Jared Eliot Society. I acted in productions of Restoration comedies staged by my college, Berkeley. I examined Shakespeare folios at the Elizabethan Club, which served afternoon tea and Ritz crackers with peanut butter. One of my friends there, Hendon Chubb, would pick up a little round cracker sandwich, press the two sides carefully together, remove the peanut butter from the rim with his index finger, and replace the cracker on the tray. I shouldn't criticize, for Hendon had an interesting mind in a dilettantish sort of way (learning Japanese, taking up painting), and he gave me the second best bottle of wine that I ever drank, a Romanée Conti 1959, as a wedding present. He was, however, a bundle of eccentricities, which showed that not everyone at Yale was cut from the same cloth, though in those days the diversity came more from temperament than race or class.

In my senior year I took up night-climbing, an activity borrowed from Oxonians, which consisted of climbing the neo-Gothic spires and towers on campus without using any equipment such as ropes or flashlights. Night-climbing was completely antithetical to the values that Yale instilled, such as winning a letter in a varsity sport, getting tapped for Bones or Scroll and Key, and becoming a Big Man on Campus. Night-climbing was surreptitious and illegal, and getting caught by the campus police could have meant expulsion or worse. The only reward of this secret diversion, more than a game and less than a sport, was the risk and difficulty of doing it. My partners in crime were Strode Purdy, Ed Sparn, and Harry Coulter. We climbed Calhoun College, the Sterling Library, and a number of other buildings, usually after midnight. I have never been so scared before or since, but I got through it, not because I was brave, but because I was more terrified of backing out in front of my friends than I was of performing a trapeze act without a net. Purdy continued to climb after graduation, in the venues where he taught, and eventually fell and broke his back. Coulter became, I think, a Soviet expert. Sparn, recruited on campus by the CIA, was sent to Thailand. When I asked him what his cover was, he said, "Mendicant friar."

WHEN I graduated from Yale in 1954, I looked for something to do. I didn't want to be a diplomat like my father, Gabriel de Gramont, who once told me, "Diplomats are sent abroad to lie for their country," or a businessman like my uncle Dimitri. He worked for Niarchos, whom he called "the bandit." Medicine and the law meant being at the beck and call of patients and clients. I was, however, drawn to journalism after reading a phrase of Camus: "The journalist is the historian of the moment." That was my high-minded reason. My low reason was that I had always been a snooper, and the journalist gets paid for snooping. I had the nasty habit of going through drawers and medicine cabinets. Once when I was 12, my mother took me to visit a couple near Wilmington, Delaware, who had a beautiful daughter of about 18. She caught me in her closet sniffing her dresses. I learned the meaning of mortification. Curiosity, however, is a much-undervalued trait. That "lust of the mind" is also an engine; it keeps you going because you need to know what will happen next. Although I knew he suffered from depression and had changed his medication, I never understood how my old friend and fellow Congo correspondent, Tony Lukas, could have killed himself when he had a book coming out. *Big Trouble.* Didn't he want to see the reviews and feel the intense pleasure of cursing the reviewers?

The deeper motivation pulling me toward journalism was that I had developed an aversion to causes, however noble. I instinctively sought to remain uninvolved, an observer rather than a participant. This was the lingering aftershock of my father's death. Growing up in Paris, I remember my father as a playmate, carrying me on his shoulders or singing songs. He took me for rides on his lap in the planes he was learning to fly, which had open cockpits, one for the pilot and one for him. I figured it was easier for him to revert to my age than for me to reach his. He had a smile that lit up his face. Only once did I see it darken, when I snuck into his office and spilled a bottle of ink over papers on his desk.

The word his friends affectionately used to describe him was *quixotic.* Once he got an idea into his head, he was inflexible. At the age of 15, after reading Voltaire's essay on the Lisbon earthquake, in which he repudiated a deity that could allow such a catastrophe to occur, my father told his mother: "I have lost my faith." Accustomed to his pronouncements, she replied lightly, "Where did you lose it?" as if he had misplaced his wallet. "At the Gare Saint-Lazare," he said, realizing that she did not take him seriously. But he was serious—he had stopped believing in God.

When he was 18, he fell in love with a 16-year-old Greek girl at a sanatorium in Switzerland, where he had been sent for treatment of a spot on his lung (Mariette was there with her tubercular mother). In those Magic Mountain surroundings, he wanted to get married immediately, but his mother insisted that he go to South Africa for two years and work on a ranch, hoping that he would get over it. He didn't get over it. He married my mother when she was 18 and he was 20.

My father's friend Ettore Bugatti gave him one of his cars as a wedding present. When they left on their honeymoon, my father insisted, in spite of her impassioned protests, that she learn to drive the two-seat roadster at high speed. She drove it right into one of the poplars that line French roads. They spent their honeymoon in the hospital. I have a photograph of them, swathed in bandages like Egyptian mummies, holding hands across their white metal beds.

My mother soon learned that my father could not be swayed from his intended path. He was a champion golfer, with a shelf of silver loving cups in his office, and he played every Sunday at his club outside Paris. One Sunday she pointed out that it was raining very hard. "Not in Vallière," he said. When he was studying for his exams for the Quai d'Orsay (foreign office), our house was filled with relatives and their friends. Exasperated, he went outside and broke a street lamp, then called the police and asked to be arrested. He wanted the peace and quiet of a jail cell.

Our house was in Auteuil, across the street from the Roland Garros tennis club (one of my earliest memories was the snap of rackets hitting balls during the tournament season). One of our houseguests was my father's mother, Maria. Born a Ruspoli, a well-known Roman family, my grandmother had married my grandfather, the portly and walrus-mustached *duc* Agénor de Gramont, when he was 52 and she was 17. Twice widowed, Agénor had gone to Rome to woo Maria's widowed mother, but fell for Maria. After his death, Maria fell in love with a man 10 years younger than she was, as if in compensation— François Hugo, the grandson of Victor Hugo. At the age of 47 she became pregnant. My practical mother, who called them as she saw them, pointed out Maria's noticeable condition to my father, who saw his mother as the perfect woman, a saint-in-waiting. He became so enraged that he shook her until she fell to the floor. A few months later, Maria gave birth to a son, George Hugo, and married François.

When I was five, in 1937, my father brought us to Washington, my mother, my two brothers, and I, where he had been posted as air attaché at the French embassy. Two years later, when war broke out in Europe, he went to France and joined the air force. As a diplomat, he would not have been mobilized, but in his patriotic ardor, he left his wife and three sons behind to take part in the *drôle de guerre* ("funny" or "phony war") of 1939–1940. After the armistice and the fall of France, rather than take a diplomatic post in the Vichy government, he sailed to England in a fishing boat days after General de Gaulle's June 18 appeal to the people of France, and flew in the Free French escadrille of the Royal Air Force (RAF).

One day, in April 1943, when I was 11, I came home from school at St. Matthew's, next to the cathedral, to our apartment at 2040 S Street. My mother was home, which was unusual, since she worked at Elizabeth Arden's on Connecticut Avenue. I saw from her frozen expression that she was trying to control herself. "Something has happened to your father," she said. At that point I knew he was dead, but trying to keep him alive a little bit longer, I said: "He's been wounded."

"No," she said, "his plane was shot down over Frankfurt in a bombing raid and he was killed." At the time, my grief was tinged with pride that he had died in combat and killed some Germans, for I had been obsessively following the course of the war, not only in the papers and on the radio, but in movies such as *Thirty Seconds Over Tokyo* and *A Walk in the Sun*. In one of them, Alan Ladd, playing an OSS agent in Paris, is caught by the Gestapo by the way he eats his steak, not knife in the right hand and fork in the left hand French style, but cut your meat, put down the knife, pick up the fork, and chew. Later on, I was stirred by *Stairway to Heaven*, in which David Niven, playing a downed RAF flyer, gets a second chance at life.

But that was not to be, nor did the heroic image I had of my father endure. I later learned that my mother, in an attempt to make my father's death conform to my expectations, had made up the story of the bombing raid. The truth was that my father had been killed in a crash at his air base in England. The plane he was piloting had run out of gas a few miles from the runway as he tried to land. What a stupid way to die, I thought, by running out of gas. As a result of a banal accident, I was left fatherless and rudderless. My grief turned to anger. So this was where it all led, the patriotism, the commitment, the compulsion to get involved—to a wooden cross in an English cemetery. He would have been better off staying with his family in Washington.

But as it turned out, the year of my greatest sorrow became the year of my personal liberation. My bereaved and overwrought mother couldn't handle three boisterous boys and a full-time job. She took her resentment out on me, and every other day I had to pull my pants down and get whacked on the butt with a hairbrush. When the '43–'44 school year started, she arranged to send me to New York for a year to stay with my aunt and uncle and attend the French lycée. I was glad to get away from my grieving mother and my two whining, snot-nosed, tattletale younger brothers. New York beckoned, full of promise.

My aunt and uncle, Catherine and Dimitri Negroponte (he was my mother's younger brother), were an attractive couple in their twenties. Dimitri was a Valentino type, dark and brooding, with a mane of oiled hair brushed straight back, while Catherine was a rare blue-eyed blond Greek from Sparta, a fine-boned and elegant beauty. They lived in a splendid apartment at 130 E. 75th Street, with a fresco by Jean Pagès in the dining room. I was given the tiny maid's room off the kitchen, where I was glad to be, since I could raid the refrigerator. Their four-year-old son John (later to become President George W. Bush's somewhat irrelevant ambassador to Iraq, since there was no Iraqi government to be accredited to, and then the Director of Intelligence), was in another section of the house with his nanny, seldom seen, but often heard, since he was something of a crybaby.

CATHERINE AND Dimitri were out most nights at El Morocco or Larue (where the band played "Stay As Sweet As You Are" whenever she made an entrance), and I was left to my own devices. Far from my mother's nitpicking, I felt an exhilarating sense of freedom, which at the age of 11 was matched not by a sense of responsibility but by what I could get away with in a vacuum of parental and school authority. The lycée at that time was located in a mansion on 95th Street, off Fifth Avenue. Attendance was loosely enforced, and my friends and I played hooky, exploring the great hub of 86th Street, where a few years before, brown-shirted Bundists had goose-stepped and *heil*-Hitlered. The great attraction of 86th Street, aside from Prexy's, "The Hamburger With the College Education," with its smiling, mortar-boarded burger over the door, was that it had three movie theaters within two blocks—Loew's Orpheum, RKO, and the Grand, a seedy dump that showed old movies. It was there I first saw *Gunga Din* and *The Four Feathers*, films extolling heroism and the colonial ethic. All three showed double features, and what with short subjects and the Movietone news, for the price of a quarter (if you were under 12) you could spend much of the day there instead of attending boring classes.

When I got home I listened to *The Green Hornet* and *Henry Aldrich*, stole loose change whenever I could find it, and dropped water-filled paper cups from a window of the eighth-floor apartment. This was the one time I was reprimanded by my uncle Dimitri, when one of the doormen complained about "that crazy kid." In the evening when they were out, I played their albums of scores from Broadway musicals. In a song from *Bloomer Girls*, with lyrics by Yip Harburg, I found my personal anthem. It was called the "Eagle and Me," and it went something like this: "River it like to flow, Eagle it like to fly, Eagle it like to spread its wing against the sky. Possum it like to run,

Ivy it like to climb. Bird in the tree and bumblebee want freedom in autumn and summertime. Free as the sun is free, That's how it got to be, Whatever is right for bumblebee and river and eagle is right for me. We gotta be free, The eagle and me." Such was the synchronicity of New York, that capital of brilliant people, I thought, that Yip Harburg could have written those great lyrics a few blocks from where I was mapping out my territory. I played that song, which was actually a civil rights anthem before its time, over and over, and ever since, I have associated Manhattan with freedom, freedom to shrug or smile, freedom to groan and moan, freedom to sink or swim. I also feel like a New Yorker "down to the last capillary," as Yip Harburg described himself.

A ND SO in the fall of 1954 I enrolled in journalism school at Columbia, which had the advantage of taking only one year, so that I could start earning my living recording printable events. My frustration with the school was that it pretended to be a newspaper. We were sent out on stories that were never printed. Once I was sent to the United Nations, where the French ambassador, Charles Lucet, had been a friend of my parents' before the war. When I stopped by to say hello, he told me: "Something terrible has happened. Vyshinsky died during the night." The notorious prosecutor of Stalin's purges was dead, but his death had not yet been announced. I had a scoop, but I couldn't do anything with it.

In those days, newspaper editors across the country came to Columbia to look over the graduating class and perhaps hire a young reporter at a beginner's wage. I was picked by the managing editor of the *Worcester Telegram*, Frank Murphy, one of those tightly wound, dyspeptic Irishmen whose mocking sense of humor concealed a bedrock kindness. He was the prototype of the crusty editor and actually wore a green eyeshade and cuff restrainers in the city room.

In Worcester, Massachusetts, I rented a room in a boarding house and bought a beat-up Studebaker. I was paid $55 a week, and I spent my days off in Cambridge, where I had friends of both sexes attending the Harvard summer school. My real joy was my work at the paper, which seemed more real than the little city itself, as a distillation of its anatomy. I was as happy as a clam at high tide, loving the bustle of the city room, the reporters and the rewrite men at their typewriters banging out stories, the desk men red-pencilling their copy, the city desk sending it down to be set, and at seven you had the finished product, still warm from the presses. You could hold in your hand the result of this combined effort to which you had contributed.

The staff was the usual mix of the mundane and the eccentric, of bright boys and retreads, of the ambitious and the pension-bound. Ernie Labranche, a copy editor, had written a World War I novel, *Immortal Sergeant*, that was made into a movie starring Pat O'Brien. Jack Kelso, who was from Kentucky, had covered the 1948 Truman convention, when Alben Barkley was picked as vice president. He liked to intone his lead as if reciting a line from a Shakespeare sonnet: "Alben Barkley wept as the band played 'My Old Kentucky Home' . . ." And then there was the guy in the morgue who said: "I started as a file clerk and in two years I became assistant file clerk."

As a newcomer, I was given an assignment that nobody wanted. Each morning on the front page, there was a box with a graph or two under the rubric "There's Always Good News." It's a truism that most news is bad news—accidents, murders, wars, financial chicanery, an endless array of humanity's misdeeds. I scratched my head to come up with anything positive, resorting to hoary old chestnuts such as "The Sounds of Summer," and stealing a line from Andrew Marvell for the kicker: "All the live murmur of a summer day."

To me, the flimsiest story was a delight, because we weren't pretending, as we had been in J-school. I interviewed a man who owned a valuable stamp, and the story made the front page on a slow day. He called the city desk to complain that his wife was mad at him because I had quoted him as saying, "I'd no more sell this stamp than I'd sell my wife."

Another assignment that no one wanted was to interview the parents of a boy who had drowned at summer camp. I rang the bell, feeling like the meddlesome violator of their grief, but to my amazement they greeted me warmly, offering me a beer, and showed me albums of photographs. I couldn't tell if they wanted to share their sorrow or whether their innate sense of hospitality had overcome their desire for privacy.

In August, torrential rains fell and parts of the city were flooded. Several reporters could not make it to work, so I was sent out with a photographer to cover the flood. We found an old canoe and paddled around the tree-lined streets of Worcester, talking to people who had moved to their attics, above the water line. For the first time, Frank Murphy commended me for my work. When I pointed out that my byline had been misspelled, he said: "Who will know but you?" My name was a problem, and I changed it to Ted Morgan (an anagram of de Gramont) when I got my citizenship. My first name, Sanche, was an abbreviation of *St. Charles*, which everyone pronounced "Sanchee," whereas it rhymed more or less with *paunch*. My last name, *de Gramont*, was often spelled with two m's. "By the way," Frank said, "the French consulate in Boston called to get your address."

A few days later, I received a letter ordering me to appear on September 3 at 9 AM at a barracks in the town of Vernon, in Normandy. The long arm of conscription had reached across the Atlantic and grabbed me. Conscription was not the draft. France had a system of national service. Upon his twentieth birthday, every young man was obliged to serve his time in the army. There were, of course, student deferments, but the army had caught up with me, at the age of 23.

The reason was that the army needed men. The Moslem rebellion had broken out the previous November in Algeria, and the army was casting a wide net. France had a professional army, but it did not suffice. The conscripts and the reserves had to make up the shortfall. Conscription went back to Napoleon's excursion into Egypt. Would we never be done, I fulminated, with these infernal African adventures?

I wondered what to do. I could easily have ignored the summons and stayed in Worcester. I was not drawn to the military. I disliked taking orders as much as giving them, and I shunned regimentation.

I did not want to leave the working democracy of the city room, nor did I feel impelled to defend the *colons* of Algeria from rebellious Arabs. But something was pulling me in the other direction, and that was the memory of my father. Avoiding conscription would betray a debt of honor owed to a man who had served and died for a free France, even though the war in Algeria was a question mark, while his war had been a just one. I didn't believe in an afterlife, but I always felt that my father was watching over me. I knew that if I did not go, I would bear the guilt of having disappointed him. It was irrational, but there it was.

When I showed the conscription notice to Frank Murphy, he said: "I've lost a lot men for a lot of reasons, but this is the first time I've lost one to the French army." He asked me to send him some copy when I got to Algeria. I said that would be frowned on by the authorities. "We won't use your name," he said. "We'll use *Pierre d'Alzon*. He was the founder of the Assumptionists."*

---

*Emmanuel-Marie-Joseph-Maurice Daude d'Alzon (1810–1880) founded the Order of Augustinians of the Assumption (or Assumptionists) in 1864. At the Vatican Council of 1869–1870, d'Alzon drafted the definition of papal infallibility. Where Murphy got the Pierre from I don't know.

Les Classes

On september 3, 1955, at the train station in Vernon, a quaint town of thatch-roofed houses with apparent beams, trucks were waiting for the 100-odd recruits assembled on the platform. On the way to the barracks, I listened to urgent discussions on ways to flunk the physical.

"If you eat a can of sardines in hot oil," said one of the conscripts, "you'll look like you have jaundice."

"Or wrap your hand in a towel and bang it with a hammer. You'll break a finger or two," another said.

"I've got a chronic liver problem," said a third. "I think it's hereditary. I wonder if they'll reject me if it's hereditary."

The conscripts were not showing a great deal of enthusiasm for what lay ahead.

We arrived in front of a massive arched pig-iron gate that seemed built to keep the inmates from escaping. Inside there was a courtyard with paving stones as big as an officer's head. All over France were scattered antiquated barracks such as this one, built during wars of centuries past, and seeming to go back as far as the Hundred Years' War. The courtyard smelled of cold coffee and urine. We were led in single file into a low hangar where men in white smocks were lined up behind desks.

"All right, everybody," a topkick shouted, "down to your underwear." As our names were called out, we stood in front of the white smock who ran the x-ray machine and asked us to cough. Then on to another white smock in front of an eye chart, a third standing in front of a scale, and a fourth who stamped your file.

One fellow was limping. A white smock asked, "So you limp, do you?"

"Only when I walk, sir," he replied. "I brought my medical records. I brought photographs. I was born this way." The white smock stamped his file "Good for the Armed Services."

The men waiting in line were chattering. "I'm going to tell them that even with glasses I can't read the eye chart."

"You must be dreaming. My cousin's a hunchback, but they took him."

"How did he carry his knapsack?"

"On his chest."

"Did you see the one with one leg shorter than the other?"

"They'll put him in the infantry."

"And the midget?"

"They'll send him to officer's school."

"I had a student deferment, but they canceled it. And just before exams."

"What, you don't want to give your life for your country?"

"Shit, no."

"I'm engaged. What is my fiancée going to do without me?"

"Don't worry. If she's pretty, she won't be lonely."

When my turn came, the white smock said, "You can see, you can hear, get the hell out," and stamped my file "Good for the Armed Services."

We moved on to another hangar where we stood in line for uniforms. With the ill-fitting uniform came a slip of paper with a barracks number: room 21, staircase 5, building C. As I was leaving the hangar, a topkick shouted: "Can anyone here speak English?" I raised my hand.

"Then take this broom and sweep the yard."

It was a useful lesson: Never volunteer.

An hour later, I returned the broom to the sergeant, who had my file on his desk, where it said I'd gone to college in the United States. "So you're the intellectual with the little pink ass," he said. He took a rubber stamp from the drawer and stamped my file ANALPHABETE ("illiterate") in big block letters.

In the barracks, about 80 metal beds with thin mattresses rolled up at one end were lined up. I picked one out and threw my gear on it and sat down, thinking, I could be in Worcester covering the flood in a canoe. I noticed a sandy-haired, round-faced, pug-nosed recruit who was smiling at me. "I was going to raise my hand," he said in English, "but you beat me to it."

It turned out that I was not the only conscript who had arrived at Vernon from America. The other one was Alain Seznec, the son of a professor of French literature at Harvard. While studying at the Sorbonne in 1950, he had married an American girl, Janet, and together they returned to Cambridge, where by 1955 they had two children and he was an assistant professor.

"When I got my conscription notice," he said. "I went to the French consulate in Boston, and they told me I'd only have to serve twelve months. They said I'd be an officer in four weeks and I could live with my wife and children."

"I went to the consulate too," I said. "I didn't have the money for a plane ticket. They told me my travel expenses would be reimbursed upon arrival. What crap! They don't want to be bothered with anything that would interfere with their three-hour lunches. We'll be lucky if we get out of here in eighteen months."

"The funny thing is," Seznec said, "that Janet and I spent our honeymoon in Vernon, and now my wife and kids are in Paris and I can't go and see them."

"Well, we'll be here for three months of basic training," I said.

"The worst thing is the monotony. Life becomes a series of reflexes. Salute, present arms, attention, at rest, heads right, heads left."

"The usual values are turned inside out," Seznec said, as he made his bed. "Shining your boots is more important than the complete works of Descartes."

"So now we're in the *intendance*," I said, "whatever that is."

"It's the quartermaster corp. It's where they put all the misfits. You know what de Gaulle said: "The *intendance* will follow.""

Someone yelled, *"Fixe!"* And we all stood at attention. A pudgy captain strode in, wearing his kepi. "I'd like to welcome you to the regiment," he said. "You have been assigned to a building in good condition. Make sure it stays that way. When my sergeant comes by in the morning, I want to see your beds properly made and your gear stored away. I want the johns always clean, not a sheet of toilet paper on the floor. And now, in formation in the courtyard, on the double. Do you think you're at the beach?"

And so it went, that robotlike schedule of marches, gymnastics, target practice, and drills. As sensible Seznec advised, "it's something you get through. Just do what everyone else is doing."

At target practice, we learned to take apart and put together machine guns blindfolded. There was always someone hovering over you, barking orders: "Flat on your stomach! Lower your sight! You're firing above the target! Spread your legs more, so that your rifle forms a forty-five-degree angle with the axis of your body. The stock hard against the hollow of your shoulder. Your cheek hard against it to muffle the recoil. Exhale normally and then hold your breath. At my command . . . fire! Lift the bolt, eject the cartridge, and move toward the target."

This particular gunnery instructor once made an observation that stuck with me. "Where," he asked, "does the bullet go when it leaves the barrel of the rifle?" The answer was: "Into the domain of ballistics."

And we, the conscripts, seemed to be in the domain of some unfathomable buffoonery. Our regiment was made up partly of university graduates who'd come to the end of their deferments, who played bridge and discussed Sartre, and partly of younger men with a sixth-grade education at best, who played *belote* (a Spit-like card game) and talked of nooky. One of them, a farm boy who could barely read or write, asked me to help him with a letter to his girlfriend, to tell her he was coming home on leave. He began to dictate: "Prepare your ass," he said. "My cock is arriving."

"Are you sure that's the way you want to put it?" I asked.

He said that was what she wanted to hear.

Seznec had struck up a friendship with a hoodlum from Belleville, a working-class section of Paris, who acted as his bodyguard. When the sergeant shook him awake at reveille, shouting, "Wake up, you nun's fart," his new friend said, "Don't touch Seznec or you'll deal with me."

In October, our general routine was interrupted by the news that the quartermaster-general was coming to review the regiment. I had never seen the officers so agitated. They knew that their promotions hung in the balance. We were all put to work cleaning up the barracks, washing the tile floors, painting cracked walls, scrubbing the johns. In the courtyard, they planted a flowerbed, and in the kitchen, the big copper pots shone.

On the appointed day, the entire regiment stood in formation on three sides of the courtyard, expecting the arrival of the general, who kept us waiting for more than an hour. Punctuality, like everything else, was a matter of rank. Finally he arrived, a thin, long-nosed man with close-set eyes, wearing his braided kepi and his decorations on his chest.

The captain shouted, "Present arms!" which we did, and the general filed past the rows of soldiers, asking each one his name and civil status. Seznec, who was standing next to me, said, "Married, two children, my general." I said, "Bachelor, my general." The spindly little fellow on the other side of me, no more than five feet tall, shouted out: *"En concubinage, mon général."* To each conscript the general said the same thing: "Very good. Continue." I should have realized that *concubinage* (having a common-law wife) was a legal status in France, but I couldn't help stifling a laugh, and the general gave me a dirty look.

After reviewing the troops, the general spoke. "Many of you," he said, "will be called upon to protect our compatriots in Algeria. Some of you will advance to higher rank. Never forget that a good private makes a good officer and a good officer knows he was once a good private."

In November, as our days in Vernon were winding down, we heard that we would all be sent to Algeria; 1956 was going to be the year of the big buildup. We were alarmed to learn that even those who had completed their military service a year or two before were being called up again. Stories appeared in the newspapers about these *rappelés*, as the callbacks were known, who refused to board trains and lay across the tracks. In Rouen on October 7, the *rappelés* refused to leave the barracks and had to be forced at gunpoint into the trucks. The *rappelés* felt that they had done their time and shouldn't have to leave their wives and jobs for a war they didn't believe in. Those who refused to board the train were taken by truck to Marseilles, where the boats left for Algeria. In another incident, near Bordeaux, the men of the 401st Anti-Aircraft Regiment, who were being kept "under the flag" an extra nine months, were sent on a training operation on the beach, where they took off their clothes and went swimming. Pamphlets began to appear in barracks saying: "We who have lived under a foreign occupation learned to hate the occupiers. We are not cowards or defeatists, but we refuse to fire on our Arab brothers, many of whom served in the French army in World War Two."

In Vernon, the conversations turned to how to avoid being sent to Algeria. "It's simple," Seznec said. "All you have to do is go to the École de Caporal in Metz. Once you're a corporal, you apply for École de Sergent in Versailles. And when you become a sergeant, you apply for the EOR [École d'Officiers de Réserve]; and that takes five months. By the time you're an officer, you've served most of your time."

"You don't have to worry," I said. "You've got two children."

"Maybe so," he said, "but they keep changing the rules. Look at the *rappelés*. By the middle of next year, they want to have half a million men in Algeria. I'm not taking any chances. I'm going to Metz."

Another fellow I'd gotten to know, Jean Aslanian, was an Armenian who'd been a tool-and-die worker at the Renault plant in Paris. He had thick black hair and a bushy mustache, and he seemed to get along with everyone. "I don't mind the army," he said. "In a way it agrees with me. I like the order and the discipline. So I make my bed, I salute the officers, I peel the potatoes, and on Sundays I go dancing in town. They say girls like men in uniform, but I've never had any luck."

When I asked him what his plans were, he said, "I don't want to go to Metz. I'd rather remain a private. I don't want to lose my pals, and I don't like to order people around. It changes you to wear stripes."

But when he thought about it some more, he realized that he had a choice between Algeria and Metz, and he chose the latter. In December, in the dead of one of the worst winters on record, all those who had applied to be corporals left for Metz, a city in northeastern France on the Moselle River, near the German border, and the scene of many battles in three wars with the Huns. We left for Metz in groups of 12, so as not to create bottlenecks upon arrival, traveling third class on the train for the five-hour trip. My dirty dozen included Seznec and Aslanian, who climbed into an overhead luggage rack to stretch out. "I used to do this when I had a girlfriend in Lyon," he said. "If you don't lie just right, the metal divider cuts into your ribs."

If the Vernon barracks were nineteenth-century, the Metz barracks were medieval, surrounded by a 20-foot-high wall, and above the wall, rolls of barbed wire. In the courtyard men were marching in rows of six with rifles on their shoulders, as a corporal yelled, "Hup hup, one two." We stood under a veranda shivering in the cold, hopping from one foot to the other and slapping our hands, but there was not an officer in sight. The place seemed to be run by corporals and sergeants.

"If Vernon was a prison, this is an asylum," Seznec said. Finally a sergeant came toward us. He seemed to have trouble walking, as if his shoes pinched his feet. He was short and round and red-faced, with a head too big for his body and the long, crooked yellow teeth of an old horse.

"Where did this bunch of shit-heads come from," he said to no one in particular. "What are you, in transit?" Seznec explained that we'd come from Vernon to be trained as corporals.

"I don't know what to do with you," the sergeant said. "You were supposed to be here on the fourth."

"Hey," Aslanian said, "if you don't want us, we'll go home."

"Oh, a comedian," the sergeant said. "I've already found a job for you. You can clean the johns with a toothbrush."

"We were five hours on the train," Aslanian said. "When do we eat?"

"You think we're going to feed you?" the sergeant said. "Now shut your filthy mouth and follow me." He led us into a room where a corporal sat with his feet on the desk reading *Tintin at the Beach*. He interrupted his reading to unlock a cupboard of field rations. "Hey, you shit-eaters, you didn't salute, so you're not getting any." I thought to myself, Why should I salute a fucking corporal when I would soon become an officer?

When we had eaten our rations, the sergeant took us to get blankets and winter coats. "I'd forgotten these guys," he told the corporal on duty. "Bring me the files." He sat at the table with the stack of files on it and examined them while coughing and burping and scratching his bald spot. "Looks like we lost one," he said. "Must be the one who was run over by a truck." He assigned us to companies in different barracks, to break up those who seemed to be pals, and said: "Now get out of here, assholes. How can I run a training camp when I'm being constantly interrupted?"

In Metz, I experienced the French propensity for living in the past. In 1940, Metz had been on the Maginot Line. Fifteen years later, you could still get arrested for taking snapshots of the city. The army was always one or two wars behind. Why did we have to learn to use gas masks, as if the Algerian rebels were going to fire mustard gas at us?

"I have a small head," Seznec said. "I can't keep mine on."

"You can use it to scare your kids," I said.

The first month, we were restricted to quarters. Both Seznec and Aslanian seemed dejected. "Vernon was a piece of cake compared to this," Aslanian said. "I need to find a whore and get laid." But the one time he bribed a sentry to slip out for an hour, it was too cold even for whores.

My God, it was cold, and it snowed all the time. If you did two hours of guard duty at night, you froze. In the unheated classrooms, we sat in our overcoats and couldn't take notes—the ink in our Bic pens froze. In the dorms, we were ten to a room with a puny coal stove that we took turns stoking. One morning I ran into Seznec in the courtyard, filling his helmet with snow. "The pipes in our building froze," he said. "The only way I can shave is by melting snow over the stove."

In Vernon Seznec had been the model soldier. Now, holding his snow-packed helmet, he cursed the army. "The lunatics are running the asylum," he said. "These corporals and sergeants don't want to instruct, they want to humiliate. They hate our guts because we'll soon be out of here, but they're stuck here." Each morning there was a room inspection, and the men stood at attention while a noncom inspected their beds, clothing, and weapons. The noncom who inspected Seznec's room had fastened on him. His bed sheet was not tight enough, there was a scuff mark on his boots. "It's completely arbitrary," Seznec said.

He had just found out that his wife, Janet, had an abdominal problem that would require surgery, and he wanted to be by her side in Paris. He was planning to ask for compassionate leave. But that morning at the inspection, his nemesis found a speck on his rifle and placed him under arrest with the citation "Neglects the care of his weapon, compromises the progress of the instruction." With the citation came four days of prison.

Seznec found an officer to whom he felt he could appeal. But the officer could not grant leave, since he'd been put under arrest. He did, however, reduce the sentence to four days of guard duty.

Seznec was beside himself. "My wife could die under the knife, and I won't be there with her," he said. "Up until now I've gone along. I'm no lefty. France has been in Algeria since 1830; I thought it was worth keeping. I was reconciled to going. But now I'll do everything I can not to go. I hate this fucking army, its sadism mixed with cretinism."

As it turned out, Janet had her operation and did fine. Seznec was on guard duty at the entrance of the barracks when a pregnant woman came by and decided to give birth on the sidewalk. Seznec brought her inside the guard post, and since there was no doctor around, he helped in the delivery.

I had my own problem. At morning assembly, my platoon was under the command of the red-faced sergeant we had met on the first day whose name was Bouvard. Each morning he took the roll call, and we replied, "Present." One morning when he got to my name, he repeated it several times, insisting on the particle, *de*, which was supposed to be the mark of nobility. "De Gramont, de Gramont," he said, then added, "*de Gramont de mes deux couilles*" ("de Gramont of my two balls"). During the drill, he was on my case: "So you're the only one who's marching in step, turnip head?" At the obstacle course, he was on my case: "Move, you imbecile! Push your grease! Do you think you're home in the castle?"

I sat at the dining hall table with Aslanian and Seznec, my chin in my hands, wondering what to do.

"Bouvard is a dog," Aslanian said, his mouth full of boudin (blood sausage). "When he pisses, he lifts his leg."

"I can understand that he has every reason to dislike me," I said. "He never went beyond the sixth grade, and he'll be a sergeant for the rest of his life. So because he outranks me, he's going to make me sweat blood. That doesn't mean I have to take it."

"Be patient," Seznec said. "As Pablo said in *For Whom the Bell Tolls*: 'I do not provoke.'"

"Why can't you pretend to be an idiot like the rest of us," Aslanian said.

The next morning at roll call, when Bouvard came to my name, his face was about an inch from my chest, and it was so cold that puffs of white smoke were blowing through his nostrils, like a Labrador's. *"De Gramont de mes deux couilles,"* he snorted.

I replied, *"Présent, Bouvard de merde"* ("Bouvard of shit").

Bouvard dropped the roll-call list on the ground and said, "Pick it up."

"Pick it up yourself," I said.

"Eight days of prison for insulting a noncommissioned officer and refusing to obey an order," Bouvard said.

The prison was one long room with, instead of a floor, a wooden platform on an incline so you couldn't sleep lying flat. I slept rolled up in a blanket with my overcoat on. At one end of the room there was a Turkish toilet, two corrugated porcelain feet with a hole in between, and a sink with frozen pipes. I was the only inmate. My bread-and-water diet was improved, thanks to my friends. Through the six-inch square grill in the prison door, I made a deal with the guard. "Hey, you can have my Troupes" (the 10 packs a month of free cigarettes we got from the army). "My friends will give them to you when they come by." Aslanian pushed some chocolate through the grill and Seznec brought a copy of Simone de Beauvoir's *Les Mandarins*, which he said was "riveting," and a flask of prune brandy—one of the guys in his room came from Alsace and had a steady supply, and it sure helped ward off the chills. When I got out at the end of eight days, I was filthy and unshaven. I looked like one of the hobos who hang around the Paris Halles, picking at the garbage. My main concern was that my "insubordination" would be part of my record, which might affect my admission to officers' school. On the other hand, the army had an urgent need for officers.

THE FIRST week of February 1956, Seznec and I left Metz for sergeant's school in Versailles. But Aslanian decided to remain a corporal and was shipped off to a supply depot in Algeria, where he was put in charge of blankets. He knew how to stay out of trouble. The two months in Versailles were a breeze. As soon as you had your first stripe, things were more relaxed. You were no longer a *bleu*, as raw recruits were called. You got the hang of it. You learned how to get along. The quality of the instructors improved. Every barracks had its personality. Metz had been toxic. Versailles was relatively benign.

Most of us, however, felt a disconnect from the situation we were in. As soldiers we had to follow orders and go where we were sent, but at the same time, we wanted to delay our departure for Algeria as long as possible. Among the conscripts, there was little enthusiasm for the war. Why hang on to a piece of real estate four times the size of France, most of it desert and mountains, where repressive treatment of the native Arabs had led to a rebellion?

In the spring of 1956, when I was still at Versailles, there was a new wave of protests, with the *rappelés* refusing to wear uniforms and pulling emergency switches to stop trains. The *rappelés* of 1956 were up in arms by the thousands, but it did no good—they got their notice and reported to a barracks, and a week later, were in Algeria. By the end of 1956 the buildup reached 400,000 troops. Most of them were assigned to protect *colon* property, to keep the roads and railway lines open, to protect the port facilities and power stations, the telephone and electric lines. About 1 in 10 of those 400,000 was actually in combat. It was no longer a war of professionals but a war of citizen soldiers from the mainland who could be divided into three groups—two fringe minorities resolutely for or against the war, and a vast majority who didn't want to be there but who were ready to carry out orders and get it over with. They did not buy into the myth that they were fighting a war *for* France *in* France but preferred doing their duty to insubordination. Of course, as in any war, a soldier's behavior depended on the situation he was in. A peace-loving slacker could turn into an Arab-hating warrior overnight. A few were so scarred by combat that they killed themselves. Mostly they clamored for *la quille*. A *quille* is a bowling pin, but in military slang it was the day of liberation from service (from the expression *trousser ses quilles*, "to pack up and be off"), ardently longed for, and every day there were cries of "quickly *la quille*" and "*la quille*, dammit." Also heard was *coincer la bulle*, or "squeezing the bubble," which literally meant positioning the bubble on the mortar sight, which was like a level, until it was in the middle, but in slang it meant to take it easy, to goldbrick, to be horizontal. Still another phrase on many lips was *la planque*, which means "a hiding place," but for us it meant a cushy job out of harm's way. One of my cousins had a *planque* in the navy, working at a desk in the admiralty offices in Marseilles. A friend of mine from the Sorbonne days, Jean Legouis, had a *planque* at SHAFE (Supreme Headquarters, Allied Forces in Europe) outside of Paris. He said I should apply for a position as a translator, since I was bilingual in French and English. I applied, and the test was a cinch, but I was passed over. I figured it was because of having done prison time in Metz.

There was nothing left but officers' training, which would keep me out of Algeria for another five months. After Versailles, Seznec and I parted ways. I went to the infantry officers' school in Saint-Maixent, a sleepy little village off the maps and unknown to tourists in central-west France, near Poitiers. Seznec opted for the artillery officers' school near Paris and ended up in a regiment stationed in Germany. As a second lieutenant, he was able to bring his wife and two children with him. By that time Janet was pregnant with their third child, which helped him stay out of Algeria when his regiment was shipped over.

The Saint-Maixent barracks were nothing like the ancient wrecks in Vernon and Metz. The buildings were of recent vintage and the toilets flushed. Saint-Maixent had an Olympic swimming pool, a state-of-the-art gym, and a harrowing obstacle course with rows of barbed wire, horizontal beams over mud, a hedge of upright logs to climb over, and ropes that you had to swing on, Tarzan-like, over a wide ditch studded with sharpened bamboo sticks, a souvenir of the Indochina War. The officers were fit and smart and came from elite regiments such as the paratroopers, with none of the bloated and vehement retreads we'd seen before.

General Faure, the school commander, was himself a blue beret, and in his opening address he told us: "Gentlemen, we are going to do whatever it takes to make officers out of you." There were 300 of us, assigned to barrack rooms of 30 with double-decker bunks. Saint-Maixent was the feeder for infantry regiments all over France and Algeria. We went through grueling 12-hour days, a mix of classes on the Arab mind, which was described as devious and fanatical; obstacle courses, where we crawled through mud under barbed wire as a machine gun fired live ammunition over our heads; and combat exercises. We were sent out in teams of 6 on night missions in the countryside, such as blowing up a bridge. If and when we found it, an instructor was waiting with a stopwatch.

We learned to fire the light weapons that, as officers, we would be handling in Algeria: the old reliable MAT 49 submachine gun, effective at close range; the 15-pound FM (*fusil-mitrailleur*) 24-29, which fired in single shots and bursts. It was reasonably accurate at 50 yards, but you pitied the poor bastard who had to carry it in operations. We learned to bracket rounds on the 60-mm and 81-mm mortars by squeezing the bubble and to zero in on a target.

Saint-Maixent was highly competitive, for at the end of our five months, we were ranked and graded. Each of us had to choose a regiment in order of rank, so that those with the top grades had their pick, while those at the bottom were left with the least desirable regiments. Our instructors hoped to transform us into gung-ho warriors, but it didn't turn out that way. In my barrack room of 30, there was only one fellow who wanted to join a para combat regiment. Jean Berger was a little over five feet tall, but muscular, with big arms and legs, and a thick neck. He had been a militant Communist who mixed it up with the Paris police in the early '50s. To him, the paras were like the party, a band of brothers with camaraderie between officers and men, one for all and all for one. He wanted to jump; he loved *baroud* (combat). He wasn't at all a boastful tough-guy type; he was thoughtful and mild-mannered, but he had a passion for action.

My own strategy was to try and rank high enough to be able to pick a regiment still stationed in France. This was no guarantee, since any regiment, and particularly infantry regiments, could swiftly be transferred to Algeria. I liked the physical stuff, the obstacle course and the combat training, but some of the classes made me laugh. Since I was too stupid to keep my mouth shut, I got a reputation as a *rouspéteur* (griper).

On graduation day at the end of August, we were given a yearbook with several blank pages where the men in your barracks wrote what they thought of you. I looked at the program recently and reread the judgment of my peers. I was of course known as "the American" at a time when the graffiti on Paris walls often said "U.S. Go Home." So one comment said, "Don't say U.S. Go Home, for you would miss knowing a good-hearted fellow, in spite of his often difficult personality."

Other comments were:

"We often saw him go to war against everything and nothing."

"I hope he will maintain the agreeable aspects of Cervantes' hero, which bought him the friendship of everyone."

"An enemy of the banal and commonplace, which earned him the enmity of mediocrities."

"His tongue was the best and the worst, according to whether the words came from his heart or his head."

"Above all, he loved his bed. We taught him to squeeze the bubble, and he taught us *le 'relax.'*"

My favorite comment was: "He wasn't the best, and he wasn't the worst, but he was the tallest." That was exactly where I wanted to be, in the middle.

The traditional graduation ceremony in the only lecture room with rising bleachers, where all 300 of us could fit, turned out to be a suspenseful drama. Each of us had a list of the available regiments, about 40 of which were in France, a few in Germany, and the rest in Algeria, and a list of our ranks. A tall, athletic para colonel named Murat, a veteran of Indochina and Algeria, clad in the combat uniform known as the *tenue léopard* (camouflage pattern), strode on the stage to the lectern and told us that when he called out a name, that person should stand at attention and shout out what regiment he had picked, while the rest of us scratched it off our list.

He called out the names in order of rank, starting with the best and the brightest. They rose and shouted out regiments in Paris, in

Lyon, in Bordeaux. It was obvious that our months of competitive striving to attain a high rank had everything to do with staying out of Algeria and nothing to do with wanting to fight the war. In the first 20, only my dorm mate Berger opted for a para regiment located in the Aurès Mountains of eastern Algeria, a zone of heavy combat.

I could actually see Colonel Murat getting red in the face under his blue beret. Finally he exploded. "You're all shit-heads. France is completely corrupt! You'll see what happens to this government of cowards—we don't even have to take power, we only have to pick it up." I never forgot those words: *"Le pouvoir n'est pas à prendre, il est à ramasser,"* predicting a military coup d'état, which in fact took place in May 1958, bringing General de Gaulle to power.

The colonel's outburst did not change matters. The men continued to pick regiments outside of Algeria until there were no more. I was ranked eighty-second out of 300, and by the time my turn came, the choices were limited. I chose a regiment stationed about 50 miles south of Algiers, the 1st Regiment of the Colonial Infantry. I was intrigued by this corps, which recruited its troops from France's remaining colonies, mainly from Senegal in West Africa, though the noncoms and officers were mostly French. The Coloniale had a legendary reputation for being full of surprises. I had the feeling it would be less regimented, less by the book, perhaps a bit exotic, a renegade among regiments, as in one of their songs: *"Et j'ai fumé du kif sur les pitons du Rif, O Sarazine aronde"* ("And I smoked hash on the peaks of the Rif mountains, Oh swallowlike Saracen maiden").

A few days later, wearing the single silver bar of a second lieutenant on my epaulets and the forage cap of the *colo* with a tiny anchor sewn to the hem, I was on the train to Marseilles, where the troop ship would take me to Algeria. In Marseilles, however, the longshoremen were on strike, refusing to load Algeria-bound ships in protest of the war. I had to go down the coast to the smaller harbor of Fréjus and spend the night in filthy barracks with lice in the mattresses and rats running through the halls. On the bunk next to mine, another departing conscript said: "I'm already sick of Algeria, enormously."

At dawn, in single file, the men went up the gangplank of the

Ville d'Alger, weighed down by their *barda* (gear), and it was obvious from the smell that the old tub had brought back from Algeria a cargo of sheep.

"Hey, storm coming up," one man said.

"What are you, a fucking barometer?" the one behind him snarled. The well-known good humor of the French soldier was lacking in this crowd.

On deck, a naval officer said: "Install yourselves in the *transats* [folding chairs], if you can find one, with helmets between your legs, so you can throw up if you're seasick."

In the sky, dark clouds clustered, and on the horizon, I saw the curve of the roiled sea. Then, the engine noises, waves breaking against the keel, and we were off. I watched the coastline disappear through the morning haze.

When we got to the open sea, all along the deck heads leaned over the railing. If they threw up against the wind, the vomit flew back into their faces. The naval officer whose order had been ignored said: "You could get sick just watching these guys."

It wasn't quite up to the standard of ocean liners, I reflected, with bow-tied stewards in white jackets offering bouillon, as in the Cunard line poster: "Getting there is half the fun." Tired of the smell of vomit, I climbed a ladder to a higher deck where an army jeep was tied down. Its seats were dry and quite comfortable. I struck up a conversation with a crew member who was checking the lifeboats. He said he'd been to a brothel on his last night in harbor. "I had a black girl. They're just like the others, pink on the inside."

It took two days to reach Algiers, with the men bitching that they had to sleep in the hold, with its sheep stink, and that they were being treated no better than sheep. The toilets were backed up, and when the ship rolled, the urine on the floor rippled and splashed.

We steamed into the Bay of Algiers on a sunny morning. In the distance, the white city rose steeply from the sea, and the light streamed in rivulets through the palm trees down the façades of the buildings. On the right, a stand of Aleppo pines gave off a faint smell of resin. Under a dusty blue sky, the city in early September was a sponge exhaling humidity. A long line of children in rags begged for coins. My first impression was the difference between the beauty of the landscape and the squalor of the Arabs. So this was France?

A jeep from my regiment was waiting for me, driven by a non-com who said: "Now you're in the *colo*. Be proud."

In the Bled

I HAD ONLY A glimpse of Algiers before we drove south into the *bled* (countryside), past the low coastal hills that protect the rich wheat fields of the Mitidja plain from the sea winds. Algeria's landscape, like its people, went to extremes, from stony mountains to idle desert, divided by narrow bands of arable land, while along the thousand-mile coastline with its profusion of beaches, the Mediterranean acted out its moods.

My own mood mingled dismay with curiosity. I was now headed for combat in a war I had no stomach for. Clausewitz wrote that to win a war, you must hate your enemy. I found it difficult to hate an enemy who had as much right to independence as the Americans when they threw out the British.

The village of Champlain, where my regiment was stationed, lay in wooded hills 50 miles south of Algiers. To get there, we passed through Médéa, a long-time garrison town, with a square that featured the usual obelisk honoring the dead of Algerian campaigns past. My driver, Sergeant Lavigne, suggested we stop for a drink. Stocky and sandy-haired, he looked a little like the corporal who had been on my case in Metz. There I had been punished with jail time; here they had to salute me.

We ordered beers at an outdoor café on the square, which had a mixed clientele of *spahis* (cavalry in Turkish-like uniforms) who were barracked there, *colon* families drinking Orangina, and robed and turbaned Arabs sipping mint tea. Arab children came up selling oranges and little cakes, but Lavigne waved them away. He was a veteran of Indochina and called all natives "Viets." "The same ones who sell you oranges with a friendly smile are out to kill you," he said. "Once I was driving an *auto-mitrailleuse*" (a jeep with a machine gun mounted in back), "and two *gamins* jumped in the back to dismantle the machine gun, but the jeep behind mine shot them. One of them was the baker's helper who sold us bread every day."

From Médéa, we headed south through well-tended orchards and vineyards. Every few miles there appeared a pretty village with red-tiled roofs and a church steeple. It did seem like the south of France, except that most of the women carrying shopping baskets were veiled. Soon we reached the Chiffa Gorges, over a picturesque one-lane blacktop flanked by the steep sides of the ravine. Below us the waters of torrential rapids roared. The ravine, six miles long, was famous for the tribe of monkeys that nested in small caves and shrieked at tourists, when there were tourists. Lavigne stepped on the gas. "It's not monkeys up there now," he said, "It's *fels*" (*fellaghas*, or rebels).

Champlain was too insignificant to be mentioned in the *Guide Bleu.* At one end of the unpaved main street, a few gnarled olive trees enlivened a drab square, which was overlooked by the town hall and the school, now occupied by the third company of the 1st Regiment of the Colonial Infantry. The post office remained open, mainly to pay out the money orders that Arabs working in France sent home to their families, and there was an Arab-run grocery store and a café. The small church was abandoned, since the *colons* had fled. Behind the ochre cubes where the villagers lived, a tent city for the troops had sprung up.

The third company consisted of four platoons of about 30 men each, armed with no weapons heavier than a mortar, and provided with a few jeeps and trucks for transportation. The men were mostly Senegalese and the noncoms were mostly French, though we did have one from Pondicherry, a French enclave in southern India. The Senegalese had cheerful dispositions and were known as highly disciplined soldiers who stuck to the letter of the law. The oft-told tale has Napoleon crossing a footbridge during the Russian campaign, when he is stopped by a Senegalese sentry who refuses to let him pass, since he doesn't know the password. "But I am the emperor," Napoleon says. The Senegalese utters the immortal words, *"Tu ne passeras pas,"* using the familiar *tu* in addressing the commander-in-chief.

Our Senegalese in the third company were Moslems, and I wondered why they had no objections to fighting Algerian rebels, also Moslems. It was explained to me that black Africans detested the Arabs, who had been slavers. As fighters, the Senegalese had one idiosyncrasy, which was cutting off the ears of the enemy killed. Their faces were etched with tribal scars, which gave them a fierce expression. They wore amulets called gris-gris around their necks, and they had perfect white teeth, maybe from the twigs they chewed.

The colonial infantry was known as *l'arme poubelle* ("the garbage pail corps"), attracting misfits and drunks, officers with no hopes of promotion, and noncoms with a stain on their blotter. Our company was commanded by a major and his chief of staff, a captain, while the platoons were led by second lieutenants like me.

Upon arriving, I was shown to my pup tent, which was furnished with a metal bed, a table, and a chair. We did our washing in the school building, where the major and the captain resided and had their offices. I went over to report to Captain Henri de Lastours, the chief of staff, whose office was decorated with a portrait of World War I hero Marshal Foch, and the stuffed heads of an antelope and a boar.

What first struck me about Lastours* was that he wore a monocle, which seemed out of place in the *bled*. On his desk lay an ivory-headed stick and a pack of Players, one of which he was smoking in

---

*I have followed French army usage, which is to drop the particle when mentioning the name.

an ivory holder. Other officers, disdaining the Troupes, which tasted like sawdust mixed with horse manure, smoked Gauloises or Gitanes.

Lastours rose to greet me. He was about five foot seven and wiry. The parchmentlike skin of his face and his creased brow were animated by blue eyes so narrow that they reminded me of slits in a medieval helmet. Over thin lips and a mustache that ended in points, there protruded a nose with a knob on it. His graying hair was cut short enough to reveal a tonsurelike bald spot, which gave him a monkish air, but not of a monk from one of the contemplative orders, for he conveyed an impression of restless energy, that of a man waiting for a train that was always late.

As I stood at attention before him, he stared at me with those strange narrow eyes and said, "At ease. De Gramont, de Gramont— one *m* or two?"

"One *m*," I said. "The two-*m* Grammonts are arrivistes who took the name quite recently."

"I knew a duc de Gramont, Armand, who invented a bomb sight," Lastours said.

"He's my uncle," I said.

"His brother, Louis-René, always shook hands with his left hand."

"He caught some shrapnel at Verdun," I said, "and lost the use of his right hand."

"Well, here in the *premier* RIC [our regiment]," Lastours said, "we have mostly troops from Senegal, good boys, if they like their officer."

I realized that since the captain knew members of my family, I was in what the French call *pays de connaissance*, that tiny principality where everyone knows everyone else. So I said: "I hope I can confide in you, Captain. Since childhood, I have always disliked giving orders. I shy away from any relationship in which one human being constrains another."

"Then why did you go to officers' school?" Lastours asked, furrowing his narrow brow.

"To avoid being sent to Algeria," I said.

Lastours jumped out of his chair, and his monocle fell out of his eye and hung by its silk cord. "And you come from a family that gave France two marshals!" he boomed. "A fine example you are! Don't you see that the job of an officer is to give orders? What if the imperative mood was removed from our grammar? Sometimes it is necessary to say, *'Feu à volonté!'* ['Fire at will!']."

"And some people still believe in the divine right of kings," I replied, realizing that I was overstepping my limits in speaking to a superior officer. At the same time, I felt that he was humoring me.

"Don't be absurd," he barked. "That has nothing to do with it. We have a mission. We must complete it. I need people I can count on."

"For some reason," I said, "I feel I can speak to you frankly. I probably should have asked to be an ambulance driver or a stretcher-bearer, something like that."

"Good God," he exclaimed. "We don't have stretcher-bearers in this regiment." He paused and then went on. "Well, since I know your uncle, I see we have an opening for a transportation officer. You'll only have to give orders to trucks and jeeps."

I thanked him and saluted, prior to making my exit, but he stopped me. "Wait a minute," he said. "Since you spoke to me frankly, I will speak to you frankly. You are wondering why I, a graduate of Saumur [the elite cavalry school], am still a captain at the age of forty-eight, stuck in a hole like this. In 1942, I was a young captain in Syria when the Gaullists came in. I refused to fight them and I refused to join them, so I asked to be placed on the inactive list. I returned to my wife and children and my property in the Gironde. But by 1950, I was so bored that I asked to be reinstated, at the same rank, knowing I would never be promoted."

Despite his affectations, his monocle, his walking stick, and his brusque manner, Lastours had the simplicity of the wellborn. He preferred garrison life to his vineyard in the Gironde, which provided 100 cases of Saint-Émilion a year, and to his wife, a pious Catholic devoted to good works. His passion was the hunt. "The woods around here are teeming with partridge and rabbit," he said, "but there is an appalling parallelism in my lack of success with animal and human game.

"Now," said Lastours, "let me take you to meet the major. Don't be surprised by anything he says. His favorite saying is 'We are all in the same boat and we must row together or we will go around in circles.' "

Major Fourcade was all puffy dewlaps and no neck. On his cheeks, tiny red rivulets traced their deltas, and his hands were covered with liver spots. A Gauloise hung from the corner of his mouth, and his glass eye was noticeable because the other eye was bloodshot. He was an old soldier who belonged in another war, reminding me of one of Napoléon's paunchy generals, who had to be pulled in carriages because they could no longer ride a horse.

"Ah, our new transportation officer," said the major, after Lastours had introduced me. "The last one knew nothing about vehicles, wasn't capable of reading a map, on his cot most of the time with his ear glued to his transistor. He was a partisan of the least effort."

"I don't have a transistor," I said.

"And remember," the major said, wagging an index finger, "you don't command because of your stripe; you command because of your presence, even in your bathing suit. At the same time, I never forget that a conscript army is a republican army, a reflection of the civilian society."

"There may not be the same level of competence in a conscript army," I said, while thinking, Level of enthusiasm.

"Very true, very true," said the major, and, turning to Lastours, he added, "This young man may not have invented the two-seated chamberpot, but he's far from stupid."

"As for me," he went on, putting out his cigarette against a pock-marked drawer of his desk, "I fought in 1940. I was wounded." He pointed to his glass eye. "I fought in Indochina. I was wounded. I hope this time not to be wounded. But I confess that I don't understand this war at all. It's the politics of the dead dog bobbing on the water, as General Navarre used to say. We'll win battle after battle until we lose the war."

"This is a dirty war," Lastours interjected, "but we'll fight it and win it to preserve the idea of France."

"If you say so, my dear captain," said Fourcade, lighting up another Gauloise. "You know, when I was young, I was a steeplechase rider. I had a good horse who knew how to take the obstacles. I let him think he was running the race. It's the same thing here. We have to convince these people that they should help us by letting them think it's their decision. We don't want them all hating us. We have to change our habits. When you are out on patrol, talk to the villagers, shake hands with them. We must create a climate of trust, reassure people. The trick is to keep repeating it like an advertising slogan. You know, those billboards in the Paris metro showing the four Mariannes with their Phrygian bonnets, and the slogan 'The Republics pass, but Ripolin paint remains.' "

"And what's out slogan?" I asked.

"Army equals peace equals prosperity," the major said.

I could see that Lastours was covering his lower lip with his mustache to suppress a smile, and I thought, If only we were launching a brand of paint.

"All right," the major said. "I'm not a mind-reader, but I can see what you're thinking. I'm sure they gave me this godforsaken company because no one wanted it. I'm a fifty-five-year-old major, and in five years I can retire. But I still know how to draft victory reports." Fourcade gazed off into the distance. This was the French officer's atavistic facial expression, a faraway gaze known as "looking at the blue line of the Vosges," where the Germans had repeatedly invaded.

Once we were in the courtyard, Lastours said: "That's his standard disquisition to every arriving officer."

I spent an hour walking around Champlain. I had to get used to men saluting me, which I found faintly embarrassing. I still felt out of place in uniform. In a vacant lot I found a modest open market offering old clothes, dates and oranges, kohl for women's eyes, and various other unnamed potions. A barber and tooth-puller stood behind his chair, next to which lay a cotton cloth where he displayed the rotten teeth he'd pulled.

That evening I attended my first meal in the officers' mess, or *popote*, in the lobby of the *mairie* (town hall). One wall was covered with a fresco often seen in provincial *mairies*, representing a scene from the war of 1870, a desperate band of French soldiers surrounded by Germans, called *La Dernière Cartouche* (the last cartridge), exalting heroism in hopeless situations. On the right there was a makeshift bar, a long table bearing an assortment of aperitifs, wines, and cognacs. About a dozen junior officers sat at square tables, which between meals were used for playing cards and chess.

When I walked in, they all stood up and began to sing the traditional song of welcome, *"Il Est Cocu le Chef de Gare"* ("the stationmaster is a cuckold"). Then it was my turn to offer a round of drinks and propose a toast. Raising my glass of Pernod, I said, "Being an imbecile, I am happy to find myself among equals." They applauded and rousingly sang another classic: *"Et on s'en fout, d'attraper la vérole, et on s'en fout, pourvu qu'on tire un coup"* ("And we don't give a fuck if we catch the clap, as long as we get our rocks off").

I heard a booming voice call, "Hey, *marsouin*, over here. Sit down." (*Marsouin*, or porpoise, was the nickname for men of the *Coloniale*). The voice came from a burly lieutenant with thick blond brushed-back hair, a handlebar mustache, heavy-lidded blue eyes, and a face as round and rosy as a Bayonne ham. His name was Boris Dourakine. His parents had fled Russia during the 1920 famine and settled in Paris. Sitting with him was Lucien Cossard, smaller and sparer, long-faced, sallow-skinned, with a high forehead and chestnut hair parted in the middle.

Crushing my hand with his great paw, Dourakine said, "I've heard about you. You're an exile like me. I had to leave Russia, you went to America. We are both air plants, rootless." Actually, as I learned, he had been born in Paris in 1925, five years after his parents' departure. His father, once an important czarist bureaucrat, had started out as a taxi driver and saved enough money to move to the rue Daru, the heart of the Russian colony, where he opened a shop selling specialties such as blinis and borscht. They lived above the shop.

"Can you imagine me, Boris, a shopkeeper?" he asked. "And Paris, that city of *gagne-petits* [nickel-and-dimers]? Not for me. I have the steppes in my blood."

"And Pernod in your veins," the morose Cossard interjected.

"Better than the Vichy water in yours," Doukarine responded.

At the age of 25 he had enlisted and been sent to Indochina. "Ah, Saigon," he recalled as he wiped his mouth, "from the terrace of the Pagoda, rue Catinat, you saw the prettiest girls in Cochin China wiggle their asses as they strolled down to the river in their high heels. And Cholon, with its taxi-girls and whores at three piasters, and the Arc-en-ciel, with the best girls of all, from Shanghai. Their slit dresses revealed golden thighs and small breasts like ripe apricots. I was so much bigger I fucked them standing on the floor with the girl standing on the bed."

"And when you fell on her she died from the smell," Cossard said.

"Don't confuse me with your donkey," Dourakine bellowed.

When I mentioned that I had met the major, Dourakine slammed his fist on the table and said, "I hate all hierarchies."

"Then what are you doing in the army?" Cossard asked.

"I don't want a life of routine with wife and kids," Dourakine said. "I want surprises."

"Routine is just what I want," Cossard said. "I've got two weeks left. Do you think I want to get killed in my last days of service?" Cossard taught math in a lycée, and his wife and four-year-old son were waiting for him in Lyon.

"Well," I said, "the major told me to be good to the villagers and create a climate of trust."

Dourakine snorted and emptied his glass. "Too many people here talk to no purpose and like to give sermons. I don't want the correct answers of the good student with his hand up. I want to win."

"I don't give a shit about winning," said Cossard, scraping the metal chair he sat on along the tile floor. "I want to go home to my wife and son."

"Ah, you filthy petit bourgeois," Dourakine said, grabbing the nape of his neck. "Let me buy you a Pernod. Lucien is our intelligence officer," he explained, "though we all wonder whether he knows which way is north. As for me, I lead my platoon to glory."

"You just want *bananes* [decorations] on your chest," Cossard said.

"Like Napoleon, I despise those 'scraps of silk,' " Dourakine said.

He saw himself as a leader of men, though he didn't think much of his Senegalese troops. "As far as I'm concerned," he said, "they're good enough to shine my shoes."

"But are you good enough to shine theirs?" Cossard asked.

"Look, I know how to handle them. Last time out, there was one who was running ahead of the others. Let's calm him down, I thought; let's give him the machine gun. With the tripod, it weighs eighty pounds. He wasn't running ahead anymore."

"What about the Algerians." I asked. "After all, it's their country."

"I can't stand the Arabs either," Dourakine said. "They're all jackals, always looking for the how and the why. Christ, they're re-pugnant! When anyone in my platoon fucks up, I tell them, 'That's Arab work.' Anyway, there's only a handful of *fels*. The masses are pro-French."

"I guess that's why we have four hundred thousand men here," I said.

"And my sister's hand in a *zouave*'s pants," he roared. That was his expression for showing extreme disgust.

Dourakine was mercurial, leaping from topic to topic. It was hard to follow his associative process. He said that all the noncoms in his platoon were Indochina hands and then burst out, "I hate the smug-ness of these Indochina hands," even though he was one himself. He needed a little anger-management training. There was always some-thing to hate. At the same time, I found him immensely likable, be-cause he was completely uncensored, while I tried to go along to get along. Perhaps anger was the exile's form of regret, a way of mourn-ing a lost society.

The officers at the *popote* were a hard-drinking bunch. After beer and wine with our chicken and French fries, it was Pernod and co-gnac.

Dourakine and I walked back to our tents, past a grove of eucalyptus trees. He stopped for a moment to watch their branches waving in the night breeze and said, "Don't those branches remind you of a woman's hair when she's taking her bath? Come with me," he said. "I want to show you something." In the corner of his tent there was a locked trunk. He opened it and pulled out a Colt revolver. "She's a beauty, isn't she," he said. He spun the cylinder. "This is the way to find out if you have the *baraka*." *Baraka*, the Arab word for luck, was perhaps the most important word in the platoon leader's vocabulary, for it meant luck in battle.

"I have one cartridge in the chamber. I spin the cylinder. I place the barrel against my temple, and I pull the trigger," he said, suiting action to words. There was a click. "Aha," he said. "I'm still alive. Do you want to try it?"

"Hey," I said, "I'm only the transportation officer. My worry is that a truck may break down."

"My dear Gramont," he said, "life is not worth living if you do not take risks."

It seemed to me there were enough risks in our day-to-day activities without asking for more, but I didn't want to get him excited. In any case, I'd read somewhere that when you spin a cylinder loaded with one cartridge, the weight of the cartridge makes it drop down, away from the barrel.

As I returned to my lumpy metal cot, under a tent lit by an oil lamp, on my first night in Champlain, I had that rare feeling of having found a friend, a feeling of recognition. Although Dourakine had been in the army for six years, his was the exact antithesis of the conventional military mind, expressing the contradictions and excesses of an anarchist. His was a temperament I admired but could not emulate. I didn't want to ruffle any feathers or be singled out. I retained like a mental amulet my mother's words on my first day of school: "And try not to make yourself remarked." It was in a sense a tribute to the French army, known as the great leveler, that someone like Dourakine could not only survive but reach officer rank. Here was an officer who hated authority but led a platoon. He was recklessly brave, not for self-advancement, but out of a deep personal need to express his disregard for all conventions, including the wish to stay alive. He had to be always testing himself, staring at the precipice. He held the military in contempt, but hated the constraints of civilian life even more—*boulot, metro, dodo* (job, subway, sleep)—that wretched triumvirate that turned men into lemmings, as he put it. His sense of the tragic was turned inward and became a line of conduct.

T HE NEXT morning at eight, somewhat hung over, I was alone at the *popote*, drinking bad coffee, when Lastours rapped his stick at the side of my table. I rose to salute him, but he said, *"Repos"* ("At ease").

"There is something I neglected to tell you yesterday," he said. "One of the duties of the transportation officer is to lead all convoys out of Champlain in a jeep. This includes moving troops and supplies and one other matter. Permit me to read you Article 46 of the Colonial Infantry regulations: 'Colonial troops are entitled to have sexual relations once a month in the nearest available military brothel.' "

"I haven't come across one in Champlain," I said, while thinking, Unless it's the company itself, *bordel* being slang for "pandemonium."

"Precisely" the captain said. "The army has traveling brothels, called *bordels militaires de campagne,* or *BMCs.* Usually four whores and a madam who keeps the accounts, under contract to the army. The cost is two francs fifty [50 cents]. But since we are close to the garrison town of Médéa, which has its own brothel, we take one platoon there each week to comply with the regulation. Today is Wednesday, brothel day. You should leave in an hour for Médéa in your jeep with a driver, followed by two trucks with fifteen men in each truck. Here is your *ordre de route.*

"Oh, one other thing," he added. "The officer in charge of a convoy must remain standing in the jeep on distances of less than twenty-five kilometers, which this is."

"I'll find Diallo," I said, while thinking, Another senseless regulation.

My driver, Diallo, was a Senegalese sergeant but not a regular soldier. Tall and athletic, he was the son of a cocoa broker in Dakar, who sent him to study at a commercial college in Paris. Diallo enrolled but rarely attended. He was a talented dancer and found a job at the Folies Bergère, in the corps de ballet. "It was paradise," he said, "getting paid to lift and carry those sumptuous beauties each night, not to mention after the show." But after a year, his student deferment was canceled and he was conscripted. After graduating from sergeant's school, he was sent to Champlain.

As it happened, it was the turn of Dourakine's platoon that morning, but he was not interested in going and left the men in charge of two hard-bitten sergeants, Lavigne and Laroche. Because Diallo was the only Senegalese noncom, they kidded him mercilessly. They called him Banania, after the popular children's drink that ran ads showing a caricatural, thick-lipped black saying, in West African patois: *"Ya bon, Banania."*

"Say, Banania," Lavigne asked Diallo as he herded his men into a truck, "is it true you've got three wives back in Dakar?"

"Banania tells you to go fuck yourself," Diallo said.

Lavigne laughed and asked, "Say, Banania, is it true you've got pink balls?"

"Nah, he's got balls like coconuts," Laroche chimed in. Diallo drove the jeep out of Champlain and headed north on the road to Médéa, followed by the two trucks. I stood in the jeep as I had been told. We passed through the Chiffa Gorges, over that one-lane road flanked by high stone walls. In the middle of the winding, six-mile stretch, shots were fired from above. I sat down, telling Diallo, "I'll be damned if I stand while we're being shot at."

When we reached Médéa, the trucks parked on the main square near the brothel, a nondescript whitewashed house on a side street. The men were led in five at a time. I went in to have the madam sign my *ordre de route* and got a glimpse of five or six opulently large women in loose slips, easily between 250 and 300 pounds. I figured I had a free hour in front of me and I decided to have a beer on the square. I asked Diallo to join me, but he said, "I think I'll join the men." They were lined up by rank, and as sergeant he would have first pick with Lavigne and Laroche.

It was a warm September day, and the blue bowl of the sky cupped the copper sun overhead. I sat at a table, observing the life on the square, Arabs standing in clusters chatting, *fatmas* (women) feeling and smelling the melons in the stands of the open market, shoeshine boys looking at your feet as they moved from table to table. As I sipped my Kronenbourg, I heard my name called. It was a childhood friend I had not seen in years, André Bayens, resplendent in the red cap and cape of the *spahis*, with a first lieutenant's two bars on his epaulets. Our fathers had been posted to the French embassy in Washington before the war. On weekends they took us to the Chevy Chase Club, and while they played golf we swam and played Chinese checkers. I had seen him from time to time since then, but it was startling to run into him in a place so completely out of the context of our former lives.

Husky, with oily black hair brushed back, merry blue eyes, and thick eyebrows that joined over his turnip nose, André had a tendency to put on weight, even on army rations. "My God, what are you doing here?" he asked.

"As you can see, I'm a second lieutenant in the colonial infantry, stationed near here, and I'm escorting my Senegalese to the *bousbir* [Arab for "whorehouse"]. What about you?"

"I'm in the Third Spahi Regiment in Blida, but we have some men here," he said. "We're armored now, no more horses. Last week we mopped up a band of *fels*. Spotted them in a riverbed marching single file, called in the T-6's for strafing runs, then moved in for the kill—twelve dead, five wounded, five prisoners."

"Were you in on it?" I asked.

"No, I'm at headquarters, but I was in on the planning, and I'll probably get a citation. I'm going to join the Quai d'Orsay when I get out, and my war record will help. I could be named military attaché in Washington, with a jump in rank to captain."

André was binational like me. His mother was an heiress from San Francisco, and he was well connected on both sides of the Atlantic. He had the convivial, back-slapping manner of the born politician. To demonstrate his cosmopolitan nature, he liked to tell bilingual jokes, which were understood by only a few. One was about a famous racing car called the S-car. During a race, a spectator keeps shouting, "Look at the S-car go." And therein lies the humor, for in French, *escargot* means "snail."

His self-assured account of a battle in which he had not taken part annoyed me. Maybe I was a little bit envious that his future was so well planned. Partly to provoke him, I said: "I can't see the point of this war, since eventually we'll have to leave, just as we left Indochina."

André put on his serious expression, the one he had during exams when we were both at the French lycée in New York, and said: "Don't you understand? It's the crusades in reverse. It's Islam on the march, after our loss in Asia. It's reverse racism, reverse expansion. The Arabs want to take back all the lands they lost to the *colons*."

Now I was really annoyed with my old playmate, and I said: "These fucking *colons*. On the beaches working on their tans while we're risking our necks."

"They're not on the beaches; they're trying to save their farms."

"Making the *burnous* sweat," I said, which was a common expression used to describe the exploitation of the Arabs.

At this point, Diallo joined us, being one of the first out of the *bousbir*. To put a stop to my argument with André, I told Diallo: "I don't know how you were able to fuck those three-hundred-pound whores."

"Well," he said, "when you've been fucked, you *know* you've been fucked."

André laughed heartily and said, "Look at that S-car go." Which was what he said, more to himself than to anyone else, when he heard something funny.

When we got back to Champlain, I told Diallo that before reporting to Captain de Lastours, I was going to ask Dourakine what he thought of the standing-in-the-jeep regulation.

"Dourakine," Diallo said with disdain, "he's just another *moujik*."

He told me that he had served in Dourakine's platoon. One night, when they were out on a two-day operation, Diallo was caught napping on sentry duty. In front of the entire platoon, Dourakine announced: "There is a shit-head among us. Diallo, step out of the ranks. Last night on sentry duty, you were sleeping. Let me show you what could have happened." He stepped behind Diallo and took out a hunting knife and placed it under his chin and made a slicing motion. "Now you're dead," he said. "The way is clear."

"Dourakine reported me," Diallo recalled, "and that cost me my annual leave back home to Dakar."

I found Dourakine in the *popote* and told him about being shot at while I stood in the jeep. "You're over six feet," he said. "You make a good target. Pay no mind to these idiots. Just ask yourself, 'Is it worth getting killed taking these apes to get laid?' For my money, this whole company is a brothel. Look at Lastours."

He asked me if I'd seen the stuffed head of the wild boar.

It was hard to miss, I said.

Dourakine said Lastours had been out on an operation in the forest when he spotted some boars. He called in the Alouette helicopter and took it up with a bagful of grenades. Two boars, frightened by the chopper, trotted into the open, and Lastours dropped grenades on them. "One for you and one for me," he told the disgruntled pilot. "Now land and help me load the beasts." They hauled the boars aboard, and the pilot said, "You've gotten my cabin all bloody."

"Don't bust my balls," Lastours said. "I've already radioed the company that we've got game for dinner."

"Do you think he was following regulations?" Dourakine asked. "In any case, the boar was so tough you could hardly eat it. Boar has to be marinated for at least a week."

The following Wednesday I had the brothel run again, with a different platoon. In the Chiffa Gorges, on our left, there was a steep, almost vertical cliff of gray stone with deep horizontal cracks, out of which thorny bushes poked. On our right, the ground sloped down to the torrent below, and across the torrent stood the far side of the ravine. As we passed an abandoned military post perched on the other side of the ravine, firing came from men hidden in a bend of the slope that dropped to the stream.

Of course, I thought, they know our Wednesday schedule and they're waiting for us with automatic weapons.

I told Diallo to step on it. I was worried they'd cut the road. The truck behind us followed. The men inside were firing and throwing grenades.

But where was the second truck? Its driver, a big, lumpy corporal I didn't know, had panicked and braked, and his truck skidded so that it found itself crosswise in the road. The corporal had opened the cab door and jumped in a ditch. The Senegalese sitting next to him saw that the truck was sliding backward toward the slope. He grabbed the steering wheel and pulled the hand brake. The men in the second truck jumped out and directed a hail of fire at the *fels*, who retreated down the slope. My jeep and the first truck had driven about 50 meters past the site of the ambush. I told Diallo to stop. There was no more firing. All this had taken no more than five minutes. We reconnoitered the slope where the *fels* were hidden and found patches of blood on the ground, but no bodies. Amazingly, we did not have a single dead or wounded. Diallo counted five bullet holes in our jeep, and the second truck had two blown tires and a bullet in the gas tank and would have to be towed.

I asked the driver of the second truck why he had braked and jumped out. "Put yourself in my place," he said.

I told him that that was difficult for me to do. I had to report him, and he served 30 days of prison *ferme* (no time off).

I told Diallo to ask the men if they were still up for Médéa or would they rather return to Champlain. A minute later, he reported that "they said if they have to go back, they'll riot." So we limped into Médéa with our disabled truck. "We had the *baraka* today," Diallo said.

Back in Champlain, I reported the ambush to Lastours and asked for a change of assignment. "It doesn't take an officer to do this," I said. "Diallo can do it. He likes his weekly outings to Médéa. But you've got to mix up the schedule, or they'll be waiting for us."

"Either that or I could order some protection," Lastours said, "a couple of half-tracks or *auto-mitrailleuses*. Or tanks. The *spahis* in Médéa are armored."

"Tanks for the brothel run," I said.

"It's the regulation," he said. "However, sometimes we have to improvise." He sat at his desk, across from his boar's head, rubbing his chin with his hand as if it was sandpaper. "It's true that you could be more useful somewhere else."

"Give me a platoon," I said.

"All four platoons presently have officers. However, Cossard is leaving at the end of the week, and you could replace him as *officier de renseignement*" ("intelligence officer").

"Anything is better than what I'm doing," I said.

C OSSARD SAT at his desk. The rays of the late September sun shone into the windows of his office, giving some color to his waxy face. One wall was lined with file cabinets. On the wall behind him, there was a snapshot of his wife and a drawing of a steamship by his young son, the ship that would bring Cossard home, with big puffs of smoke coming out of its three stacks.

"It's fairly simple," Cossard said. "Each day I get the BRQ [*bulletin de renseignement quotidien*] from sector headquarters in Médéa, listing actions of the previous day with enemy losses plus a summary of recent intelligence. The BRQ relies on human intelligence and aerial photographs." He showed me a couple of photographs with white arrows indicating a camouflaged camp or changes in the look of a forest or village.

He got up from his desk and paced the room, like a teacher lecturing his class. "I also have some sources; I'll leave you the files," he said, pointing to the cabinets. "As you saw today, the *fels* are active in the area. They chop down telephone poles and set fire to isolated farms. They collect taxes from the Arabs and protection money from the *colons*. One of my best sources is a tax collector for the FLN. That shows you the complexity of the situation. You know Morin, who runs the bus service to Médéa. When he failed to pay his monthly tax, his bus was torched. The rebels ambush our patrols, booby-trap the bodies of their dead, and hide their weapons in Moslem cemeteries."

Cossard went to the window, stood there with his hands folded behind his back, and looked out at the two stunted olive trees in the square. He then turned, bent his head, and joined his hands as if in prayer against his brow. He seemed to be trying to phrase what he had to say next. Finally he said, "Let's say you take a prisoner who knows that a farm will be attacked and the farmer will be murdered. If that happens, you may wish you had questioned him more forcefully."

"I hope I never have to make that decision," I said.

"Yes, but you may have to decide which is worse." Cossard paused, frowned, and shook his head. "It's really funny," he said, "with the things I've had to do in this job, that I've been criticized for not being enthusiastic about the war. All I can say is 'Thank God it's over.' The dogs bark, the caravan passes."

A couple of days later, I took over from the departed Cossard. Lastours looked in on me as I was reading the BRQ and asked me what was new. "A *colon* named Legros had his livestock slaughtered," I told him.

"Oh well, he was about due," Lastours said. His way of dealing with the horrors of war was to brush them off as fated. I wondered whether some of the Koranic *mektoub* ("it is written") had rubbed off on him.

"Anything else?" he asked.

"Two jeeps collided on the Chiffa road and a *spahi* was killed. What a stupid way to go."

"Death is always stupid," Lastours replied.

That afternoon, Dourakine, who'd been out on a two-day operation, brought in a prisoner, a kid who didn't look more than 15, spindly and narrow-shouldered. Part of my job was to interrogate prisoners.

"He's the brother of a section chief we killed this morning with most of his band," Dourakine said.

The prisoner wore khakis that hung loosely on his small frame, and his hair was matted with dirt.

"How old are you?" I asked.

"Seventeen," he said.

"What are you doing with the *fels?*"

"I was in school in Médéa. My brother needed a secretary to write reports. He can't read or write. I can write French and Arabic."

I offered him a cigarette, but he shook his head. I handed him a glass of water and asked if he'd been armed.

"My brother gave me a uniform and a pistol. The supplies came in at night, by mule."

"How many were you?"

"About twelve. This morning we heard the French coming, and my brother and I hid in a cave near the riverbed. They would never have found us but, when they walked by the cave, my brother said he didn't want to be caught like an animal in its burrow. He jumped out firing, and the French killed him. One of them came into the cave and saw me and said, 'it's not a man—it's a boy.'"

"He's a boy, but he's a rebel," Dourakine said. "Maybe we should have shot him."

The boy was chewing his lip. "Look," I said, "if you want to be a rebel, I'll send you to a POW camp. If not, you can be back in school tomorrow."

Next day, he was back in Médéa.

One drawback of my new assignment was that I usually spent the day in my office, and I was at the mercy of Lastours, who popped in half a dozen times a day to find out, to lecture, to question, and to advise. He had all the instincts of a *pipelette*, a concierge in Paris apartment buildings who makes it her business to know everything about the tenants, who are expected to call out their names when they come in at night, after the curtains of the concierge's loge are drawn. Malraux exacted his vengeance on all gossipy concierges in *Man's Fate*, when one of his characters brought in a horse through the carriage entrance and yelled, "*Cheval!*"

One afternoon as usual, Lastours burst in and said, "We've got to do something about Ouakrim." He was the fellow who ran the produce store and was giving information to Cossard, while suspected of being a tax collector for the FLN. I had been over to his shop, with its bags of dates and orange crates piled helter-skelter, to introduce myself. Ouakrim was a compact man with a lean face and a mop of coarse, black, disorderly hair. His deep-set eyes had crows'-feet at the corners, and his smile, skewed to one side, revealed yellow teeth. When I came in at noon, he was eating couscous from a big clay bowl at a low table, and he invited me to join him. He poured *harissa* sauce, and we ate with our fingers.

He was clearly making an effort to be welcoming and friendly. "The one before you," he said, "he was a *grosse tête*" (fathead, meaning full of himself).

"I hope we can work together," I said.

"I am attached to France," Ouakrim said, "even though I have suffered many humiliations. Imagine I'm in line to buy a train ticket. A Frenchman cuts in front of me as if I don't exist. When I had a job at the post office, a Frenchman who did exactly what I did was paid more. My brother wanted to enlist in the air force, but Moslems weren't allowed in their air force or in officers' school."

"I realize that Arabs have not been treated fairly," I said. I wondered where his real loyalty lay, or whether he had any. Men like Ouakrim, who played both sides, had nothing left but their cunning. I also wondered why he was laying out his grievances when he professed attachment to France.

As if divining my thoughts, he said, "I only want to help you understand the situation here. You will go from surprise to surprise. Nothing is simple. Before the French left Champlain, we had a *colon* schoolmaster. One day he came around crying that his 403 Peugeot had been shot at. There was a bullet hole in the trunk. 'The bastards,' he told me. 'They did that to me, to me who teaches their children.' What he didn't say was that in the summer when there were no classes he supervised the seasonal laborers during the lentil harvest, when entire families worked fifteen hours a day for three francs."

And now, Lastours was in my office and seemed agitated. "We know something about the way he operates," he said. "He collects taxes in a series of villages. He supplies the rebels with food and recruits *choufs* [sentries], usually young shepherds, to protect passing *katibas* [large units of rebels]. He travels with a briefcase filled with bills. He's deeply involved with the *fels.*"

"But he says he's deeply attached to France," I said.

"That's his game. He said he would work for us. He gives us the names of Moslem notables who pay taxes to the FLN to buy insurance. In any case, I meant to tell you, this morning I had his shop searched and we found fifty thousand francs hidden in an orange crate. Soiled bills that didn't come from a bank teller. We think he's embezzling some of the funds he collects for the FLN. I've got him locked up in the shed."

"And then what?"

"We'll keep him there for a few days, feed him once a day. He can sleep on the floor."

When we went in to question him a couple of days later, Ouakrim was rolled up on the floor in his brown burnous. Lastours kicked the huddled form, and Ouakrim turned over, bleary-eyed and unshaven. He looked at me and said, "I thought you were my friend."

Lastours kicked him again and said: "Will you talk, my *lascar* [thief], *oui ou merde* [yes or shit]?"

Ouakrim knelt before us, with his head bowed and both hands flat on the ground, as if in prayer, and said, "Kill me, kill me. Put a knife to my throat."

"We don't want to kill you," I said. "We want to give you couscous and a warm bed."

"France is good," Ouakrim said.

"We'll be back tonight," Lastours said.

Back in my office, Lastours said, "He won't talk, because he doesn't want to admit taking the collection money. He's in trouble with the FLN. The solution is to release him and let the FLN take care of him." We let him go the next morning, and two days later, he was found in his produce store with his throat slit.

"You see," Lastours told me, "I was right. There aren't any fifty percent collaborators. They're either for us or against us."

"There are degrees," I said. "Some do the fighting, some help those who do the fighting, some collect the taxes, some act as lookouts."

"No, it's all the same outfit with different jobs," he said.

It occurred to me that the true nature of war is that your declared enemy is not your only enemy. Your superior officers, who place you in high-risk or reprehensible situations, are also your enemy, and so are some of the soldiers you have to work with, like the corporal in the Chiffa who jumped in the ditch. You had to be on your guard against everyone.

OUR PLATOONS were out every day hunting *fellaghas*, and sometimes they brought back intelligence that I sent to headquarters in Médéa. One morning in mid-October, platoon leader Robert Amand, a Marseillais who was known for singing Tino Rossi ballads and for making a credible facsimile of absinthe in the town hall bathtub, ambled in with his customary greeting: "*Alors*, are you fucking or are you catching a train?" He unfolded a map and showed me the location of a village in the *djebel* (mountains). "We were near there yesterday," he said, "and some informants told us it was a passage for *fellagha* bands. But we couldn't get there. There's no path, just masses of huge boulders."

"I wonder how the *fels* do it," I said.

"They've got goat blood," Amand said. "I sent a couple of men up, but they didn't get far. I tell you, I was so disgusted I lost my appetite for dinner."

"I'll see what I can do," I said. I radioed the coordinates to headquarters, and I soon received a reply that they were mounting a helicopter operation with black berets, and that since it was my bailiwick, the commandos would pick me up in Champlain.

It was in Algeria that the French army discovered the combat uses of helicopters. In a mountainous and roadless landscape, the choppers could reach places that no other units could. In the Indochina War, choppers were used only to evacuate the wounded. Finally, some bright general figured out that they could also carry troops into combat. In 1956, the black berets, or airborne commandos, were formed, all volunteers, and already they had a reputation as hoodlums. In their Sikorskys, the H-34 that could carry 12 men (known as the big bumblebee) and the H-19 that could carry six, they conducted lightning raids in terrain that was inaccessible to the infantry.

"Ah yes," Lastours said when I told him I was going for a ride in an H-19, "helicopters are the latest fad, aren't they?"

The next morning, its rotor whirring over the town square, the H-19 picked me up. Five seats were taken, and I dropped into the remaining seat. I realized later that the commandos had placed me so that I would be the first to jump, in case we were fired at upon landing. So often in these encounters, everything depended on who fired first. I had my map and my sidearm, a 7.6-mm automatic. The black berets were armed with MAT 49 submachine guns and hand grenades. Their leader, a swarthy sergeant who wore dark glasses, said, as we flew south toward the *djebel*: "I like grenades, they don't take up much space, and in case of trouble, it's not a weapon you leave behind."

Soon we reached the Arab village, on a high, scrubbed mesa, seven or eight bedraggled *mechtas* (houses), with coops where they kept their chickens and goats, surrounded by thorny hedges. The Sikorsky hovered about four feet above the ground, its rotor raising dust, and I was the first to jump, followed by the other five. I had a sinking feeling that this was a wild goose chase.

"Search the *mechtas*," the sergeant told his men. He kicked open the door of a shuttered house, and in the half-light I could see a young woman sitting cross-legged on some blankets in the corner.

"Maybe she's hiding a weapon," the sergeant said, and started groping her. "Look at the layers she's wearing. Good God, it's an entire wardrobe."

"Hey," I said, "that's enough. She's not hiding anything. Do you want me to report you?"

"Make me laugh," the sergeant said.

The conduct of the black berets was founded on the rationale that since they were doing highly dangerous work, they permitted themselves every excess.

I heard shouting and stepped out into the bright day. I saw the four other black berets gathered around an elderly Arab, turbaned and robed. I pulled him aside. Trying to put him at ease, I gave him the Arab greeting, "*La bess?*" ("How goes it?"). "*Chouia*" ("All right"), he automatically replied, then added that the black beret who had searched his *mechta* had taken 300 francs he'd received that month from social security—about $6. I asked the Arab to point to the black beret who had conducted the search, and he raised a quivering finger and pointed at a swaggering, bushy-mustached commando, who threw himself at the old man and started slapping him, punctuating his words with each slap: "Call me . . . a thief . . . you son . . . of a whore."

I pulled the old man away and said to the sergeant: "All right, search your man and see if he has the money."

"There's going to be trouble if we don't find anything," the sergeant said.

Before he could be searched, the accused commando reached into his pocket and threw a handful of change on the ground. "This is all I have on me," he shouted. "Is this what I took from you, you filthy liar?"

At that, two other black berets grabbed the Arab and told him: "You're coming with us." They started pushing him along the path that led away from the village. Seized with panic, the old man made a run for it, holding one arm straight up with index finger extended, as soccer players do when they are being replaced during the game. He had gone about 20 feet when the black beret accused of stealing fired a burst from his MAT. The Arab still ran, his burnous flapping and his turban unraveling, but a few feet further he fell. It all happened too fast for me to react. I wondered what I should have done. I should have handled it differently. Instead of ordering the black beret to be searched, I should have taken him aside and talked to him man to man: "If you have the money, give it back to him and we'll say no more about it." But would that have worked? These black berets had regressed beyond constraints. I wondered whether a criminal record was a condition for their recruitment.

On the ride back to Champlain, the commandos were laughing and joking.

"Did you see that old guy with his arm up?"

"I guess he was waving good-bye."

They liked to reminisce about their feats of battle the way marathon runners constantly check their stopwatches for their times.

"Remember that twelve-year-old boy?" the sergeant said. "He told us he'd never fired a weapon. And we gave him a rifle and said we'd give him one hundred francs for every beer bottle he hit at fifty meters. And this kid could really shoot, like clay pipes at the fair. We gave him five hundred francs and a good spanking." It seemed to me he told the story to show that sometimes they acted in a humane manner.

"You must be proud of your work," I told the sergeant.

He shrugged. "Why should terrorists be spared if it means that our men will be killed?" To him, every Arab was a terrorist.

Back in Champlain, I reported the outing to Lastours. "And so the result of our brilliant helicopter operation is one dead Arab civilian," I concluded. I said I wanted to file a report.

"No report will be filed," he said. "You cannot fight a guerrilla war with humanitarian principles." Lastours rapped his stick on the table and said: "What has war become but a sordid butchery? We have completely lost the chivalric ideal, when war was a sport."

"War was never a sport," I said. "At least in a sport like mountain-climbing, the only life you risk is your own."

"Don't get me riled," Lastours said. "It's bad for my arteries."

I was feeling disgusted, and it was time for a sundowner, so I went over to the *popote*, where I found Dourakine, already on his first Pernod (according to the saucer on the table, one with each drink). "Over here, you revolting paper-pusher," he called. "I'm back from my leave." He was in high spirits, and I didn't feel like talking about the chopper operation, so I let him pour it out. He had blackmailed

Lastours into giving him a 48-hour pass by threatening to reveal some of his hunting forays to divisional headquarters, or so he said.

"I hit the gong" (a French expression for extravagance), he said. "I went to Algiers and took a room at the Aletti" (one of the two first-class hotels, along with the Saint-Georges). "You know, if I don't have a woman every week, I go nuts. Can you understand that?"

"Easily," I said.

"In the army you're constantly around men—you yearn for the company of women."

One of his favorite topics, which he began to expound upon again, was the connection between sex and death. "After all," he said, "we call the male orgasm *la petite mort* [the little death]. You know, when you have trouble coming because you've drunk too much, but you work hard at it and you shoot your wad, then you roll over completely spent and you lie there in total stillness, as if your soul had left your body. But it's a deathlike spasm that gives life. Out here, we're surrounded by death, we smell death, we breathe death, day and night, and the antidote is sex, the affirmation of life, the procreative urge."

"Well," I said, "did it go well?"

"You know, whores depress me. It's so predictable. They wash your dick over the sink like they're doing the laundry, and then I feel like I have to hurry up because I'm wasting their valuable time. Years ago, I found one I liked, young and pretty, and I took my time, and she said, 'Listen, you, I'm not your fiancée.' That's why I went to the Aletti. I was looking for an opportunity. In the bar. On the first night, nothing, just two of the regular fat old Aletti whores. On the second night, again at the bar, I saw these two French *gonzesses* [broads] in their late thirties, not bad, not beauties, clean-looking, good skin, good hair, smoking Camels. I went by their table on the way to the men's room, and one of them dropped her lighter. I picked it up, and we started talking. They were nurses at the Maillot hospital."

I didn't say anything. I didn't want to interfere with the flow.

"I wanted to buy them a drink, but the bar was closing, and I said, 'It's too bad we can't have a nightcap.' One of the nurses, the one with the tight chestnut curls covering her head like a helmet, said, 'Why don't you come and have one in our room? We've got a bottle of cognac.' Well, I knew the nurses at Maillot were barracked in dorms, so they must have taken a room for a little recreation. We got to the room, a big room with twin beds, and the other one, the reddish-blonde with a fringe across her brow, went straight for the bathroom, and when she came out she was naked as a worm. Not much astonishes me, but I sat there astonished. Then the second one went into the bathroom and she came out naked too, and she said: 'Are you a sissy or something?'

"No, madam, I'm no sissy," I said. "I pulled off my tie and took off my uniform, and the blonde said, 'Come on. Help me get these two beds together. Remove that night table, and watch out for the lamp.' Good God, she was bossy. They hopped on the bed and started going at each other. I felt like the referee at a wrestling match, walking around the bed, dropping my head to get a good look at a hold and see if it was legal. Then they said, 'Come on,' and we went at it, the three of us, and there's nothing we didn't do. I stayed there until four in the morning, humping them both. They said, 'We'd been in that bar since ten, waiting to get picked up.' "

I was glad to see Dourakine so relaxed, for usually he was pumped up like a tire with too much air and ready to burst. In Algiers, he'd let some of the air out.

"Tomorrow, I'm visiting my pet project," he said, "in a *douar* four klicks from here. I've hired an Arab carpenter to build a one-room schoolhouse. I pay him with my own money, and I gave him a gun just in case. Sometimes you have to trust these bastards."

At dawn the next morning, he left with his platoon for the *douar*, where he found the schoolhouse torched and the carpenter and his wife riddled with automatic fire. The villagers told him that a band of 30 *fellaghas* had come through only an hour before. When they set fire to the schoolhouse he had labored for months to build, the carpenter tried to stop them. One of the *fels* grabbed the carpenter's wife, and when she fell, he dragged her by the feet into an alley. The carpenter pulled out his handgun and shot the *fel*. The carpenter and his wife were taken to the village square and executed in front of the villagers and the children for whom the school had been built. Their leader then warned the villagers against accepting help from the French, before marching his men off into the hills.

Dourakine led his platoon in the direction the villagers had showed him and set a brisk pace, hoping to catch up with the *fels*. Two kilometers farther, the point man saw footprints going off the trail into the brush and followed them. "There's a bush moving," he called out.

"Take five men and search the bushes," Dourakine told Sergeant Lavigne. "If you find anybody, I want him alive."

They found a wounded *fellagha*, left behind by the others without a weapon. He was the one shot by the carpenter, hit in the shoulder and bleeding profusely. The medic patched him up and gave him some food and water.

"We'll use him as a guide," Dourakine said. "He can still walk."

The Senegalese point man tied one end of a rope around the *fel*'s neck and looped the other around his waist. The prisoner-guide slowed them down, stopping every 100 feet or so to look for footprints and mule dung. When the *fel* complained that he couldn't go any farther, the point man poked him in the back with his rifle. "You can't treat a wounded man this way," the *fel* called out to Dourakine. "I'm protected by the Geneva Convention."

"Write them a letter," Dourakine replied.

The trail narrowed into a corkscrew goat path, steeply rising to the top of a 100-foot-high cliff. After reaching a eucalyptus grove at the top, the platoon stopped to rest. Some of the men sat on the ground, cradling their weapons. Others leaned against the scrawny eucalyptus trees. The prisoner stood at the edge of the cliff, looking down, with the rope around his neck. Then, without saying a word, he jumped. He would have dragged the point man with him, who still had the other end of the rope tied around his waist, except that the point man was sitting with two Senegalese friends, who were able to cut the rope, even as the weight of the fallen *fel* pulled the point man toward the edge of the cliff. Luckily the *fel* weighed about 130 pounds, while the Senegalese was a big, husky man. "You can't trust these bastards for one second," Dourakine said, "but what should I write in my report—that he jumped to his death or that he hanged himself?"

Moving off the top of the cliff, the trail meandered downhill into a scrub-covered plain. To the right of the scrub, cascades of boulders were surmounted by slabs of flat rocks with overhangs like huge upside-down frying pans with no handles. The point man saw some movement on top of the flat rocks and cried out, *"Embuscade! Planquez-vous!"* ("Ambush! Take cover!").

From the slabs of flat rock came heavy automatic fire. Dourakine and his men were caught on the plain. In the bedlam of battle, a mix of machine-gun bursts, rifle shots, grenades exploding, and men yelling and cursing, Dourakine called out, "Regroup, regroup," and led the way across the open ground to the woods beyond. He was known for standing while the bullets were flying. "I don't like to get my hands dirty," he said.

Most of the platoon made it to the woods, running or crawling. When Dourakine surveyed the open space through his binoculars, he saw two Senegalese lying there. One was hit in both legs and couldn't move, while the other had crawled near a boulder at an angle that was out of the line of fire from above. Dourakine did not want to risk further losses by trying to retrieve the two men. The *fels* had at least one 50-mm machine gun up there and could cut down anyone trying to reach the wounded. He told Lavigne: "I'll call in some choppers." In the meantime, he ordered the platoon to start the descent back to Champlain. There was some angry muttering among the Senegalese, for whom there was no worse military blunder than leaving wounded men on the field. As it turned out, choppers were a precious commodity in the French army, and none were available to pick up the two wounded men, whose bodies were never found.

That evening, I went by Dourakine's tent, and he gave me an account of the day's events. I asked him if he wanted to get a drink. "Yes," he said, "but not at the *popote*. Let's go to the Spaniard's." Pepe the Spaniard, for some reason marooned in Champlain, ran a café where you could get tapas such as olives, chickpeas, and anchovies, and the usual drinks.

When we sat down at a table in the small room decorated with old bullfight posters, we saw, a few tables away, Lavigne and Laroche, both Indochina veterans. Dourakine sat with his back to them, but they had a good start on us in terms of drinks, and as soon as we sat down, they raised their voices to make sure we could hear.

"There's all kinds of officers," Lavigne said, "good and bad. I had one who pulled me out of a rice paddy in the Mekong Delta when I was hit in the knee."

"And I had one," Laroche said, "who found some Meo stretcher-bearers when I had two ribs and a leg broken from shrapnel at Bong-Hong, and took me through the jungle for three days until we reached the hospital at Pleiku."

Dourakine, silently working himself into a fury, placed his hand crosswise against his chest and said: "The mustard, it is here," meaning that his anger was rising.

"And then there was that captain at Ban Me Thuot who sent us into artillery fire and we had fourteen killed," Lavigne said.

Dourakine's face was beet red. He put his hand to his throat and said, "The mustard, it is here."

"Yes," said Laroche, "and that night someone lobbed a grenade into his tent. It could happen again."

Dourakine leapt out of his chair, pulled his .45 automatic from its holster, lunged over to their table, and said: "Let's settle this right now."

"Lieutenant," Lavigne said, smiling broadly, "we were just talking."

"About the rain and the sunshine," Laroche said.

"Get out of here right now," Dourakine said. "I don't want to look at your ugly faces. I'll settle your bill." They slunk off, cackling under their breaths.

"God's whore," Dourakine roared, "I'll never forget anyone who died following my orders. But I'm running a platoon. I'm not here to blow their noses. I want to transform this bunch of ragtails into a combat unit."

"Good luck," I said.

Three days later, Dourakine took his platoon out again to look into a report in my BRQ that a political commissar nicknamed Ali Baba had been spotted in a warren of caves in the Chiffa ravine. In the late afternoon, Lastours came into my office and said, "I'm sorry to tell you that your friend Dourakine was killed." I felt bewildered, for I had convinced myself that he had the *baraka*.

"Dourakine was leading his men into the ravine," Lastours said, "when a *fellagha* emerged from behind a tree, shouldering his rifle. Dourakine beat him to the draw, and the *fellagha* dropped his rifle, spun around, and leaned both hands against the tree. Dourakine fired another round into the man's back, and his hands slid down the bark of the tree and he fell, folded in two. Then Dourakine fell, and they thought at first that the *fellagha* had hit him. But here's the odd thing. Like the *fellagha*, Dourakine was shot in the back."

"Are you saying that he was shot by one his own men?"

"Well, it's suspicious, but there's not much we can do. They brought his body back, but even if we retrieve the bullet, the *fels* have weapons they steal from us. We can't examine every rifle of every man in his platoon."

Holy hell, I thought, he doesn't really care enough to investigate the possible murder of one of his officers by his own men. That's the attitude: Don't rock the boat—it will make the company look bad. I had lost a friend, though our views of the war were miles apart. Dourakine saw the war as a form of self-expression, of his valor and vitality, and also of his pride and love of strong sensations. For me the bird of war was not the eagle but the stork, clumsy and ungainly. It was also deadly, and my main purpose was to survive. Although I did not take the Hobbesian view that war is the natural state of man, I saw its fascinating aspect. It heightened and magnified the knowledge one had of oneself and of others, all caught and observed in extreme situations.

"In any case," Lastours said, "the two sergeants, Lavigne and Laroche, took over. They found a cave and threw in smoke grenades. Two men came out firing, and they were killed. Inside the cave they found another man, coughing and teary-eyed, with his hands up. We think he's the political commissar, but there were no papers on him. I've got him in the shed, tied to a beam. We're going to interrogate him. We need to know who he is and what operations he has planned in our sector. He's obviously an important catch, and it's vital that we find out why he's here."

The *fellagha* had been strung up with his wrists tied over a horizontal beam, so that his feet didn't touch the ground. He wore a khaki uniform without rank or insignia. His coarse black hair was cut short, and he had a bushy beard and a mustache. His gaze was more defiant than fearful.

I asked him his name, but he did not reply. "Ask him the location of his base camp," Lastours said. I asked him, and he did not reply.

"Ask him a bit more forcefully," Lastours said.

I punched him hard in the stomach.

"*Hakarabi. Makache,*" the man said. "I swear I don't know." I hit him again. "*Hakarabi. Makache.*" Then something happened to me. I started to lose it. I was in an altered state, where my mental processes broke down. It was as if the scene had been rehearsed and choreographed. My role was to punch him, and his role was to repeat his line. This went on for about two minutes, and then he stopped repeating.

Lastours felt his pulse and said, "He's dead. And he didn't talk."

I was horrified by what I had done. I had killed a defenseless man. I had not intended to kill him, but that didn't make him any less dead.

"Place me under arrest," I said.

"Don't be ridiculous," Lastours said. "When you go to the *hamam* [steambath], you sweat, and in war there are losses. It's the logic of things. I'll find a couple of men to bury him."

Now that I reconstruct the event almost 50 years later, I tell myself that nothing was simple, that there were wheels within wheels. I tell myself that I was blindly striking out at a war I hated, that I was sick over the loss of my friend, that I was assaulting my mirror image and the man who was giving me orders as much as the prisoner. But then I ask myself, Am I looking for excuses post facto? Would a judge and jury find extenuating circumstances? I've been my own judge and jury, and I can't let myself off. I never protested. I never said, "I refuse to do this." It's a form of inner disfigurement that I've had to live with.

L ATER, I TOLD Lastours, "I can't do this OR job anymore. I'd like to take over Dourakine's platoon." I felt the need to take the risks a platoon leader takes, though my main concern was not to lose any of the men.

"Well," Lastours said, "Dourakine must be replaced, so it might as well be you."

It was in the first week of November 1956 that I took over Dourakine's platoon. I had to take stock, sit down and think, assess what I had learned. With his blustering assurance, Dourakine had scorned the rebels, who were not to be scorned. They had a better knowledge of the terrain, and most of the time they picked the site of battle. Their officers lived the same way as their men. No *popote* or weekends at the Aletti. Smoking and drinking were banned and severely punished. Austerity prevailed. The *fellaghas* could march and fight on a handful of dates. They carried out surprise attacks on small detachments, to raise our body count and retrieve our weapons. When they mutilated our dead, it was not an act of rage but a directive from the FLN high command, to spread terror in the ranks of our troops. The rebels routinely executed pro-French Arabs, even (or particularly) if it was an elderly veteran who wore his World War I decorations on his burnous. They cut off his ears and his nose and put out his eyes— *pour l'exemple.* Their aim was to capsize the colonial order by getting rid of the *beni oui-ouis* (Uncle Toms). That way they could control the Arab villages and name tax collectors and political commissars who gave them the names of those who didn't play along.

The 1st RIC was a combat regiment, not part of the *quadrillage,* the grid of occupation units that protected farms and roads. Our platoons were sent on missions of various kinds—*bouclage et ratissage* (search and destroy), ambushes, visits to outlying villages to keep them pro-French, and patrols on the road to Médéa to stop buses and verify ID cards. Just the previous week, a patrol had stopped a bus and asked the passengers to get off. One of our men spotted a suspiciously muscular and hairy leg on a veiled woman as she climbed down. When he approached her, she pretended to trip toward him and stabbed him in the stomach. "It's not a *fatma*," he shouted. "Fire, for God's sake!" A burst dropped her, and as she fell, her veil slipped off, revealing a bushy black beard. Sometimes we had to open a road with frying pans (mine detectors). Sometimes we visited the few remaining *colons*.

As platoon leader, I was given a monthly ration of kola nuts imported from West Africa, which the Senegalese considered a great delicacy. I kept them under my bed in a locked box and handed them out like decorations, for valorous conduct. The reddish kola nut, about the size of a big walnut, is one of the ingredients of Coca-Cola. I tried one, and it was so bitter I spit it out, but to the Senegalese it was candy. They had a special diet of rice with meat and hot sauce, and at meals they lined up with their *gamelles* (mess kits) in front of the *roulante* (field kitchen), and never complained about the sameness of their menu. They were good soldiers, well trained and easy to get along with, as long as you didn't fuck them over.

My first assignment was to win over the sergeants, Laroche and Lavigne. Noncoms, who knew they would never be officers, had their own abrasive style and mentality. They had seen combat and had a chest full of decorations to prove it. They viewed conscripted officers like me with bemused detachment at best, and at worst, contempt. They knew the routine, the army's arcane web of rites and obligations. In combat, they could save your life or get you killed. I needed them on my side.

Both men were in their forties and had served in World War II and Indochina before Algeria. They had lost their health, their buddies, and their wives. When I asked Lavigne why he stayed in, he said: "It's habit. What would I do in civilian life?" I knew it was more than habit, though I wasn't sure what it was. Lavigne looked a little bit like actor Jean Gabin, sandy-haired and fleshy-faced, with hard blue eyes. He was blunt and crafty at the same time. Laroche was tall and lanky with a dark complexion that hinted at Caribbean origins. His face was mottled with acne scars, but a carefully tended mustache gave him a veneer of urbanity.

Since they weren't allowed at the *popote*, I took them to Pepe's, where we ate grilled brochettes with a pimento mustard that raised beads of sweat on the brow, washed down with liters of Médéa red. They wore their decorations, as a way of showing me what they had been through, row upon row of campaign ribbons studded with metal stars for citations. Laroche had a purple one encased in a gold-colored frame. It didn't look French, and I asked him what it was. *"Ca, c'est la Distaignwish,"* he said. He'd served in the French battalion in Korea and had been awarded the Distinguished Service Cross by the Americans.

"Look, I know I'm a novice," I said. "I've never been in combat. I'm going to have to rely on the two of you."

"We'll do our jobs," Lavigne said.

"I was at Dien Bien Phu," Laroche said, as he stared at the ceiling. "And now I have to take orders from little boys who never heard a rifle fired off the target range. When they were in diapers I was doing my fifty klicks a day. Of course, I don't mean you, lieutenant."

"Of course not," I said. "Look, you know the men. You know the drill. You've got to teach me."

"Dourakine was arrogant," Laroche blurted out. "He thought he knew it all."

"And look where he ended up," Lavigne exclaimed with disgust.

As the evening wore on, they loosened up. Lavigne took the position that just as in Indochina every native was a Viet, in Algeria all Arabs were *fels.* "After all," he said, "they don't wear uniforms, they choose the hour, the day, and the place, and they ambush you and shoot you in the back."

"After all," Laroche chimed in, filling his glass, "they're practicing terrorism, mutilating corpses and all the rest, and we're supposed to fight according to the rules of the marquis of Queensberry."

I could sense that their mistrustful mood had changed when they started to tell war stories. It was partly the wine, but it was also the beginning of inclusion. I wasn't yet an equal, but I was no longer an adversary. The conversation revolved around battles fought and venereal diseases caught. "We always carried a vial of penicillin in our back pocket," Laroche said, "just in case." He described in gruesome detail a strain "unknown in Europe," which they dubbed "the cock's comb."

"What the Viets were good at was inflicting pain," Laroche continued after pausing for thought. "When they caught you, they made small cuts in your back and chest and rubbed the cuts with wild honey. Then they tied you to a tree, and soon the red ants came, attracted by the smell of honey."

"On the beach at Da Nang," Lavigne recalled, "they dug a hole at low tide and sank you in it so only your head showed, and the tide came in and covered your throat, your chin, and finally went over your head." Lavigne and Laroche were like one-time visitors to a foreign country reminiscing about points of interest, such as the romanesque churches of France or the Uffizi in Florence, and recalling the experience with evident relish.

Our first time out, our mission was to visit a supposedly friendly village in the hills about 10 miles south of Champlain. Trucks drove the platoon to a point where we had to start walking, and it took a couple of hours to reach the *douar* over a treeless and rocky terrain. When we came down the single dusty street, skinny chickens ran across our paths and children in rags scurried down alleys. The boxlike clay houses had small windows covered by blue shutters, and the *douar* smelled strongly of olive oil. On the square, our interpreter, armed with a megaphone, summoned all the men over the age of 15. About a dozen appeared, all of them either very old or very young. The women stayed out of sight behind their blue shutters.

It was my job to give the villagers a pep talk: "We want peace in your village, but you must help us. Keep us informed. Confide your anxieties and suspicions."

A heavyset man in his fifties approached Lavigne, whom he

seemed to know, and said his horse had been stolen by rebels. Lavigne ignored him. "I swear it's true," the man said. "Why don't you believe me?"

"Didn't I believe you when you said you hadn't seen any rebels?" Lavigne said.

The village elder, a white-bearded man in a spotless white burnous, came up and gave me a military salute. "Can you take me to Médéa?" he asked in Arabic. "I need to see a doctor. I don't have an ID card."

"Ask him how old he is," I told the interpreter.

"He says he doesn't know. He's lived like a pebble in a stream."

"Type up an ID card for him," I said. "Just put an approximate age on it."

The old Arab bowed in thanks and said to the interpreter: "Look how things are here. There's no school. The road is in such bad shape vehicles can't use it. Why build a road for Arabs? We can't go to town for supplies; the rebels stop us on the way back and take what we've bought."

"When you see rebels, you should tell us," I said.

"How long are you here for?" the old man asked.

"What he's really saying," Laroche said, "is that if they give us information and then we leave, the rebels will kill them."

We had brought along some buckets of whitewash and brushes. I was under orders to paint Major Fourcade's favorite slogan on the walls of the houses: ARMY=PEACE=PROSPERITY. As the Senegalese applied the whitewash and the villagers looked on in stony silence, Lavigne said: "This reminds me of the Viet slogans we used to see on the walls in Hanoi: 'Death to the French Colonialists. Long Life to President Ho.'"

"The way this works," said Laroche, as he slapped a fly on his cheek, "is that there are always a few villagers who have marginal jobs with the *fels*. They serve as mail-drops, or they store supplies in their cellars, or there might be one who can't resist firing at us from a safe distance. Our objective is to show them that there is no way to be neutral. We have to come by and show the flag so they will know we are in control. You give the standard speech, we are here to help you bla-bla-bla, and the village elder replies we only want peace bla-bla-bla."

Some children had rolled up scraps of cloth into a ball and were kicking it around on the other side of the square. "You see those kids?" Lavigne said. "They count us, to see how many men we've got and what weapons we're carrying. When we're here, they seem friendly. But when we're gone, they help the *fels* cut down telephone wires and dig trenches in the road."

And so I fell into a routine of patrols, some lasting only a few hours and some several days. When you're out on patrol, time becomes warped, slow motion when marching under a leaden sky, fast forward when shots are fired, and space becomes four-dimensional, the fourth dimension being the palpable expectation of death. I tried to avoid high-risk situations, and the sergeants agreed with me that it wasn't always wise to seek contact with the rebels. Sometimes, in an exposed position, we fired a few bursts in the hope that the noise would scare them off if they were close by. Once on night patrol, the platoon was resting behind an embankment when we heard marching feet and twigs breaking. I could make out what one of them said—"*Djib el mas*" ("Give me some water"). There were too many of them. We stayed put.

Another time, in the bed of a dry *oued* (river), Lavigne said: "I'm getting the ticklish feeling that I'm in someone's sights." A few seconds later, firing came from the far bank, and the din was stomach-churning, the bursts of gunfire and exploding grenades, men hit, men running, men yelling, "Where's the *lance-patate*?" ("potato thrower," or grenade launcher). "Where's the medic, where's the sergeant?" I was afraid that when the time came, I might panic, but there was too much to think about, the correct orders to give for the deployment of the platoon, the correct tactics to adopt, whether to call in aerial support, finding the coordinates on the map, attending to the wounded. It was like slaloming without hitting any gates. In the end, it was one more of our inconclusive encounters.

In the week between Christmas and New Year's, my platoon was in its first big battle. The rebels were on the Moslem calendar and did not abide by the holiday season. Our intelligence told us that a band of about 30 *fellaghas* were entrenched in the El Habous mountains southeast of Champlain. The trucks, when we left at dawn, took us past the last *colon* vineyard. The rows of vines were as neatly aligned as the strands in an Arab rug and the spotted trunks of eucalyptus trees lined the road. The sun rose, a scoop of orange sherbet, giving no warmth, its pale light flickering between the trees.

At the base of the mountain lay a narrow valley where groves of cork trees grew. The patrol advanced on the stunted, thick-barked trees. I was armed with a MAT 49 submachine gun, a reliable weapon with few moving parts. Its handle also held the 24-bullet clip, and it was effective up to 20 feet, though it tended to swing to the right. We also had two 24-29 FMs (*fusil-mitrailleurs*), which could be fired in single shot or in bursts, from the hip or lying down and lowering the attached tripod, as well as a 30-mm machine gun and two 81-mm mortars.

Coming up to the cork forest, I wanted to see if my MAT was in good order, and I fired a burst into a clump of laurel bushes. The bushes fired back, and the platoon ran for cover in the trees, returning fire. About six rebels made a run for the path that snaked up the El Habous ridge, and one was hit. I sent a man out to search the body. "Be careful," Lavigne called out. "He may not be completely dead." The *fel* had pulled the pin from a grenade and held it under him so that when he was rolled over it would explode. The Senegalese dragged him by the feet so that when the grenade exploded it was still under him. Nonetheless, the Senegalese caught some shrapnel in his legs. "It's an old trick," Lavigne said. "The Viets used to do it."

Laroche, who was operating the radio, told me the field guns were in position. Before we shoved out, I had asked for artillery preparation.

"Orange to green, are you receiving me?" Laroche asked the gunnery officer.

"Five out of five" ("Roger").

"We're under fire. Hard to tell how many."

"We can see activity on the mountain. Maybe twenty or thirty."

"Are you ready to fire?"

"Affirmative."

The 105-mm howitzers started blasting away, but the first shells fell short, at the other end of the cork grove, where there was an ancient, untended Moslem cemetery with moss-covered graves.

"You're hitting the Moslem cemetery," Laroche told the gunnery officer.

"Today, it's the turn of the dead," he replied.

"They can only die once," Laroche said.

After the field guns had hammered the rebel emplacements, we started up the narrow track cut into the side of the sun-scorched mountain. I already had one wounded, and I thought of T. E. Lawrence, who said that the art of war lay in getting as few as possible of your men killed. The sundry ways of seeing a landscape also crossed my mind. The geologist saw strata; the geographer saw meridians; the naturalist, flora and fauna; the painter, a picturesque cork forest with a pretty stream winding through it and a mountain in the background; and the soldier saw firing zones and places to take cover, a drop cloth for battles.

Up the steep, four-foot-wide incline we marched, in single file, at ten-foot intervals, except for Laroche, who was right behind me with the field radio strapped to his back. At a hairpin turn in the path, with an almost vertical wall of rock on my right and on my left the yawning void to the ground 100 feet below, I came face-to-face with a rebel armed with a rifle. I had the MAT in firing position. I fired a burst, and he fell, dropping his rifle, a World War II Mauser with a Nazi eagle on the stock. I was shaken by a wave of relief at having fired first. That body on the ground with the thin stream of blood coming out of its mouth could have been mine. The incident was not in the least dramatic. It was casual, as if bumping into someone in the street, except that we were armed and my reflex was half a second quicker than his, and I had a better weapon.

"You've got the *baraka*, Lieutenant," Laroche said, as he pushed the body off the path with his feet to the ground below.

"I think he was the lookout for the main bunch," I said.

"They're dug into holes up there behind the rocks," he said, "and they've got at least one FM."

"Lob some mortar shells up," I said, as the slope grew more gradual, "and bring up your FMs in cross fire, and the machine gun at the highest point you can reach, a ledge if you can find one, and move the men through the thorn thickets. Don't follow the path."

The Senegalese scrambled up, looking like armed mountain-climbers, grabbing at bushes and slabs of rock, protected by the heavy fire of the FMs, mortars, and machine guns. I saw a rebel rise above a boulder to aim his rifle. A burst from one of our FMs knocked him backward, and his rifle slipped from his hands and bounced from boulder to boulder.

We reached a kind of clearing, with the rebels dug in 30 meters above at the top of the ridge. "The high command sends us out on an operation after looking at a map," Laroche said. "They have no idea what the terrain looks like."

The platoon took positions in the clearing, which was like a narrow, sloping Alpine meadow, with no grass, just bare earth. A rebel sniper hit a Senegalese five feet to my left. He cried out in pain and fell behind a clump of bushes as the medic tried to reach him. Lavigne ran past me, saying, "I'm going to get that bastard." He was a fine shot and carried his bolt-action MAS 56 with a scope.

Lavigne crawled from bush to bush until he could see, 80 feet away, a small square of khaki, about six inches wide, in the space between two boulders. He aimed and fired twice and the khaki square disappeared.

Shaken by the artillery barrage and our automatic fire, the rebels started climbing out of their holes as we approached. One wounded *fel*, limping, tried to run. A Senegalese chased him down and shot him. He turned out to be their FM gunner, and the Senegalese brandished the FM above his head, knowing that a weapon recovered meant a citation.

Another rebel lay on his back with blood streaming out of an ugly gash in his stomach. Lavigne stood over him. "Don't kill me," the rebel said. "I'm a lieutenant in the ALN" (National Liberation Army). "If you evacuate me by helicopter, I can give you important information." Lavigne gave him the coup de grace. "He was too far gone," he said. "He'd have died before the chopper got here." As for the rebel sharpshooter between the boulders, Lavigne found his body slumped backward with two bullets in his chest.

We recovered seven bodies, which we carried down to the clearing and lined up, for a chopper to evacuate for burial. As they lay on their backs, their faces had the contorted look of men trying to squeeze one last breath from their lungs.

Back in Champlain, I reported to Lastours, who greeted me warmly. "What a splendid *tableau de chasse*" ("hunt tally"), he exclaimed, rubbing his hands. "Seven dead! This will improve my weekly report immeasurably. I'm putting you in for a citation."

"Don't forget that we have two dead and one wounded," I said. "In any case, I don't want a citation. What I want is to get out of this hole for a few days."

"Granted," Lastours said. "A forty-eight-hour pass in the first week of January 1957."

PART II

Introduction: How the War Moved
from the Bled *to Algiers*

WHY DID THE rebels turn from war in the *bled* to the urban terrorism that became the Battle of Algiers? The brunt of the war had been borne by the peasant masses. The FLN had to get the apathetic and divided urban population involved to show world opinion that they represented all the people. By November 1955, Abane Ramdane, known as the Robespierre of the rebellion for his intransigence, was back in the Casbah after four years in French prisons. The Casbah had one of the highest population densities in the world—80,000 Arabs on 45 acres. Abane was recruiting teams of commandos and distributing pamphlets in baskets of vegetables that said "Arise, people of Algiers." Abane was a small, sinewy man with a deeply lined face who won the respect of his jailers by going on a 40-day hunger strike. He was tenacity made flesh, as well as a fatalist who predicted that he would never see independence, for he would be dead by then.*

---

*In December 1957, he was murdered by other FLN leaders in a struggle for control of the movement.

Abane recruited Yacef Saadi, a child of the Casbah. Yacef worked in his father's bakery. In 1955, he was 25 years old, dapper and voluble, with big brown eyes in a face where one could still see the mischievous child, despite his mustache. Yacef was a bit of a posturing braggart, but he had organizational ability. He was a proponent of urban terrorism and told Abane he wanted to turn the Casbah into a fortress and send teams of bombers into the European city. One bomb in the rue Michelet, he said, was worth five battles in the *bled*. But for the moment, he focused on the political cleansing of the Casbah.

Yacef recruited Ali Amar, known as Ali-la-Pointe, because he came from the beach town of Pointe Pescade. Ali's schooling had been the Casbah streets. He was one of the semiabandoned children known as *yaouleds* who sold single cigarettes and chewing gum by the stick or lottery tickets or who carried little wooden shoeshine boxes. Ali grew up tall and athletic, and his good looks and wavy hair predestined him to pimpdom, with the required brutal streak and tattoos: *Tais-toi* ("shut up") on the top of his left hand and *Marche ou crève* ("March or die," the motto of the Foreign Legion) over his heart.

Arrested for pimping in 1954, Ali was sentenced to two years in Barberousse prison, located above the Casbah. Since common-law criminals were thrown in with politicals, Barberousse became a recruiting ground for the FLN. Ali's fallow mind was fertilized by militants who told him it was because of colonialism that he still signed his name with an *X*.

When he was released in 1956, he met Yacef at the flea market on the Boulevard de Verdun outside the prison, and said he was ready to help. Ali was a catch. He was violent by nature, and he knew the players in the Casbah milieu of pimps, gangsters, and drug dealers, their names and hangouts, and which ones were informers.

In late 1955 and early 1956, urban terrorism was limited to killing Arab police informers. Yacef's next move was to declare war on the *pegre* (gangsters). He became the strict enforcer of Islamic morals—no smoking, alcohol, drugs, or movies. The tactic was intended to bring the Casbah population under the control of the FLN.

Yacef had informers inside Barberousse, an ancient fortress with high, thick, whitewashed walls and a great entrance door painted black. In mid-May 1956, he was told that a van had brought sealed cases into the prison containing the parts of a guillotine: the blade, the scaffolding, the basket. In the basement of Barberousse there was a death row, two rows of narrow cells with tiny openings in the doors. Word got out that two of the men on death row, both FLN rebels, would be guillotined on June 19.

One of the men was Ahmed Zabana, an FLN officer, captured near Oran in the first month of the war, November 1954. Trapped in a cave and wounded twice, Zabana had shot himself in the temple, but the bullet exited from his left eye without touching his brain. He was hospitalized, then tried by a military tribunal, and sentenced to death. The second man, Ferradj Abdel-Kader, was a farm worker in the Mitidja plain. A neighboring farm burned down, and soldiers found an old bicycle in a ditch. Ferradj admitted it was his but said it had been stolen. He proclaimed his innocence before a military court. Although there was no other evidence against him, and although he was not given a lawyer to defend him, he too was sentenced to death.

In France, of which Algeria was supposedly a part, the death sentence was rarely carried out. When the executions were announced, the highest religious authorities in Algeria—the grand mufti, the Protestant pastor, and Monsignor Duval, the archbishop of Algiers—pleaded with the governor-general, Robert Lacoste, to exert his influence over President René Coty, who could pardon the two. Lacoste replied, "Blood must be answered with blood." Privately, Lacoste told his aides that if he wanted cooperation from the ultras, he would have to throw a few Arabs to the wolves.

On June 19, guards walked down the death row corridor, closing the shutters of all the cells, so that none of the inmates would know who was being removed. As soon as the men heard the clap of the shutters they began to shout, "*Tahya el-Djazair*" ("Long live Algeria").

Zabana was taken out first, manacled, with ankle chains, wearing a shirt with no collar. Guards led him across the courtyard to the guillotine, with its scaffolding, slanted blade, pulley system, and basket for the head to fall into, where a hooded executioner waited with the prison warden. At the foot of the guillotine, he cried, "I will die, but Algeria will live." He knelt and placed his neck in the semi-circle below the blade. The executioner pushed his torso forward. The heavy blade dropped, and the basket with his head in it was removed.

A few minutes later it was the turn of Ferradj, who did not go quietly. He screamed that he was innocent and let himself go limp, and had to be half-dragged, half-carried into the courtyard, as the *you-yous* of the Casbah women rose like rolling thunder.

In ordering the executions, Lacoste broke the unwritten compact that the FLN would not kill any Europeans in Algiers as long as its men on death row were spared. Yacef Saadi was now obliged to carry out reprisals. On June 22, handguns were distributed to his teams of young men. They were told to place on their victims' bodies a flyer saying, "Zabana and Ferradj, you are avenged." For three days the reprisals continued, and there was blood on the sidewalks of downtown Algiers. In the summer of 1956, Algiers was no longer a serene European capital. In July, there were so many attacks on police stations that they were ordered to place sandbags at the entrances.

Yacef was running five armed teams under Mokta Bouchafa, a daring rebel who received information that in the swamplike summer heat, the politicals in Barberousse were being beaten with iron bars and given salt water to drink. The next day his men ambushed the head guard on his way home and killed him with two bullets to the head. The day after that, two other guards were killed, then four more. Conditions inside the prison quickly improved, and life became bearable for the dozens of FLN inmates.

It was Bouchafa who had the idea of recruiting young Arab girls as couriers. Moslem women were kept in such a subservient state that they did not arouse suspicion and could move in and out of the Casbah without being searched.

Now that he had couriers, Yacef launched his bomb-making operation. He found a 24-year-old Jewish Communist chemist, Daniel Timsit, who was an intern at Mustapha Hospital, in his fifth year of medical school. Timsit had been radicalized by the anti-Semitic decrees of the Vichy government, which forced his expulsion from school. He knew something about explosives, and Yacef found him a villa in the European suburb of Birkadem, where he worked on making fulminate of mercury for detonators, of which he produced 300 grams.

Despite his precautions, such as carrying his MAT 49 under his armpit, fixed by thick rubber bands, Moktar Bouchafa was arrested on August 3 in a routine search on the rue Marengo. Another blow came three days later, when the police raided the villa in Birkadem, though Timsit was not there at the time. Then, on the night of August 9 came a harsh ultra reprisal in the upper Casbah. Four houses exploded on the rue de Thèbes, and 60 bodies were found in the ruins. Firemen did not arrive until two hours after the explosion, and the police did nothing to find the bombers.

Later that month, Abane Ramdane, who was in Algiers with other FLN leaders, left to attend the Soummam Congress (August 20 to September 10). Enraged by the rue de Thèbes massacre, he urged that the war be brought to the capital with the use of bombs in the European quarters. The FLN leaders approved the formation of an Algiers front and made Algiers an autonomous zone apart from the *wilayas* and headed by Ben M'Hidi, one of the top five leaders, who was already in the Casbah.

It was after the bombing at the rue de Thèbes that Yacef began to use bombs in downtown Algiers. Making bombs was no simple matter. The personnel included welders to make casings, artificers to connect the detonators to alarm clocks, chemists to prepare the explosive, transporters to convey the bombs, and European-looking agents to place them. The lab equipment came from sympathizers at Mustapha Hospital. Yacef's bomb team worked 10 hours a day, led by a 24-year-old chemistry student, Taleb Abderrahmane. Three more Arab girls were recruited, Zohra Drif, the daughter of a *caïd* (Moslem judge) from Tiaret, blond and pale-skinned; Samia Lakhdari, a 22-year-old law student; and Djamila Bouhired, green-eyed with light brown hair. All three could pass for European.

On September 30, 1956, a Sunday, the first bombs were ready, nine-inch-long cylinders with heavy cast-iron casings. Yacef summoned Drif, Lakhdari, and Bouhired, all French-speaking and wearing European clothes, and carrying beach bags. It was still summer in Algiers, so what could be more normal? He gave them their destinations. The Cafeteria and the Milk Bar, both near the university and popular with students, and the Air France terminal. The girls looked nervous. Who wouldn't be? "Any questions?" Yacef asked.

"But in those places," Samia Lakhdari said, "it's not just soldiers, it's women and children."

"Look at it this way," Yacef said, "the French have killed tens of thousands of our women and children, through famine and disease." The era of suicide bombers was yet to come. In Algiers, the bombs were always deposited in public places by couriers who left before they exploded.

The timers were fixed for 6:30 PM. Zohra Drif arrived at the Milk Bar on the rue d'Isly at 5:00, with an hour and a half to kill. The terrace was crowded with young people, and she entered a long, narrow room. Inside, she found a little table, ordered a sherbet, and paid as soon as she was served. When the clock on the wall said 6:15, she pushed her bag under a chair and left.

The Cafeteria on the rue Michelet, across the street from the university, was packed with the golden youth of Algiers. In a breach of security, Samia Lakhdari brought her mother with her for comfort. They sat near the jukebox to the right of the entrance and stuck the bag between the jukebox and the wall. At the Air France counter in the Mauritania building, Djamilah Bouhired asked for a flight schedule, sat across the waiting room in an armchair, and placed her bag beneath it.

The Air France bomb failed to detonate. The casualties from the two other bombs were 2 dead and 10 seriously wounded and requiring amputation, their ages 13 to 20. A French sympathizer told Abane Ramdane on the night of September 30 that random attacks on civilians would only deepen the divide between the two communities. "I don't see any difference between a girl placing a bomb at the Milk Bar," Abane said, "and a French aviator bombing an Arab village or firing napalm into a *mechta* [house]."

The *colons* of Algiers were badly shaken. If a car backfired, people jumped. Samia Lakhdari told Yacef that her fiancé didn't want her carrying any more bombs. She got married and left for Switzerland. Daniel Timsit was arrested on October 22. Ben M'Hidi, a short, slender man who wore wire-rim glasses and had a scar over his upper lip, took command of the Algiers Autonomous Zone. He was a man of the people, willing to take the same risks as his men. Algiers was now a super-*wilaya*. Where else could so many enemies of the French be found crowded together?

Ben M'Hidi's strategy was to make life as unpleasant as possible for the European population. They had to think twice about taking the bus or going to a café. In November, more weapons, smuggled in from Morocco, came into the Casbah, in fruit and vegetable trucks. They included plastic explosives, powerful enough to reduce the bombs to the size of a pack of cigarettes.

Ben M'Hidi asked Yacef to carry out some targeted assassinations. Spreading fear in the population was not enough. *Colon* leaders, who shaped the anti-Arab mentality that filtered down to the masses, had to be held accountable as well. Yacef drew up a list of "French notables to assassinate." At the top of the list was the number-one reactionary, the head of the Federation of Mayors and mayor of Boufarik, 74-year-old Amédée Froger, who clamored for the death sentence for all arrested rebels. In Boufarik, he had a gang of bodyguards who hunted down FLN militants and tied them to trees and shot them. Froger kept an apartment in Algiers, at 108 rue Michelet. On December 28 at 9:50 AM, he left the building to get into his gray, chauffeur-driven 403 Peugeot. An Arab approached and fired three shots at close range. Froger, sitting next to his driver, slumped over, and the killer fled in a waiting car. The funeral of this rabid enforcer of the status quo on December 29 turned into a riot. Crowds of young *pieds-noirs* ("black feet," as settlers were called, supposedly because the Alsatians arrived in Algeria with black shoes) vandalized Arab stores and beat up or shot Arab passersby. The police did nothing to decrease the body count of 4 dead and 50 wounded.

By December 1956, Yacef had 1,400 armed men in Algiers and its suburbs. Lacoste complained that "we're fighting terrorists, and we don't know how." The war had spread to Algiers, and the police were ineffective. They could not penetrate the FLN networks and rarely made an arrest. Lacoste realized he had to put the army in charge of security in the capital. He wanted an Indochina veteran who had fought the Viets.

The job went to a 58-year-old five-star general, Raoul Salan, whose life had been shaped by the wars that France had fought in the twentieth century. Born in 1899, the son of a tax collector, he grew up in the southern city of Nîmes, with its Roman ruins and Spanish bullfights.

Salan's career was spent in colonies that France eventually lost, in a succession of costly efforts followed by failure. His mentality and personality in large part were an amalgam of those experiences. In the French protectorate of Syria, he was wounded fighting Islamic rebels. Sent to Indochina in 1924, he ended up spending 17 years there, broken up by other assignments.

At that time, the enemies were smugglers and pirates, not Viets. Salan commanded troops but also administered a Laotian province. It wasn't a bad life, and it was certainly picturesque. French officers were tempted to go native. Salan smoked the occasional pipe of opium, a pleasantly harmless form of relaxation, which earned him the nickname *Le Chinois*, according to the malicious tattle that opium-smoking made your skin turn yellow. He took a Laotian common-law wife, who bore him a son, François, in 1932.

When he went back to France in 1937, assigned to the Asian desk at the Ministry of Colonies, he took his son with him, but not his wife. On the boat going over, he met a young woman, Lucienne Bouguin, whom he married. His career advanced, but not by leaps and bounds. He was promoted to captain in 1929, and to major in 1940. He joined de Gaulle as a colonel in the 10th Armored Division of the famed "King Jean" (Marshal de Lattre de Tassigny). In 1945, he followed de Lattre to Indochina, where the Viets had taken over from the Japanese occupier and a war was on. Salan stayed until 1953, and was briefly commander-in-chief, during which time he ordered a counterattack on a strong point captured by the Viets, called Dien Bien Phu. He had left Indochina by the time the counterattack took place and thus had nothing to do with the final battle, except for contributing to Dien Bien Phu's becoming ingrained in French military thinking.

Three years later, now a five-star general and the most decorated soldier in the French army, he was summoned to Algiers. Salan was of medium height but stood ramrod straight. He had a full head of white hair, which some said was blued, thick brows, large, deep-set brown eyes, and the strong nose of a Roman proconsul. His years in Asia had given him an oriental calm. He was courteous, elegant, reserved, and known as a political general. But though he had learned to stay on good terms with the revolving-door politicians, he believed, as did the other Indochina hands, that the military had done its job there but the politicians had not. Now, in Algeria, he would not let that happen again.

Salan arrived in Algiers on November 15, 1956. The ultras thought of him as the man who had lost Indochina, even though he had not been there at the end. They revived the rumors that he was a Freemason and an opium addict, not to be trusted, and that he was so vain that he slept with his *bananes* (decorations) under his pillow. Salan, who had fought in a dozen countries since 1917, always honorably, and who carried scars seen and unseen, did not at first grasp the dimensions of the Algerian dilemma, though he continued to believe that France without her empire was not France.

Lacoste went to Paris on January 4, 1957, for a cabinet meeting. He had picked up rumors that the FLN planned a general strike in Algiers later in the month, to be timed with a debate on Algeria in the United Nations. The strike, intended to paralyze Algiers for a week, to show that the FLN controlled the Moslem population, had to be stopped.

Three days later, back in Algiers, Lacoste summoned General Jacques Massu, commander of the 10th Paratroop Division, and asked him to take over the security of the city. Recently returned from the failed Suez expedition, Massu was 49, a fourth-generation soldier who had graduated from Saint-Cyr in 1930 and been sent to Morocco as a second lieutenant in a regiment of colonial infantry. In 1940, he joined de Gaulle and served under General Philippe Leclerc de Hautecloque, whose 2nd Armored Division liberated Paris on August 25, 1944. Massu walked into the Hotel Majestic, on Avenue Kléber, which was occupied by the German high command, with a single soldier, who was killed in the street by a sniper. He yelled "Raus," and 50 officers and 300 men surrendered. "I didn't even have to take my Colt out of the holster," he recalled.

One of the nurses and ambulance drivers in the division, Lieutenant Suzanne Rosenberg, was attracted to the strapping, no-nonsense six-footer. She was married to a much older man, the well-known Paris lawyer Henri Torrès, but she divorced him in 1948 and married Massu. She helped smooth the edges of this rough diamond, one of whose maxims was "When you're not fighting, you're training."

Massu followed Leclerc to Indochina, where the French were using tanks in the Mekong Delta. But in this kind of guerrilla war, paratroopers were the answer. He tried his first jump at the age of 39, landing clumsily, and soon took command of a para regiment. It was then that he came to the attention of Salan, when he established order in a French neighborhood of Saigon, after a Viet massacre.

Massu left Indochina in 1951, convinced that his men were fighting without the backing of the government or the people of metropolitan France. From 1951 to 1954, having ruffled some feathers in the ministries, he was relegated to staff jobs in West Africa, and in 1955, still a colonel, he was sent to Tunisia.

That June, however, he got his general's star and was transferred to Algeria to take command of the 10th Paratroop Division, which he had to create from the ground up. A year later, with four regiments in place, the division was given its first assignment: Suez.

To Massu's disgust, the Suez expedition was aborted, for he was convinced that if they could remove Nasser, the war in Algeria could be quickly won, since Nasser was supplying the FLN with funds and weapons. The 10th Division returned in December, just in time to take over police powers in Algiers. On January 7, 1957, Lacoste told Massu: "I am going to entrust you with order in Algiers. You will have full powers. With your division, you will get this city under control."

Upon returning to his headquarters at the Orléans barracks, Massu told his chief of staff, Colonel Yves Godard: "I've just been given police powers." Seeing Godard's glum expression, Massu said: "The news doesn't seem to please you."

"It's not our job," Godard said. "We're paras, not cops."

"We've got to do it," Massu said. "That's all. We've got carte blanche to get rid of the killers and the bombers."

Massu thought it over. Obviously, Lacoste, back from Paris, had acted with the blessing of the prime minister, Guy Mollet. Obviously, the Algiers police were a flop and had too many ultra connections. Obviously, they needed a para division, with experience in guerrilla warfare.

Massu went to see Salan, who congratulated him and urged him to conduct night patrols in the Casbah. The key to success, he said, was intelligence. One link in the chain of command would lead to another.

Serge Baret, the prefect of Algiers, was a prudent man, thought of as too passive. He was relieved to sign over the delegation of powers, the most important of which were the power to detain those arrested instead of having them arraigned before a judge, and the power to search without warrants. The methods Massu could use remained undefined, but as he put it, he had carte blanche. He made two appointments for "special tasks" outside the chain of command. Lieutenant Colonel Roger Trinquier had spent so many years behind Viet lines that he looked Vietnamese, with slanting eyes and a tea-colored complexion. His mazelike Asian mind saw enemies everywhere and sometimes seemed on the verge of paranoia. He was named head of the DPU (Urban Protection Disposition), which drew up a census of the Casbah and was denounced by its critics as Massu's GPU. Major Paul Aussaresses, a veteran intelligence officer who had worked with Trinquier in Indochina, became the head of the torture teams.

Massu had formed the 10th Paratrooper Division by grouping four regiments that came from other corps—the 3rd RPC (*Régiment de Parachutistes Coloniaux*), who wore red berets and were commanded by Colonel Marcel Bigeard, were in charge of the Casbah. Colonel Fossey-François and the 1st RPC took downtown Algiers. Colonel Meyer of the 1st RCP (*Régiment de Chasseurs Parachutistes*, mountain troops, or blue berets) and Colonel Jeanpierre of the 1st REP (*Régiment Étranger Parachutiste*, the Foreign Legion, or green berets) divided the suburbs. If you added the police, the gendarmes and the 9th *zouaves*, already implanted in the Casbah, Massu had roughly 6,000 men under his command. Each para regiment maintained its autonomy and had its own intelligence officers and interrogation centers.

Of the four para colonels, all veterans of Indochina, Bigeard had a legendary reputation, compiled from the hardships he had suffered and survived. At 40, he was a chain-smoker, tall and lean, with an angular face, a high brow, a jutting nose, sharp blue eyes, and sandy hair cut short. He despised desk-bound officers, and his superiors had to win his respect. His legend was the armor that insulated him from the chain of command.

His feats of arms in Indochina were such that he was quickly promoted to battalion commander and called upon whenever there was a troublesome assignment. In March 1954, Bigeard commanded one of the two airborne battalions that were dropped on the encircled fort of Dien Bien Phu.

The Viets in the village opened fire while Bigeard and his 650 men were still in the air, and 11 died and 52 were wounded. The planes had dropped them from a high altitude to avoid General Giap's flak. But such was Bigeard's reputation that the 10,000 men in the fort and its strongpoints took heart. Bigeard had walked out of tough spots before.

In the checkerboard plain, the French fought for a month to hold an area the size of a single rice paddy. It was there that Bigeard developed the commando tactics that would serve him well in Algeria. Small units in night raids climbed steep slopes after an artillery barrage, and one company equipped with flame-throwers torched Viet bunkers. By April, Bigeard was holding one of the five strongpoints named after girls, Eliane 2, and using the piled-up bodies of Viets as sandbags. Giap burrowed under the French barbed wire and dug a network of trenches. Stethoscopes hung around the necks of French officers as they picked up the clank of picks and shovels.

On May 7, 1954, Dien Bien Phu surrendered. That was the day France's colonial reign in Asia ended. Bigeard was one of the 8,158 survivors taken prisoner at Dien Bien Phu, after burning his personal papers and rolling a silk escape map around one of his ankles. The Viets asked him to reenact his surrender by coming out of his bunker with his hands up, so that he could be filmed by a Soviet cameraman. "I'd rather croak," he said.

He almost did croak on the nightmare 45-day march through the jungle to the prison camp of Tuan Giao, walking with his hands tied behind his back with telephone wire. Dehydration and dysentery were fatal to many, and Bigeard dropped 80 pounds.

At the camp he had to appear before a people's tribunal for self-criticism. What did he think of American aid to France, he was asked. What did they think of Chinese aid to the Viets, he replied. His rice ration was cut. Bigeard noticed that the Algerian prisoners were separated from the French and congratulated for their fighting spirit. Peking-trained Algerian "instructors" then told them, "Since you're such good soldiers, why don't you fight for yourselves? Why fight for the occupiers? Why don't you take back your country?" Here among the captured prisoners of Dien Bien Phu were his future enemies. Bigeard also learned from the Viets. He learned ruthlessness and brainwashing techniques, both of which were useful when he arrived in Algeria in 1955.

At first, he commanded a para battalion in the mountains of eastern Algeria. He developed a combat mystique, according to which each danger you survived gave you a reserve of capital to survive the next one. He led his men unarmed on operations, with faith in his *baraka*. The man standing a foot away from him would be shot, but not him. In July 1956, in an operation near the port of Bône, in the Nemencha Mountains, his luck ran out. He was shot in the chest just above the heart. Evacuated by chopper, he was operated on in Constantine. A month later, he was in the port city of Bône, recuperating, jogging every morning along the oceanfront, unarmed and without an escort. On September 5, three young Arabs lounging against a wall across the street fired as he passed and shot him in the back. Although hit twice, he spun around and lunged at the Arabs, who fled. Bleeding down his back, his right arm shattered and a slug near his liver, he stopped the car of a *colon*, who took one look at him and said, "You'll stain my seat," and drove off.

The First Battle of Algiers

O N JANUARY 7, 1957, I left Champlain with a two-day pass in my pocket, took the train from Médéa, and reached Algiers around noon. I found a small hotel, the Oasis, where I'd been told they gave soldiers a discount. I didn't know a soul, but I had a connection. The American consul, Lewis Clark, had been a friend of my parents from before World War II. In the summer of 1939, when I was seven, my father rented a house in Marion, Massachusetts, where the Clarks also summered, and I played with their curly-haired daughter, Ann. That was the summer I discovered Howard Johnson's 57 flavors and Marvel comics, but it was interrupted by the start of World War II, and my father left for France.

When I called the consulate, Clark was cordial and invited me to lunch the next day. One of his aides gave me directions on how to get to the residence in the hills of El-Biar. It was a mild and sunny day, and I went out to get a feel of the city. Built on a slope from hills to harbor, it seemed to be sliding toward the ocean. With nearly 900,000 inhabitants, one third of them Arabs, Algiers was France's second largest city, bigger than Lyon or Marseille. I walked up a ramp from the deep harbor once so friendly to pirates. Sheltered from the sea winds and protected by a breakwater, it smelled of brine and tar. The modern city, hemmed in between the mountains and the Mediterranean, had grown east and west along a narrow coastal strip, flat land where streetcar lines were extended until year by year, the city spread to the suburbs of Pointe Pescade to the west and Hussein Dey to the east . . . a city all in length.

Along the ramp, I stopped in a hole-in-the-wall bistro that featured grilled *rouget* (red mullet). What drew me in was a small sign in the window: *Le patron mange ici* ("The owner eats here"). "It's so fresh, it's still wagging its tail," the Arab waiter said. At the top of the ramp stood the majestic Square Bresson, with the opera house at one end, flanked by balconied buildings of cut stone. A magnolia garden lined with palm trees adorned the center of the square. The flower beds surrounded a gazebo where bands played on summer evenings.

Behind the opera house was the Place de la Lyre and its open market, and behind that the Casbah began. I could see a jumble of flat rooftops and small cone-shaped windows covered by grillwork. When I strolled over to the rue Bab-Azoun, an arcaded street with square pillars and old paving stones, I saw that one end, closed with rolls of concertina wire, was guarded by steel-helmeted *zouaves*. Under the arcades were rows of shops that smelled of coffee beans and olive oil and tourist traps that sold brass tables and silver *fatma*'s hands. The 80,000 inhabitants of the Casbah were wired in like chickens in a coop.

On the other side of the Square Bresson I came upon the Place du Government, a square bordered on three sides by arcaded buildings and opening on the equestrian statue of the duc d'Orléans, made in 1845 from the melted-down bronze cannons of the Turks. Everywhere there were reminders of the occupation. The Great Mosque, Djama el Kebir, which went back to the tenth century, was now a cathedral. This was not the usual orderly French city with streets branching out from circles, it was a hodgepodge, as if a child had dropped his Pick-Up Sticks. The ancient city of the subject people was surrounded by the modern city of the occupier. Once encased by fortress walls, the Casbah borders were now boulevards, Gambetta to the south, Valée to the north, and Victoire to the west.

Wandering in another direction, I found the rue d'Isly, the Fifth Avenue of Algiers, with the chic shops and cafés. On the Place Bugeaud, the frowning marshal who had devised France's scorched earth policies stood in bronze, in front of the army headquarters where General Salan had his office. There I saw the first paras, red berets, guarding the building.

I sat at a café terrace crowded with young people and listened to the conversations. The girls were still tanned, though it was January, and the guys talked with their hands like Arabs. They were chatting about the bombs, as in normal times they would have talked about the weather. The bomb that went off and the bomb that failed to go off. The friend in the café who was hit and the friend in the other café who wasn't. What made them choose that café, they wondered. The man at a bar who saw the man next to him shot in the back. Why him? Life was a lottery.

The bombs had become a mnemonic device ("it was the day after the bomb went off in the Milk Bar"), or a way to give directions ("it's a little shop around the corner from the restaurant that blew up last week"). And yet, I reflected, they were getting on with their lives, still going to cafés, still shopping. If their lives were a lottery, the prize was not getting killed or maimed.

I went back to my hotel and showered. Dourakine had told me about a bar near the harbor called the Perroquet Rouge (Red Parrot) where legionnaires hung out. I thought it might be interesting to have a look in the evening. When I found the place, it had swinging doors, like a bar in a western, and two bouncers were in the process of throwing a drunken green beret into the street. They gave him one last push, and he fell into the gutter in a clump.

"Hey, what's going on?" I asked.

"The *salaud* [filthy bum] tried to pay for a drink with a hand grenade," one of the bouncers said.

"All these asshole legionnaires think about is *flouss*" (money), the other one said.

I went to the bar and ordered a beer. The green beret sergeant beside me raised his glass and said, "*prosit*. That guy they threw out," he said, "he wasn't a German. He was Hungarian. My name is Thomas." He spoke with a thick German accent. "I know they say we're the dregs of Europe, but we're not all alike."

He wasn't that young a man, and I asked him how long he'd been in.

"This is my third tour," he said. "I'm forty years old. They call me *Der Alte* [the old one]. I came home from the eastern front in 1945, I was a POW in the French zone, so I enlisted in the legion. I figured, I fought against the French in 1940, why not fight with them?"

"That makes sense," I said, while thinking, He has the soul of a mercenary; he doesn't care whose side he's on.

"So now I kill *fellaghas*," Thomas said, "and they call us mercenaries, but I also risk my life."

"I know what you mean," I said. "I'm stationed near the Chiffa Gorges." I nodded to the barman and raised two fingers. "Give us another round."

"I have nothing against them, except they smell," Thomas said. "And when they're dead, they smell worse."

"In my unit," I said, "we were responsible for a sector, so we took prisoners to get information."

"We're an intervention unit, in and out, so we don't give a fuck about prisoners," Thomas said. "In combat you do things you shouldn't do. We used flame-throwers in the caves, but that's banned. And sometimes we go into a *douar* where none of the Arabs speak French, and some of the boys help themselves to a girl, since you know they're not going to turn you in."

"The misfortunes of war," I said. The mentality of these legionnaires, who with other elite units did the brunt of the fighting, was disturbing to explore. The legion had a proud tradition, but beneath the veneer of panache they were rapacious brutes, trained to kill, like pit bulls.

"Always remember," Thomas said, "there's no justice in the army." That was their rationale. Since they were trapped in an unfair system, why should they abide by the rules? So they sold their weapons to the *fels*, and deserted when they had the chance, all the while maintaining the reputation of heroic daredevils bound by tight discipline.

"One time I recovered a machine gun," Thomas said, "and it was a German make. The captain told me I'd touch the red [get the Legion of Honor]. So I decided to make a suggestion. 'We're short on mortars,' I said. 'I don't need advice on our armament from a sergeant,' the captain said. I said, 'You mean advice on wearing pants without a belt or suspenders?' That was it—I didn't get my citation."

Thomas said he had to leave. *"Gott in Himmel!* Now that we have to do this police work in Algiers, we have a curfew. Still, it's better than the *bled.* You can duck out and get a beer, and the girls seem to like us. Well, *bonne blessure."* *"Bonne blessure,"* or "have a good wound," was the way legionnaires greeted each other.

The next day at noon, I took a cab to the consular residence. It wound up the El-Biar hill past the fine villas of affluent *colons,* their balconies overlooking the bay, and reached a Moorish mansion, with keyhole windows, old tiles, and a splendid garden planted with ancient eucalyptus trees. The butler who answered the door wore a red fez and led me into an ornately carved library of faded red and blue columns and shelves, covered with finely worked lattices. On the pearl-inlaid chest of drawers stood a large bust of a turbaned Moor.

Lewis Clark, whom I had not seen since Marion in 1939, rose from a gray, button-tufted divan and greeted me warmly. He was one of those cherubic elders with a pink face, a thatch of powdery white hair, and rheumy blue eyes. In his red-striped seersucker suit, he looked like a walking Christmas tree ornament, a life-size peppermint stick.

"This is my last post," he said. "I stepped in to replace a consul who was getting foggy. He gave a press conference for the American correspondents on the Algerian economy. When he was asked about the nitrates, he said they were better than the day rates."

I said I was surprised at the crowds downtown behaving as if things were normal.

"Some of that is the presence of the paras," Clark said, lighting a cigarette from a monogrammed box on a low Moroccan painted table. "They've sealed off the Casbah. There's one on every streetcar and bus searching packages. There's a nine PM curfew. If you go to a movie, you can't leave before the show is over, and you're searched before you're seated. Still, people are being careful. I went to see my little Spanish tailor to be fitted for a suit, and the man standing next to me in front of the mirrors was trying on a bulletproof vest."

"I've seen their patrols in the streets," I said, "strutting like barnyard roosters."

Clark chuckled and said, "They may strut, but they do a good job. Last week there was a daring daylight robbery in a jewelry store on the rue d'Isly, and people said, 'Thank God ordinary crime is making a reappearance.' Everyone wondered who the thieves were that risked being shot on this heavily patrolled street in the heart of downtown for the sake of a few diamonds. It seemed almost like a sign that things were back to normal."

"Almost," I said.

"*Bien entendu,*" Clark said, lapsing into the French that he spoke so well. "Things will get worse before they get better. I'm told there's a contingency plan to tear down the Casbah and build a housing project, but they'll never do it."

Other guests had arrived, Clark's colleagues from the consulate, and as we chatted he looked at his watch and said, "Our guest of honor is late." At that moment, we heard dogs barking in the courtyard. They were the two wolfhounds of General Jacques Massu, who got out of his Peugeot, still sand-colored from Suez. Pulling on leashes held by an aide, the snarling wolfhounds stayed outside.

"I was ambushed on the way up," Massu said as he made his entrance. "It was nothing. I pray you to pardon my tardiness." Two Arabs, later caught, had fired a burst at his car as it rounded a hairpin curve at top speed.

Massu, a towering and youthful 50, reminded me of a giant lumberjack with exaggerated features in a children's book I had once read—a bony face, a beaklike nose, a black mustache, a granite jaw—a face made to order for a warrior in any period of history. His wife, Suzanne, I later learned, called him "the Cro-Magnon man." In his para field uniform, with the sleeves rolled up, he seemed to be saying, "I'm just one of the guys—don't put me behind a desk."

Despite being Salan's subordinate, he was the most powerful man in Algiers, in command of the army and the police, able to deal with urban terrorism any way he chose. As Lewis Clark quizzed him at the lunch table on developments, his face changed from scowl to smile. I noticed that from time to time he scowled in my direction. I was in my brown infantryman's uniform, with the single bar of a second lieutenant on my epaulet, and he must have wondered what I was doing in such exalted company. In the bustle of his arrival, I had not been introduced.

After lunch, Clark took me over and said: "General, this young man has come from the United States to fight in Algeria."

Massu asked what I was doing in America.

"I was a reporter on a newspaper, *mon général*," I said, standing at attention.

"*Ah bon*," he said. "So you have some experience in journalism."

"Yes, *mon général*," I said, not adding that my experience amounted to less than four months on the *Worcester Telegram* before being conscripted.

Massu scribbled on a notepad and said, "*Eh bien*, call this number tomorrow and ask for Major de Brissac. *Repos*" (at ease).

The next morning I called Brissac, who gave me an address and told me to get there right away. I found the dead-end alley off the rue d'Isly, and pressed the buzzer marked Compagnie Atlantique. I walked up to the third floor, and Brissac opened the door, dressed in civilian clothes, a double-breasted gray pin-striped suit, gray shirt with gold cuff links, and patterned tie. He was an elegant-looking man, tall and narrow-chested, his head a half-size too small for his frame, but fine-boned, with a longish face, lively blue eyes, a mustache, a high brow, and wavy brown hair combed neatly back. A man about town, I thought, debonair, at home at garden parties and race tracks. I kept expecting him to twirl his mustache.

He grasped my hand in both of his and said, "I'm enchanted to meet you. Massu told me about you. You're just what we need."

"But for what?" I asked.

"Oh, no one explained? That's the army. I must give you my mini-lecture," which he proceeded to do in an office with two desks and two typewriters. The blinds on the windows were closed and the walls were bare, as if he had just moved in.

"Number one," Brissac intoned. "When I was in Indochina, I was awestruck by the finesse of those so-called Third World people. I sometimes felt that if I had been Vietnamese, I might have been Vietminh. Some officers came home with a visceral hatred of Communism. Others, like myself, were convinced that it was a war of nationalism, to which our mistakes as a colonial power contributed. Those who try to impose the Indochina model on Algeria fail to see that this is not Communism, it's Islamic nationalism. So, lesson number one: 'Understand your enemy.' "

"I found that out in the *bled*," I said.

"Number two. The war has moved from the *bled* to Algiers, where the classic methods of warfare don't work. This isn't Verdun or Monte Cassino. Thanks to the idiotic fiction that Algeria is part of France, we are technically not at war, we are under French peacetime law. The police and the gendarmes are paralyzed by legal constraints, the court system, and so on. But the army always finds a way. When the Méharis fucked their camels in the ass and got strange diseases, the army had to find an article of the military code they had broken. They were charged with 'deterioration of army materiel.' So now they've brought in the paras, because the regular army is about as adapted to fighting urban terrorism as a buzzsaw is to operating on a cataract. Every uniform, if you know the code, is an information bulletin. Legion of Honor, tailored suit, braided képi, that means one thing. *Tenue léopard, beret rouge,* that means warriors, veterans of other terrorist campaigns. So, lesson number two: Bringing in the paras is the first positive sign. For Massu, this is a war to the death. His troops patrol the city as they would a conquered enemy position."

"He's a marked man," I said. "He was ambushed yesterday on the way to lunch."

"He knows there's a price on his head," Brissac said. "When he goes to mass on Sunday, the priest ends his sermon with a request to his parishioners that they remain seated until the general has a chance to leave.

"Number three," Brissac went on. "Three events marked my youth. The defeat of 1940, the German occupation, and the formidable cavalcade of victorious armies that liberated Paris. I was sixteen in June 1940, and I was walking with my mother on the Place des Ternes, and we saw a soldier on a bench crying. My mother said, 'You see, he's lost everything, his regiment, his officers, his rifle, but he's still got his bottle of wine.' When the war was over, I enlisted in the hope that I could help redeem the reputation of the army. To be very frank, I'm not a flag-waver. I don't give a damn about keeping Algeria French. But I want to win to avoid any further deterioration in the army, particularly after Indochina. So lesson number three: Win for the army."

I began to see Brissac as a modern-day Manichaean who had deviated from the established faith and constructed his own religion. Its doctrine was coherent in a way. He despised the government under which he served but believed that the war must be won to save the integrity of the army. The spineless Fourth Republic did not deserve its splendid army and did not have the credibility to give it direction. It was up to the army to run Algiers, without interference. The time of the leopards (as the paras were known) had come.

We seemed, however, to be pissing around the pot. I still had no idea why I had come here. I asked why I had been sent to him.

"We are losing the information war," Brissac said. "Radio Cairo is on twenty-four hours a day, brainwashing the Casbah population. We must counter this torrent of FLN propaganda. You've heard that the FLN has called a general strike in Algiers for the end of the month. The strike will be the test. We have to do some serious perception management. Massu has asked me to bring out a weekly newspaper giving our side. It will be called *Réalités Algériennes*. Although funded and published by the army, it will appear in the kiosques with the other papers. I've found one fellow who worked on a paper in Paris, and I'd like you to join our team. It will be just the three of us."

"But do you really think the Arabs will read the paper?" I asked.

"It's in the nature of a colonized people," Brissac said, "as a refuge from their distress, to feel that there is something in them willing to be colonized. Just as the wife of an overbearing husband feels there is something in her that allows it. We have to play on that and keep telling them that the army is here to help them and make their lives normal again. We cannot simply give up and let the FLN take control of their minds and hearts."

"But the FLN is offering them independence and a better life in a country of their own, without the French," I said.

"Many of them don't want independence," Brissac said. "They are still at the stage when they need our assistance. Our role will be to show them the benevolent face of France. We must demythologize these matters. Take the 'mysterious' Casbah. There is nothing mysterious about it if we see it as a physical representation of the Arab mind, secretive, resilient, resistant to change, and teeming with a thousand twisting passages. Now, what do you say? With you and the other fellow writing the articles, we can bring out our first issue in a week or two. Of course, you can't discuss your work, or reveal the address of this office. You'll wear civilian clothes, you will not carry a weapon, and you'll find lodging in town. Are you in accord?"

I thought his reasoning was specious, and that putting out a paper would not change any Arab minds. His motive for winning the war, to keep up the morale of the army, did not concern me, since I was serving my time. My length of service, however, had been extended from 18 to 27 months, meaning that I would be in Algeria until the end of 1957. Here was an opportunity to get out of the *bled*, wear civilian clothes, live in Algiers. It was hard to pass up. Instead of being a hired gun, I would be a hired pen. I'd written junk before, in the New York office of the *Hollywood Reporter*, the summer after Yale, when I turned out paragraphs of film gossip.

I told Brissac that I would be happy to work on the paper. In spite of his pronouncements, he did not have a conventional military mind, and I found him likable.

He peeled off some bills from his wallet and gave me the name of a store where I could buy a couple of suits. "I'll arrange to have your regiment ship your gear to Massu's headquarters," he said, "since you don't know yet where you'll be staying. Take a couple of days to settle in and then check back here."

It occurred to me that there were few if any times in the army when one was given a choice, and that, having been given one, I would be a fool not to take it.

I still had my room at the Oasis Hotel, and I started looking for a boardinghouse. Lewis Clark had asked me to look up Don Davies at the United States Information Agency, and the next morning, after buying a suit, I had a couple of free hours. The American library was on the rue Michelet, at street level, with a façade that looked like a pillbox, a narrow display window just high enough to place a few books. Davies, a sunny and outgoing man, seemed glad to see me. He was tall and bald, with a pencil mustache and brown eyes that looked inquiringly out at the world without blaming it. He got coffee, and we sat down at one of the reading-room tables.

"December was the worst month," he said. "There was a lot of anti-American feeling over Suez. The press printed stories that documents found on Ben Bella proved that America was selling weapons to the rebels. The funeral for Froger [the ultra mayor of Boufarik] passed right by us, and rocks flew through our big plate-glass window. Then we had a couple of small bombs. I put in a tiny window with bullet-proof glass. Now we're hopefully bomb-proof."

I asked him if the paras were making a difference.

"Massu may help stop the terrorism," Davies said, "but he's also digging the ditch that separates the two communities a little deeper by acting on the theory that every Arab is guilty until proven innocent. For every terrorist he catches, he makes two more Arab enemies. I have an Arab working for me here who goes out and buys my afternoon paper. Yesterday he came back shaking like a leaf because he'd been threatened by other Arabs for buying a French paper. He told them he was illiterate, he was just running an errand, but he asked me to please send someone else in the future. When I'm asked how the two communities get along, I say they're like drawers in a desk, at different levels and never touching."

I looked around and saw a couple of kids and three adults reading magazines from the rack. "Attendance is down," Davies said, "but we've still got our regulars. See that woman sitting near the entrance?" He pointed to a young woman with bobbed hair, wearing a pink and gray jersey dress, with a single strand of grape-sized gray pearls around her neck. "That's Georgette Cohen. Her family's big in real estate. Come on—I'll introduce you."

When Georgette stood, I saw that she was nearly six feet tall with heels. Her thin legs made her look storklike, but she was a stork of bright plumage that covered hefty hips, a wasp waist, and a blooming bosom. Her large, appraising eyes had pupils the color of bittersweet chocolate, and her wide, full-lipped mouth was quick to smile.

"Are you any relation to René de Gramont?" she asked, after Davis had introduced me.

"We're cousins and close friends," I said. René was about my age but had been exempted from military service because of curvature of the spine.

"René is the most amusing man," Georgette said. "I met him in Paris, where I spent a year taking classes at the Arts Décoratifs. He told me he refused to go into the army because they wouldn't let him carry an umbrella when it rained."

"He spent a year lying on his back on a board to straighten his spine," I said.

"I brought back a husband from Paris," Georgette said. "An engineer from the École des Mines" (a top engineering school). "His name is Cohen too, so I kept my maiden name."

"You could call yourself Cohen-Cohen, though that would seem redundant," I said.

"Or Cohen *Bis* [Encore]," Georgette said, laughing.

"He came here with you not long ago," Davies said. "We talked about the oil they've found in the Sahara."

"He's down there now," Georgette said, "in Hassi-Messaoud, on the team that digs the wells." Addressing me, she asked, "And what are you doing in Algiers?"

"The same as your husband," I said. "My military service."

"Why aren't you in uniform?"

"I'm on Massu's staff, detached to a civilian office."

"How exciting! Do you carry a weapon?"

"I don't."

"How can I be sure?"

I opened my suit jacket wide and said, "Search me."

"That won't be necessary," she said. "Where do you live?"

"Right now, at the hotel. I'm looking for a boardinghouse."

"Don't be silly," Georgette said. "I'm managing a building for my parents at Square Bresson. They've gone back to France. I live on the top floor, and there's an empty apartment you can use rent-free."

"I don't want to be any trouble," I said, while thinking, This is too good to be true. Georgette was the managerial type. She liked to take matters, and people, in hand. "It's no trouble. Quite the contrary," she said. "I would rather have the apartment occupied. I will ask you only to pay for the maid who comes to clean it." She wrote down her address and phone number and asked me to come by with my things that evening at six.

I walked out of the American library feeling almost giddy. Wow, was I on a roll! First an assignment in Algiers, now a free apartment on the prettiest square in town, with a gorgeous landlady whose husband was in the Sahara. I needed to find a high-stakes poker game or horse race to run out my string.

At 6:00, I stood in front of a turn-of-the-century building with a high, arched carriage entrance and balconies looking out on the palm trees and the opera. Inside the courtyard, I announced my name to the concierge, whose loge was across from rows of waxed wooden mailboxes with copper nameplates. I walked up five flights to Georgette's landing and rang the bell. She came out and said, *"La politesse des rois"* ("Punctuality is the politeness of kings"). She showed me around the apartment where I would be staying, which had a balcony looking out on the square. It was furnished in the heavy late-nineteenth-century style, with a high, mirrored armoire in the bedroom and twin beds with caning at the base. The kitchen was huge, and so were the living room and the dining room. Monogrammed towels hung from racks in the bathroom. With its overpadded armchairs, Asian rugs, and academic seascapes with breaking waves, it had the kind of opulent bad taste the French call *cossu* ("substantial").

"I hope you'll be comfortable," she said. "Come over in an hour. I'm making dinner." Well, I was in the army and I was used to taking orders, and these were very agreeable orders. I unpacked my gear and took a shower in a big bathtub with feet, and I spent 20 minutes on the balcony, looking at the birds flying around the garden and the people sitting on benches reading newspapers and chatting. You wouldn't have known that there was a war on.

At 7:00, I crossed the landing and rang the bell. Georgette looked majestic in a golden caftan. She took my hand and led me into a living room decorated in the Empire style, massive and bombastic, mahogany-veneered divans with ormolu mounts, tables with winged-lion supports, and, in a corner, a pilaster with a sphinx at the top. On a low table with feet like hooves, there was a bottle of Veuve Clicquot, two glasses, and some pâté.

"I thought we might celebrate your arrival in Algiers," she said.

"I'm overwhelmed."

"You can't live constantly in a state of anxiety. At school, the kids are taught to lie down if they hear an explosion. After all, it's the luck of the draw. *Au hazard, Balthazar.*"

"When I was in the *bled*, I believed in *baraka*," I said, clicking her champagne glass.

"I've lived in Algiers all my life. I learned at an early age that the communities all judge one another. After passing my exam in the *sixième*, I had a choice between two languages, Arabic and German, and my mother said, 'What good will Arabic do you? Take German.'"

"That's what mothers are for, to give us bad advice," I said as I poured more champagne.

"She went on so about the Arabs that when I was a little girl and I saw one, I started crying."

I asked if she had any Arab friends at school.

"There was a girl in *quatrième*," Georgette said, digging into her pâté, "but the professor told her that in view of her family background she would have a hard time following and should quit school."

"Nothing like a little encouragement."

"Even so, it was a wonderful life, hours on the beach, my mother telling me I'd have wrinkles at twenty, and don't go out too far. Life was easy, and we counted our blessings. There's nothing like a sheet that's dried in the sun, or the taste of fresh sardines, or intense colors, bright sun. The *colon* world is a world without nuance. I was always struck by the names of the seaside cottages—*Douce France* [Sweet France], *Notre Bonheur* [Our Happiness], *Aile d'Ange* [Angel's Wing], while in fact they should all have been called Edge of the Precipice. . . . Well, enough of this depressing conversation. Monsieur de Gramont, dinner is served."

Hanging from the dining room's high ceiling was a chandelier of blue Murano glass. The candlelit Louis XV table was set for two, with monogrammed silver, china, and glassware. Georgette served a *daurade* with *beurre blanc*, washed down with a floral Meursault, a Pommard with the Reblochon, and a glass of Château d'Yquem with the tarte tatin. After a year of military nourishment, I thought I was drinking and eating what they serve in paradise.

We talked about her year in Paris, and how happy she had been to leave behind the troubles of Algiers. Her parents had moved there and were selling off their real estate holdings. She had met her husband, Julien, at a party. He had come with his girlfriend, and they had a stupid fight—she wanted to leave; he wanted to stay. She left in a huff, and Georgette got him on the rebound, and a month later they were married. Since he was being sent to Algeria, she came with him to settle the family business. When he got out of the army, they would live in Paris.

After dinner, I followed Georgette back into the living room. There was a phonograph on a table and a collection of albums on a shelf against the wall. She put on Charles Trenet's *"La Mer,"* threw out her arms, and said, "Let's dance." She kicked off her heels and said, "Take off your shoes. This is an Aubusson, and my parents are fussy about it." And so we danced, barefoot on the carpet, and the fit was right, so that her cheek was against mine, and she began kissing my neck. I stood there, wavering and wondering what to do next, when she said: "Well, are we going to stand here all night?"

She led me to her bedroom, and a few minutes later we were in bed. I came like a shot, for I hadn't slept with a woman since the previous August in Paris, before shipping out to Algeria. *"Sale cochon"* ("Filthy pig"), Georgette said.

"Just give me a few minutes," I said.

"What I really like," she said, "is De Falla's *'El Amor Brujo.'* It starts off playfully and builds and builds, and then at the end, there's this crescendo, this explosion of sound." She had a phonograph next to her bed and put the record on. She aroused me with her mouth, and I began to explore her body, thinking of it as a summery day on the Mediterranean, its musky warmth, the pliancy of the curved beach, the taste of salt in the crevices.

"Now, come into me," she said, "but go slow." I thought of my cock as a baton, following the pulse of the music, which gathered intensity until the explosion came, and she said, "Now," and we both shuddered and lay still. *"C'est bon,"* Georgette said.

It's odd how in the midst of passion one's mind can wander. When she said, *"C'est bon,"* I was reminded of a conversation I'd had with Dourakine, who had a wide-ranging experience with women of many nationalities. "The sensible Frenchwoman," he said, "says, *'C'est bon'* because sex fits into her concept of general goodness, as in good food or good furniture or good curtains. A Spanish girl I met in Seville said, *'Anda, anda'* [go, go], which is the vocabulary of momentum, as in bullfights and bicycle races. An Italian girl in Naples said, *'Mamma mia,'* the language of the family, and a black American girl in Paris said, 'Feed me, feed me,' which is the language of nourishment." Doura-

kine said he was working on a thesis to be entitled "Linguistic Varia-
tions in Orgasmic Phonation."

Georgette was dozing, and I was thinking. Maybe we could have
an affair of convenience. Her husband, whom she did not know that
well, was in deepest Sahara. Marriage had revealed to her a nature
that was deeply conjugal. She needed a day-to-day life with a man and
the nightly comfort of the nuptial bed. Since her husband was absent,
I was serving as a proxy, which I was glad to do. Georgette wasn't one
of those tanned hard-bodies I'd seen at café terraces. She was more
Duchess of Alba than Modigliani, opulent and deeply satisfying.

It was not only that I found her physically appealing and that I
wanted to continue living in her apartment. I also admired the way
she was capable of gaiety and enthusiasm in difficult times. She had
an eagerness to connect, to please, and she was never withdrawn or
sullen. Also, as I learned, she was caring. She put fresh flowers in my
apartment every other day. Three or four times a week, there was a
note with the flowers that said *J'ai besoin* ("I'm needy"), and I would
go over. After a couple of weeks, I broke the caning at the foot of my
bed, which was too short. When I apologized and offered to have it
repaired, she said, "It costs a fortune. I'd have to send it to France. It
would be much simpler if you slept with me." So I moved to her bed,
and at night she played *"El Amor Brujo,"* and once she observed: "As
the Comtesse de Sévigné wrote, 'we make love like animals, but a bit
better.' "

O N THE morning of January 12, I was back in the office, and
Brissac introduced me to the third member of our little team,
Bernard Brodin. In some ways he still looked like a small boy, with a
round, pink-cheeked face, straight blond hair that tended to drop
over his brow, eyes of a pale and humid blue, and black-framed glasses.
He had the disconsolate air of a child lost in a railroad station, and he
stammered a bit.

"I'm happy to meet you," he said. "I didn't want to be the major's
only victim."

"I know he doesn't look old enough to vote," Brissac said with a cackle, "but he's been writing articles for three years for a Catholic weekly."

"Our editorial position," Brodin said, "was based on Teilhard de Chardin—the human condition is very much like the way of the cross."

"Surely," I said, "we don't all die crucified."

"Of course not," Brodin snapped. "What we mean is that the suffering of millions is more important than tallying up venial sins." He had the odd habit of squeezing his eyes shut when he spoke to you.

"We're not here to discuss philosophy," Brissac said. "I saw Massu yesterday at his headquarters in Hydra [in the hills of eastern Algiers]. The strike is set for January 28 until February 2. He told me, 'We have to act before they do!'"

"The strike is timed to get the attention of the United Nations, which has Algeria on its agenda in February," Brodin said. "Colonialism is a great heresy at the UN. In their eyes, colonial powers fail to invest their capital to lift the colony out of underdevelopment."

"Massu is all too conscious of the connection between the strike and the UN debate," Brissac said. "His strategy is to use the paras to break the strike. He told his colonels, 'Gentlemen, I want you to recapture the night. The Casbah with its eighty thousand inhabitants, is the key. Conduct night raids and fire at all those who are breaking the curfew. We must show the FLN that we are as ruthless as they are.'"

"But how can they find their way around the Casbah," I asked, "especially at night?" From the little I'd seen, the Casbah seemed like the Minotaur's maze.

"Aha," Brissac burst out, pacing from one end of the office to the other like a caged animal. "Colonel Trinquier has formed a unit that will conduct a house-to-house census of the Casbah and draw up lists of the inhabitants. They will paint a number on each door and make sure there is a street name."

"He got that from Napoleon," Brodin said. "In his conquest of German towns, he always began with a census and a street map."

"Can you believe it?" Brissac exclaimed. "One of Massu's officers actually argued against a census. 'You might as well count the grains of sand in a dune,' he said. Well, the general put him in his place."

Lieutenant Colonel Roger Trinquier, the head of the grab-bag Disposition of Urban Protection, was Brissac's boss. He was an ideologue, convinced that he was defending Western civilization against the heathens. His expertise in guerrilla warfare was based on his command in Indochina of a commando unit that worked behind Viet lines. Massu described him as having "a complicated and sometimes unfathomable turn of mind, a tortuous craftiness well attuned to the job at hand."

"When is our first issue hitting the stands?" Brodin asked.

"Massu wants it in the kiosques the day before the strike," Brissac said. "Any ideas?"

"I could talk to some of the leaders of the UGTA [Algerian Workers' Union] to see if they approve of the strike."

"You must be joking," Brissac said. "Half of their leaders are FLN and are helping prepare the strike. No, we have to appeal to the needs of the Arab community, who will suffer hardships because of the strike."

"They want to shut down the Casbah schools," I said. "Why not urge parents to send their kids to school? Why should the children be involved in the strike?"

"That's it," Brissac said. "That will be our front page, with a big headline that says 'Tous à L'école.' We'll prepare other articles on how the vital services will not be affected by the strike, such as gas and electricity and transportation."

"What if they are affected?" Brodin asked.

"Massu has assured me they won't be," Brissac said.

As we got our first issue together, the para presence began to make itself felt. The deployment of the four regiments in the city was intended to create a psychological shock in the Arab population. The regiments were actually battalion strength, around 800 men each, and Algiers was divided into four sectors. Colonel Bigeard, with his rather bombastic style and contempt for civilian government, had the Casbah sector. Bigeard's experience told him that in a moral sense, one side was as good as another. The only thing that counted was that there be a winner and a loser. What he wanted was the success, not of his country, which was governed by corrupt politicians, nor of the army, most of whose superior officers he saw as rivals of small merit, but of his unit, the 3rd RPC, the red berets, who were quartered in a villa in El-Biar. Bigeard had the first accurate maps of the Casbah ever made, based on aerial photographs, in addition to the census lists drawn up by Trinquier. Houses that were found to have frequent comings and goings were marked.

At midnight on January 14, combat teams from all four regiments were briefed in front of a huge map of the city. They had 250 names and addresses, marked with red tacks on the map. At 12:30 the sand-colored trucks drove to the main Casbah exits—rue de la Lyre, Square Montpensier, Boulevard de la Victoire, Boulevard de Verdun, Rampe Valée, and rue Bab-el-Oued. In single file, the paras entered the badly lit alleyways, and by 12:45 they had verified the addresses of suspects.

Those in the lower Casbah zeroed in on the red-tack houses with a flashlight in one hand and a MAT in the other, breaking down doors, bursting in, and making arrests, as women and children screamed and the arrested men said, "You have no right." In the upper Casbah, the paras went in from above, vaulting onto flat rooftops and jumping from roof to roof, which had a dramatic effect on the inhabitants, who hid in the basement.

The number of arrests was not released, but Brissac told us the next day that it was over 1,000. "The paras have kicked the anthill and the ants are scurrying," he said. The problem was what to do with the arrested. Normally, they would have been turned over to a public prosecutor and taken through the court system, arraignment, investigation, and trial. But the paras, and particularly Bigeard, did not want "exasperating measures" such as search warrants and arraignments, which were "a waste of time." After all, this was a war, and it could not be fought if suspects disappeared into the snail-like judicial system. There was, however, the useful provision of "assigned residence." Instead of being arraigned in front of a judge within 48 hours of their arrest, the suspects could be detained by the paras for a week. The requests had to be signed by the secretary general for the police, Paul Teitgen, who got writer's cramp signing the hundreds that came in.

Teitgen was a devout Catholic who had been in the Resistance during World War II. Arrested by the Gestapo in 1943, he was tortured and sent to Dachau. It was an experience he never discussed. He arrived in Algiers in August 1956, when the city was already in a state of siege, and was told that the rebels were gaining the upper hand. He could see why. The Algiers police were in the hands of the Corsican mafia, notable for its inactivity. There were two categories, the thugs and the paper-pushers. They rarely ventured into the Casbah, which they called "the aquarium."

When the paras were given full police powers under Massu, Teitgen was ambivalent. They were definitely an improvement over the police, but the detention of suspects bothered him, though he had no choice but to sign the requests. At least, he reasoned, he knew how many had been detained. Massu was told that Teitgen and several other civil servants who had been traumatized by deportation under the Nazis were comparing them with the paras. Teitgen was shocked to see German legionnaires doing some of the dirty work. According to Brissac, he was saying, "I'm not a cop. I don't like this work."

There were so many suspects that the paras had to find camps to put them in. After the first triage, those held were sent to interrogation centers. Eventually, every company in ever para regiment had its own interrogation center. Bigeard had his team at the 3rd RPC. The rumor went around that he was drowning some of the suspects, who became known as *crevettes* (shrimp) Bigeard.

After work on January 17, I went to see Don Davies at the American library on rue Michelet, which was a prolongation of rue d'Isly. It was close to seven, and an icy rain was beating down. As I crossed from the Milk Bar to the other side of the Place Bugeaud, the yellow pavement surrounding the fountains was wet and slippery.

As a church clock struck 7, there was a thunderous explosion. Waiters with white napkins over their arms came out of the Milk Bar and pointed at the military headquarters, where General Salan worked and lived with his family. There was a gaping space on the second floor, where one of the long windows partly hidden by palm trees had been, and billows of white smoke poured out. In the street below, as the ambulance sirens sounded, the crowd was buzzing: "It's the *fellouzes* [fellaghas] for sure." "I smell the *cocos* [Communists]." I stood there like a statue, dumbfounded. It was my first explosion.

As it turned out, it was neither the FLN nor the handful of militant Communists who were known to set bombs. It was a right-wing underground group who had mistakenly believed that Salan was soft on Algeria. A bazooka had been fired at his office from a building directly across the street. Twenty minutes earlier Salan had been summoned to the office of Governor-General Lacoste. The general's aide and close friend, Major Rodier, was sitting at Salan's desk when the shell struck. Salan's 10-year-old daughter, Dominique, who was doing her homework in a room directly above the office, ran downstairs and saw Rodier slumped over, thinking at first the dead man was her father. By the time Massu arrived, a furious Salan was standing in his office in the debris. "Why in the world did I give you full police powers," he said, "if this is all you can do?"

Across the street, the police found the bazooka tube and the electric detonator. The wire came from the admiralty arsenal. The welder who had made the tube worked there and led them to the instigators of the plot. One was Philippe Castille, a right-wing hoodlum and former noncom. Another was Dr. René Kovacs, a Hungarian-born ultra intriguer with political connections in Paris. When arrested, they said they considered Salan the man who had lost Indochina. They did not want him in Algeria. Salan was in shock and found these accusations deeply wounding. He had been ordered by his superior, General Paul Ely, to preside at the ceremony of hand-over of Indochina to Ho Chi Minh. He had not realized at the time that this was a poisoned gift. The handover ceremony continued to be held against him. Castille was tried and sent to prison.

Kovacs fled to Spain and was later sentenced to death in absentia. Salan remained convinced that highly placed politicians in Paris were behind the plot.

As for me, the attempt to murder the general commanding French forces simply showed what a many-headed monster Algeria was. You never knew who was going to shoot whom. All you could be sure of was that killing was the answer—for both sides—when in fact it only made things worse . . . for both sides.

In a war, the difference between life and death was a matter of timing and luck. If Salan had not been called away from his office, he would be dead. If my father had flown into his base a few minutes sooner, he would have landed safely. I was swept by the feeling that my life was senseless and false, which I dimly perceived had to do with my father's death. I had gone to war out of a sense of obligation to his memory. But he had joined de Gaulle so that he could fight the Germans who occupied France. I was the occupier, at war with a people trying to lift their shackles. I was now a noncombatant, thanks to a stroke of luck I did not deserve.

I took the next day off, telling Brissac I had to do some library research on the schools in the Casbah. I told Georgette I detested the war and that it made me sick in the head. "You need a change of scene," she said. She offered to drive me to the Roman ruins of Tipasa, overlooking the sea, 40 miles west of Algiers. We strolled through the remains of a thermal bath, the broken rows of a semicircular theater, and the vestiges of an early Christian church with a mosaic inscription dating back to the fifth century. First Phoenician, then Roman, now French, I thought, one era piled on top of another, reminding us that all civilizations are mortal. "Oh trampling empires, and mine was one of them." Only the sea remained intact, its green-blue waves rippling on the sand below.

Georgette sat on a fragment of Roman pillar and threw her head back, lifting her face to the sun, the worshiper of a pagan god. "This was a summer resort for the Romans," she said. "Do you think they knew how to swim? Do you think they swam in their togas? When do you think swimming came in?"

"After the first shipwreck," I said.

I took her hand and asked if she was happy.

"How can I be happy," she said, "when I'm here with you and my husband is in the Sahara? I'm divided, I'm selfish, I'm lustful."

"Just think of the sea and the sun as the answer to everything," I said. "A kiss in the ruins of Tipasa is not a kiss in the Paris metro." I bent down and kissed her.

"I prefer the Paris metro," Georgette said. "Listen—it would help if I could read you one of Julien's letters," taking an envelope out of her handbag.

So now, I thought, it's not enough to be her husband's proxy—I also have to be her accomplice in sympathizing with his absence. I flashed back to the *bled*, the bodies of young soldiers blown up by mortar rounds. Her destiny was sunbathing, her flesh yielding to the sun. Why should I have to go along with her whims and listen to her husband's observations?

But she was already reading: "It's an unfortunate coincidence that the discovery of oil coincided with the insurrection. The rest of Algeria is in ruins, but in the Sahara there is unlimited wealth. The seismic and geographical teams have come in, and surveyors in broad-brimmed hats are planting stakes and taking sight lines. We use small explosive charges to auscultate the ground. Then come the drilling teams that can go down twelve thousand feet. Once a well is dug, it must be protected, with housing and supply routes, and we bring in generators for light and refrigeration. The planes supply fresh water and fresh fish. Here the Moslem workers drink beer alongside us and shout with glee when there's a Brigitte Bardot movie. There's enough oil in Hassi-Messaoud to supply France for forty years. The pipeline is still a dotted line on maps, but what it spells is 'Keep Algeria French.' There are rumors that France will sell oil to the Americans, but why should we? I flew over the desert yesterday. From the air, the Sahara looks like a great red swamp with undulating waves."

"I'll spare you the love and kisses," she added.

"I feel as though I've been peeping through a keyhole."

"Don't think of it that way. Think that for a while you are sharing my life, and I don't want to exclude you from any part."

When we got back in the late afternoon, Georgette's *fatma* was in my apartment cleaning. She always arrived veiled and cloaked but stripped down to a cotton sweater and skirt to work, an overweight, round-faced woman with crinkly graying hair and five children, married to a dockworker. They lived in a two-room apartment in the Casbah.

I asked her if her husband was going on strike on the 28th. "For sure," she said. "There's a lot of pressure on the dockers. But I'll try to come to work as usual. Someone has to feed the family."

She said she liked working for Georgette. "They say the Jews are the hardest and pay the least. But Madame Georgette is good to me. If I need a little extra, she gives it. I worked for another Jew who wouldn't let me eat bread on the Sabbath, and I worked for a Spanish woman who yelled at me when I was a little late. The best are the French from France, those who are working for the government."

"What about the *petits blancs*" (lower-class *colons*)?

"Some of them treat their *fatmas* like mangy dogs and pay them next to nothing. One of them wanted me to drink always out of the same glass, as if I was dirty. Another one set back the clock so I'd work longer hours."

I asked her if she was taking a risk by coming to work during the strike.

"In the Casbah, they instructed us not to work. I was accosted by a militant, and I said, 'You want me to stop working—are you going to pay my salary?' We'll see. I might miss a couple of days."

The *fatma* had to juggle her loyalty to Georgette, her obedience to the FLN, and her need to support her family. In this urban warfare, with the entire population of the city involved, like it or not, matters were never simple or clear-cut. As the strike approached, even Brissac began to wonder how the paras would handle it. "I was never taught at Saint-Cyr how to supply a city the size of Algiers with fruits and vegetables," he said. "I was never taught how to question a suspected terrorist."

When I told him there was abundant evidence that the paras were using torture, he said: "Are we talking about the Spanish Inquisition or a form of third degree? The FLN uses a cell system, so that when one is arrested, the paras have to act fast to find the other members of the cell. Of course sometimes it goes too far, but the civilian authorities refuse to clearly define what is permitted and what is prohibited, leaving the paras to act without directives."

SATURDAY, JANUARY 26, was one of those springlike sunny days that drew the crowds to downtown Algiers. I was with Georgette, who wanted to buy a picnic hamper for the outings she planned when it got warmer. (This was one of the ways of pretending that life was normal.) It was after 5, and we were on rue Michelet, looking for a place to have an apéritif. We passed a popular student hangout, the Otomatic, but it was packed.

Just around that time, as we later learned, a 17-year-old French girl, Danielle Minne, was finishing her Orangina and went downstairs to the ladies' room, where she placed a small bomb on the water tank above the toilet, and left. Across the street at the Cafeteria, a European-looking Arab girl, Fadila, placed her bag with a bomb in it under a table in the back room, near a window, finished her tomato juice, and left. Around the corner on rue Péguy, at the Coq Hardi, a popular brasserie, Djamila Bouazza, a 19-year-old Arab girl who worked at the post office, ordered tea with lemon at the crowded terrace. When a young man tried to pick her up, she left.

When Georgette and I walked by the Otomatic, I noticed a headline in a newspaper someone was reading on the terrace: "Princess Grace has given birth to a daughter, Caroline." A minute later, there was an explosion inside, and we saw the waiters bring out an elderly woman, her dress covered with blood. Then there was a second, more powerful explosion at the Cafeteria, across the street, followed by a third at the Coq Hardi, where the glass-encased terrace blew up and the heavy glass shattered, throwing out shrapnel-like splinters. There was the usual post-bomb bedlam, with people screaming, sirens blaring, body brigades forming outside the cafés to remove the victims, and young men chasing isolated Arabs who happened to be there, two of whom were killed. The total casualties from the bombs were five dead and forty wounded, twenty-two of whom had limbs amputated on the operating table. The general strike was two days away. This was the overture, announcing to the *colon* population that their lives were about to be seriously disrupted. I am ashamed to say that instead of helping out, I complied when Georgette tugged on my arm and said, "We've got to get home."

I later learned that Danielle Minne left Algiers after the bombing and joined a rebel group in the Constantine area. She married an FLN officer and was captured in a shootout in November 1957. Her mother was married to Dr. Hadjères, the head of a group of Communist bomb-makers. Danielle Minne was the French version of a red-diaper baby. The other two were part of Yacef Saadi's bomb team.

On Sunday, January 27, the day before the strike, Brissac awakened me out of a sound sleep at 8 AM and told me to come to the office at once. The first issue of our paper had been printed and was in the kiosques. He had a stack of them in the office and wanted me to take them over the Casbah in a chopper and drop them in the hope that the banner headline, "Tous à L'école," would make an impression.

The chopper was waiting on the parade ground of a barracks above the Casbah, and I got in with my papers. "A little reading matter for the *bougnouls*" (an offensive word for Arabs), the pilot said. We hovered over the Casbah, and the people below in the narrow alleys scattered. I started throwing the papers out, but a gust of wind came up and most of them blew out to sea. I watched them fly off, the pages flapping like pelican wings.

I went back to the office and found Brissac composing a leaflet that said: "The Algerian Communist Party says *no* to the strike. It is useless, since the United Nations will demand Algerian independence. It is unjust because it will starve the people. The FLN is leading the Algerian people astray."

"Just a little disinformation," he said. "We'll get these printed up, and they'll be all over the city this afternoon."

"It's sewn with white thread [too obvious], if you ask me," Brodin said.

"I didn't ask you."

At dawn on January 28, a chopper dropped another set of Brissac's flyers over the Casbah: "The FLN demands the closing of stores. The FLN wants to starve the inhabitants of Algiers. Have faith in the forces of order." Massu had warned storekeepers that closed shutters would be forced open and that stores would not be protected from looters.

The FLN had also made preparations. Longshoremen who worked in the Algiers harbor were asked to leave the city to avoid the expected para raids. Every street in the Casbah had a strike committee of three or four to make sure the strike was observed.

Massu's entire division was mobilized to get men to work and keep stores open. By 7 AM, thousands of paras were in the Casbah banging on doors, with lists of names from the census. They paid particular attention to employees of essential services, gas and electricity and public transportation. Brissac had asked me to observe events, and I was in a jeep full of white-helmeted military police with a loudspeaker in the back that alternated Arab music with the message "Everyone to work. The trucks are waiting."

In rue Randon, the widest street of the lower Casbah, stood rows of empty trucks, ready to take strikers to work. The paras pulled men out of their homes and threw them into the trucks. "Does so and so live here? Okay, Mohammed, put your bus driver's hat on and come with us." Those who showed the slightest resistance, a look in the eye, a "take your hands off me" gesture, were arrested and taken to the triage center in the Saint-Eugène stadium. Others were drafted to collect the Casbah garbage with donkeys. In the harbor, when the longshoremen didn't show up and ships waited to be unloaded, Massu ordered hundreds of suspects in the Beni-Messous detention center to work on the dock at gunpoint. They were paid at the end of the day. The harbormaster said he wanted to hire them because they worked twice as fast as the regulars.

In many neighborhoods, store shutters were closed shut. The paras fixed a steel cable to the bottom of the shutter, and the winch on the back of their jeep tore it off like a sheet of paper. In some neighborhoods, young *colons* looted shops broken open by the paras, taking everything from shoes to radios, and sometimes the cash register. In the Casbah, the produce market was closed. There was not a single carrot or orange available. The paras sent trucks into the countryside to requisition vegetables and fruits, and by afternoon a trickle began to arrive.

In the cafés and restaurants of downtown Algiers, on that first day of the strike, there were no waiters. On the buses and streetcars, the conductors were European. In the Clauzel open market, with its 200 stands, there was one elderly fellow selling birdseed.

Brissac was told that on the first day of the strike, 1,000 Arabs were arrested in the Casbah in cordon-and-capture operations. Two additional triage centers had to be opened to process them.

On the second day of the strike, January 29, I accompanied a patrol of red berets into the Casbah, which was built on an incline, so that the houses seemed to be on top of one another. Many of the streets were steep stone stairways, leading to a tangle of alleys and lanes. Sometimes one came upon a fountain adorned with mosaics, a secret garden, a tiny cemetery, or a wall pocked with bullets. Many of the houses had inner courtyards and private wells, good hiding places; the arabesques screening the windows were designed so that women could look out without being seen.

The patrol leader, Lieutenant Méric, brisk, short, and sinewy, banged on a door, and a man answered.

"Why aren't you at work?" Méric asked.

"It's a strike, Lieutenant."

"Did your union tell you to strike?"

"Not the union, the instruction."

"Where did you get this instruction?"

"Everywhere, Lieutenant. Everyone said it was a strike, so we obeyed."

"If you were told to throw yourself in the ocean, would you obey?"

"You can't say no, Lieutenant, or they slit your throat."

"Come with us," Méric said, and took him down to one of the trucks.

In the door-to-door check, if no one answered, Méric forced the door open, usually to find only women and children. But one door was opened by a man who said he worked at the post office. "If I go to work on my own," he said, "my neighbor will say I didn't follow the strike, and I'll get in trouble. But if you grab me, Lieutenant, and take me forcibly, I'll be all right. I'd rather go to work and pick up my paycheck." Méric grabbed him by the scruff of the neck and pushed him into the street to make it look credible. "Some say they're sick," he told me, "and one even cut off his finger. The sick ones, we pull out of bed and tell them to get dressed."

Later in the day, we were in rue Ben Chenab, near an elementary school, and saw the band from the 9th *zouaves*, who were stationed in the Casbah, followed by about 10 children. When they weren't playing their marches, the *zouaves* passed out candy. "Some of them are coming back to school," one of the *zouaves* said.

We came to the rue de Lyon, a busy commercial street, and Méric pointed out that most of the shops were open. "They can say to the FLN tax man, 'How can I pay if my store is looted?' " he explained. The *fatmas* were doing their shopping as usual in the produce markets, and the only disturbance came from the constant noise of the loudspeakers on the jeeps, playing their music and slogans.

By the third day, January 30, Algiers was almost back to normal. In the morning, on rue Randon and rue de la Lyre, workers were lined up waiting for the paras to take them to work, on the docks, to the gasworks, to the post offices. Most of the shops were open, except for a few that tried to finagle with a sign on the shutter that said "Closed due to a death in the family." Street vendors reappeared and markets were crowded.

In our office, Brissac claimed victory for Massu and the paras. "The big mistake the FLN made," he said, "was to announce the strike too soon and make it last too long. We had plenty of time to prepare, and after a couple of days the workers wanted their paychecks. And in the process, the paras got to know the Casbah."

Bernard, who had close connections to liberal Catholics, said: "I can tell you that in Hussein Dey [a suburb], on January twenty-eighth, the parish priest ordered the paras of the Second RPC to leave the church, where they had burst in during Mass looking for rebels. And then, in his sermon, the priest said that taking Moslems forcibly to work in military trucks was an infraction of their liberty."

"I wonder how that went over with the parishioners," Brissac said. "Of course, that's why they call Archbishop Duval [a steadfast defender of Arabs' civil liberties] Mohammed Ben Duval. I can tell you in strictest confidence that Massu wrote the pope to complain that Duval is a troublemaker. He got a namby-pamby reply that we should all use the gospel as an example."

Later that day, I went to a café with Bernard, whose candid opinions sometimes annoyed Brissac but whose ability to turn out a thousand or more words on any topic in record time made him an essential component of our editorial trio. Bernard said he had decided he could trust me, even though he felt I had not formed a mature political opinion about the war. Had I read Fanon's *The Wretched of the Earth*? I admitted that I had not. " 'The Arab woman's veil is a symbolic protection against the pillaging of the French,' " he quoted. In any case, he said, he was writing articles under an assumed name for *Témoignage Chrétien*, his former employer, which took a strong anti-war stance. I told him I wrote the occasional piece for my old newspaper in Worcester, also under a pseudonym.

"We could be in serious trouble if the army found out," he said.

"Bouche cousue" ("My lips are sealed"), I said.

He told me that his next article had to do with a doctor he knew, Hassan Manour, who had been arrested during the strike for not going to work at the Mustapha Hospital. He was taken into a room in the police station, where a para officer told him: "Look, it's like a card game. You played the FLN card and you lost, so now it's time to lay down your cards."

Dr. Manour sat there in silence, and the para said, "Personally I've always found it idiotic to shoot down people in the street. If the FLN killed the big boys, I'd admire them. The governor-general, for instance."

The para stepped outside for a minute, and the cop guarding the doctor told him that one of his children was sick and asked him for advice. Manour took out a prescription pad and scribbled something, while thinking, First they arrest me, and then they want a free consultation.

Dr. Manour was held in a cell and awakened during the night by the same para officer. "Enough fooling around," he said. "I want to finish with you; I've got other cats to whip." He had with him a husky cop in shirtsleeves with a nightstick, who banged the doctor around a bit. When he didn't talk, the para officer left again, and the cop who hit him said, "I've got liver trouble. Can you recommend anything?" Manour gave him the name of a medication, thinking, I'd like to prescribe cyanide.

The para officer came back and said, "Take a look at one of our prisoners." He was led to another cell where a man was lying on the ground. He was so badly burned that his undershirt was stuck to his skin. He screamed when Dr. Manour tried to pull it off. His back was a raw and bleeding wound. Dr. Manour asked for some ointment. The para officer said to the injured man, "*À poil*" ("Get naked").

"My religion forbids me to be naked in front of others," the man said, "even before my wife."

Dr. Manour was released the next morning. What happened to the other man, he did not know.

E VEN THOUGH the strike was a tactical failure, the FLN tried to give it a positive spin by pointing to the United Nations resolution. When the Algerian question came up on February 4, the French argued that the UN was not competent to judge a situation taking place in a part of France. Nonetheless, Algeria was discussed, and on February 15, the General Assembly passed one of its stale declarations, calling for the peaceful resolution of the conflict, which implied the recognition of the FLN as a legitimate independence movement.

In terms of the Battle of Algiers, the true importance of the strike was that it provided the paras with an opportunity to arrest thousands of Arab men in cordon-and-capture operations. They detained hundreds and quickly obtained tactical intelligence, thanks to systematic torture. The notion that torture is counterproductive, and that suspects will tell you what you want to hear, did not hold true in Algiers. The para methods of arbitrary arrests and torture produced immediate results. February was the month when bomb networks were dismantled and rebel leaders were captured. Those leaders who escaped arrest fled to the countryside.

Spearheading the para operations was the 3rd RPC (red berets) led by Colonel Bigeard, who gave his men directives from his villa above the Casbah, on the heights of El-Biar: "We are operational twenty-four hours out of twenty-four, with patrols, arrests, ambushes, and interrogations." He had four billboard-sized charts against the wall of his office, showing the organization of the FLN in the Casbah cell by cell, with blank rectangles that were filled in when rebels were arrested. Intelligence, Bigeard said, "is like a coil of yarn. You start pulling on a thread, and the coil unravels."

The first thread was pulled in early February, when the paras raided a housing project and arrested Hamened Abderrahmane because he was carrying a copy of the FLN newspaper, *Moujahid*. He ran a metalworks in the suburb of Saint-Eugène. One of Bigeard's officers accompanied him to his shop with a police inspector, who found some blueprints of metal boxes that looked like casings for bombs.

"And what's this?" he was asked.

"I don't know, Captain. It belongs to a fellow who comes in after hours."

They took Hamened back to the regimental interrogation center, put a hood over his head, and poured water down his throat until he gave them a name, which led to another arrest, and then another, until they had the address, 5 impasse de la Grenade. They raided the place at 3 in the morning on February 8 and found Mustapha Bouhired, a city hall employee, his niece Djamila, and two other young women, who objected so strenuously at being roused from their sleep that the paras left. When they came back the next day, Bouhired and the women were gone, but they left behind snapshots of the women aiming submachine guns at the photographer, who was none other than Yacef Saadi, although the paras did not know it at the time.

Meanwhile, the rebels struck daily. On February 9, a grenade thrown into the Joinville restaurant, on rue Tanger on the edge of the Casbah, left two dead and 12 wounded.

On Sunday, February 10, the minister of defense, Maurice Bourgès-Maunoury, who was visiting the war zone, went to see Bigeard in the afternoon and asked him about interrogation techniques. "The torture room is down the hall," Bigeard said, "if you'd like to take a look." That was Bruno—he wanted to rub the minister's nose in it.

Their conversation was interrupted by a phone call for Bigeard. "Two soccer stadiums have been bombed," he was told.

Yacef Saadi, the chief terrorist, knew every corner of the Casbah, but he cursed the paras for turning it into a concentration camp with their house-to-house searches, which obliged him to change his address every few days. He could hear their trucks arriving in rue Randon, which separated upper from lower Casbah. He could see the silhouettes on the rooftops. He could hear the rifle butts banging on doors and spent hours hiding in a closet-sized space three feet deep. And yet he still had a store of bombs in various hiding places. The problem was getting them out of the Casbah, for now the paras searched the girls and their beach bags. But the paras didn't know about the bakery whose entrance was on the Boulevard de Verdun, with a back door inside the Casbah.

One of the few things the *colons* and the Arabs had in common was a love of soccer. Yacef Saadi was a soccer player himself, and he thought, Why not bomb the soccer stadiums in the middle of a match, to show the *colons* they aren't safe anywhere, whether sitting in a café or watching soccer? He recruited four teenagers, two boys and two girls, and sent them out with two bombs through the bakery, on February 10. The sky was gray, but the day was mild and the stadium was packed. One couple sat in the bleachers of the El-Biar stadium and nuzzled each other. The bomb was in the pocket of the boy's tweed jacket. At halftime they got up and left. The boy left his jacket behind as if to save his seat. The bomb went off at 4:30 PM. The second pair went to the Belcourt municipal stadium, and their book-sized bomb exploded a bit later, also at the half. Total casualties for both stadiums were 11 killed and 56 wounded. Six of the dead were the Casanova family, husband, wife, two children, sister-in-law, and nephew.

It didn't take long to catch the teenagers. In the wreckage of the El-Biar bleachers, a police inspector found a scrap of tweed with a dry cleaner's tag. He tracked down the dry cleaner, who looked up the name of the client, Mohamed Belamine, in his stub book. Belamine was arrested and gave the names of the three others. All four were sentenced to death by a military tribunal.

Even though it was a Sunday, I was summoned to the office by Brissac, who wanted a special issue on the stadium bombings. As I walked up rue d'Isly, I could see, down the cross streets, the ocean and the ships in the harbor, and I could feel a breeze coming off the shore. I saw a woman holding the hands of her two small children as they crossed the street, and people at the café terraces, and it all seemed so normal. And yet I knew that at any moment there might be an explosion, with broken windows, flying limbs, women screaming. It was bewildering that you could get to the point where violence and death became a part of your daily routine. Only that morning, Georgette and I had driven to her tennis club, the Club des Pins, with the handles of our rackets sticking out of a bag in the backseat, and we were stopped by paras at a checkpoint—they thought we were carrying guns.

She was expecting me for dinner, but I was held up at the office. When I got home an hour later, she was fuming. "You could have called at least," she said, even though she knew that Brissac didn't want me to make personal calls from the office. "De Brissac?" she shouted. "What about me? You only think of yourself. You're just a sponge."

"At least I'm a cut-rate sponge," I said. "I don't cost you much."

She burst into tears. "It's just that when you're late, I don't know where you are. Everyone is scared and acting crazy. I was on a street-car next to a sweet white-haired grandmother who was mumbling under her breath. I said, 'Excuse me?' and she said, 'We've got to kill them all.' Again I said, 'Excuse me?' and she pointed to some Arab street-cleaners and said, 'Kill them all before they kill us.' "

Even Georgette, so practical and businesslike, so eager to connect and to please, was now liquid-eyed and upset, but at least we had the sanctuary of her bedroom, where we could forget the outside world for a while.

In the meantime, Ali Boumendjel, an Arab VIP, had been arrested on February 9 after a handgun used by a terrorist was traced to him. His arrest by the men of the 2nd RPC (red berets) led by Colonel Albert Fossey-François raised the question of how Massu would handle a well-known Moslem lawyer with political connections. He was taken to the 2nd RPC headquarters, a building with two wings, in El-Biar, and tortured so severely that he had to be hospitalized on February 12 for "attempted suicide." He admitted belonging to the FLN and heading a group of lawyers that defended arrested rebels, in the rare cases when they were put on trial instead of being liquidated.

When Boumendjel was returned to the 2nd RPC on March 4, Massu did not know what to do with him. Boumendjel was the FLN's unofficial minister of foreign affairs, with links to Third World leaders and influential deputies in France. If he were to be put on trial, the courtroom would turn into a debate on the war, which would trigger anticolonial demonstrations in Paris. Massu told Fossey-François: "I forbid you to allow him to escape. *Compris?*" On March 23, Boumendjel was told he was going to court. Two paras escorted him across a sixth-floor footbridge that connected the building's two wings. "Jumped or fell to his death" was the euphemism in the papers the next day, for he had been pushed. In Paris, his death prompted a debate in the National Assembly. René Capitant, an eminent law professor and Resistance hero, suspended his course at the Sorbonne saying that Boumendjel had been his student. In Algiers, Paul Teitgen, the police prefect who signed the detainment requests (by the end of February he had signed an astonishing 24,000) sent a letter of resignation on March 24 to Premier Guy Mollet, in which he said that he had visited the triage centers in Beni-Messous and Paul-Cazelle and seen on the detainees the same marks of torture as those that had been inflicted on him in the cells of the Gestapo in Nancy. The triage centers were holding pens where suspects were held before or after torture. Mollet replied that it was scandalous to compare the French army to the Gestapo and refused to let him resign. But Boumendjel's death was the first sign that the para tactics were having repercussions in France that could spark an antiwar movement.

On February 12, 1957, Fernand Yveton, a young Communist whose bomb had been found in his locker at the gas and electricity company, thus causing no victims, was nonetheless guillotined. Bernard Brodin was friendly with an officer on Massu's staff who attended the execution. One of the men greasing the blade told the officer, "Don't get too close. You could be splattered." The officer said the entire ceremony, the guards in black gloves, the chaplain with his nose in a prayer book, Yveton's head pushed onto the lunette and then dropping into the basket, had turned him against capital punishment. "And this was the clever machine invented by Dr. Guillotin to end suffering," Bernard said. "Killing a French Communist plays into the notion that the Algerian rebellion is inspired by Moscow in the hope that an independent Algeria will join the Soviet camp. Yveton had to be executed in order to give more weight to this thesis."

"Yveton was killed because he was a *pied-noir* who went over to the other side," I said, "and the *pieds-noirs* wanted his head."

While writing articles for *Réalités Algériennes* on the prowess of the paras, Bernard was also researching their misdeeds for *Témoignage Chrétien*. Our jobs gave us entrée to the paras and the police, and Bernard had seen the police reports and taken notes: "On

Feb. 8, 55-year-old Aisha Daoui charged that 10 red berets searched her home at 6 rue Henri Brisson and stole 150,000 francs and two gold bracelets while arresting her husband." "At 2 in the morning on Feb. 9, several blue berets broke into the store of a shoemaker, 9 rue Médée, opened the safe, and stole 450,000 francs and some jewelry. They threw the key to the safe into the street, where it was recovered by some children."

I had one for Bernard. I had gotten to know Hans Imhof, the political counselor at the U.S. consulate, a gemütlich Viennese who'd gone to America after the war and joined the Foreign Service. He lived on a dead-end street off rue Michelet, at the end of which stood a gated Moorish estate with a large garden, the Villa Sesini, taken over by Foreign Legion paratroopers—the 1st REP, or green berets. I was standing with Hans on his balcony one late afternoon when he said, "I can never find a parking space. These legionnaires all seem to have cars." I told him that the cars were stolen from the Arabs they arrested. It had not occurred to him that French soldiers would behave like hoodlums.

While Bigeard's red berets were heros, the green berets had a bad reputation. They prided themselves on obtaining actionable intelligence faster than other units. It was said that among the flower beds of the Villa Sesini (which had once been the German consulate) there was a burial ground. Their commander, Colonel Jeanpierre, told his men, "If you have qualms, ask for a transfer." No one asked for a transfer. René Gille, a police commissioner who had been deported by the Germans with Jeanpierre, brought him an album of Nazi atrocities. Jeanpierre told him: "We have to start somewhere."

Major Roger Faulques, the green berets' chief torturer, had learned interrogation techniques from the Viets. He knew how to break a man's will. Thin, gnarled, barely 30, with pale blue eyes, his body was a welter of scars. He'd been riddled by a machine gun at Cao Bang and hit in the head, stomach, arms, and legs. General Giap had sent him back to the French, saying, "He deserves to die among his own people." But he survived. His friends said that his suffering made him "a little odd," although they praised his intelligence. He used dialectics as well as the *baignoire* (bathtub) and the *gégène* (portable generators with the electrodes attached to various parts of the suspect's body). He set traps by letting suspects talk and picking up discrepancies. In the cells of the Villa Sesini basement, each cell had a nameplate, but some cells were empty. A suspect seeing the nameplate thought, No point in protecting him; he's already been caught. Faulques bugged the interrogation rooms and left suspects alone together so they could talk to each other.

Bernard had a theory that the suffering of the para officers in Indochina gave them (in their own minds) the right and the authority to make others suffer. I said the same might be true of the FLN leaders. He said no, they used terrorism as a policy, while the paras validated the use of torture with their past experience. I said the paras used torture as a method of counterterrorism but that it could not be condoned.

Talk of torture was in the air. Father Delarue, the chaplain of Massu's para division, released a letter defending torture "since civilized nations have maintained the death penalty . . . the painful interrogation of arrested criminals in order to protect innocent civilians is also permissible. What is worse—to subject a bandit caught in the act to the obstinate harassment of interrogation, or to permit the massacre of innocents who could have been saved if the suspect had talked?"

"Of course," Bernard said after reading the letter, "the para reaction will be 'If a priest says it's okay . . .' "

Brissac, who had gone to Massu's headquarters to show him our latest issue, burst into our office in a state of animation. "Hey, *bidasses* [slang for "soldiers"], you won't believe your ears. Massu wasn't in his office and no one could tell me where he was. I ran into Godard [Massu's chief of staff], who's a friend of mine, and he told me, 'He's trying out the *gégène.*' "

"That's a joke," Bernard said, "He'll try it for a minute, and they won't turn up the juice. It has nothing to do with what the suspects go through. And also, Massu has nothing to confess. And they keep it away from his private parts."

Brissac lit a cigarette and stood with his hands folded behind him, bending backward, à la von Stroheim in *Grand Illusion*. "How many generals do you know who would put themselves through that?" he asked. "For Massu, a free hand in interrogation is as crucial as the ability to shoot. But he realizes that morally it's risky for those who have to do it, so he tried it himself."

"I doubt he's any the worse for it," Bernard said.

"Don't forget," Brissac said, "the politicians told him, 'Do what you have to do. We don't want to know about it.' "

"Maybe the politicians should try the *gégène*," I said, "right up to Guy Mollet."

"Oh, I almost forgot," Brissac said. "I picked up a bit of news. Bigeard's men arrested *bachaga* Boutaleb."

Bigeard had kept pulling on his thread. Abderrahmane the metalworker, after another round of water torture, had given the name of a mason, Hassan Rabah, who was picked up and admitted building a hidden room in the home of Boutaleb, on impasse Kléber. Boutaleb was the go-between in secret talks between the French and the FLN. He worked closely with cabinet ministers in France and with Colonel Schoen, the head of Moslem affairs in the cabinet of Robert Lacoste, the Algiers governor-general. Boutaleb was part of the Arab aristocracy and owned a Moorish palace in the Casbah, though he also had an apartment in the European sector, Boulevard Bru. The title *bachaga* meant that he held a position of importance in his home town, Bou Saâda.

Hassan Rabah led the paras to Boutaleb's palace, with its gurgling fountain in the center of an arcaded courtyard. By following the design of the wall tiles in one of the reception rooms, he found an irregularity and pressed a tile. A panel swung open, revealing a small room with a cot and a ventilator, as well as nine bombs.

Boutaleb was in Paris, where he saw the French president, René Coty. Thanks to the mason, Bigeard was on a roll. Rabah led them to the address on impasse de la Grenade, where the paras had previously found Mustapha Bouhired and the three young women. This time they found a hidden room and some bombs. Bouhired was arrested and shot "while trying to flee." Between February 14 and 19, Bigeard's men found 67 bombs.

Bigeard was hearing from Colonel Schoen that Boutaleb was a special case; he had been helpful to the French in secret talks aborted by the hijacking of Ben Bella. Bigeard said, "I don't give a damn. Arrest him." He was starting to realize the extent of the bomb network in the Casbah and the amount of preparation that had gone into these hidden rooms, carefully constructed by skilled masons and carpenters.

When Boutaleb returned form Paris on February 21, he was arrested and brought to Bigeard's headquarters. Boutaleb was wearing a white *gandoura* (robe) with his Legion of Honor pinned to it. He told Bigeard's chief of staff, Captain Allaire: "I insist on being questioned by an officer of the Legion of Honor."

"Legions of Honor are a dime a dozen," Allaire said. "Here's a noncom with the *Médaille Militaire*." A tough-looking red beret came in with a blackjack that he kept slapping against his palm.

"I know nothing about the room," Boutaleb said. "The bombs were placed there by my political enemies. I am fighting the battle of Algiers in Paris." And he dropped names, including that of François Mitterand, the minister of justice (and later president). Boutaleb escaped torture but was sentenced to five years by a military tribunal.

Under questioning, Boutaleb confirmed that the top five FLN leaders had been in the Casbah before the strike but then moved to safe houses in the European section to avoid being caught in para raids. The five were Larbi Ben M'Hidi, who planned the strike; Abane Ramdane, the advocate of urban terrorism; Krim Belkacem, the veteran Kabyle warrior; Benyoucef Ben Khedda; and Saad Dahlab. These five constituted the CCE (Committee of Coordination and Execution). Boutaleb, who liked to show off his connections on both sides, said that Ben M'Hidi had stayed at his mansion on impasse Kléber. He also gave the name of the liaison agent, Hachemi Hamoud.

The paras arrested Hamoud, who was tortured so severely that he died. Under torture, he gave the address of a safe house, an apartment building on rue Debussy, in downtown Algiers. On the evening of February 23, a team of paras showed the concierge of the building a snapshot of Ben M'Hidi. "That's Monsieur Antoine Perez," she said. "He works at city hall. Very polite. Very discreet. No visitors. Third floor." Ben M'Hidi answered the door in his pajamas and offered no resistance.

The next day, Bigeard, who was not averse to publicity, gave a press conference, which I attended. He announced the capture of the top FLN leader and mastermind of the strike. I noticed that General Salan, who had not been seen much since the bazooka hit his office, was there. I struck up a conversation with Captain Allaire, Bigeard's genial chief of staff, known as Tatave, who showed me a tape recorder. "We found it in Ben M'Hidi's studio," he said. "I'm using it in interrogations."

The story that was put out in March was that Ben M'Hidi had committed suicide, but the real story, as passed on to Brissac, was not that simple. The drama of Ben M'Hidi's capture and death began with an improbable friendship and ended with a transparent cover-up.

When Ben M'Hidi was first brought before Bigeard, he was in handcuffs and ankle chains. Bigeard proposed that they be removed. Ben M'Hidi told him: "If you remove them, I will try to escape, even if I throw myself out the window." Bigeard admired his fearlessness, which was equal to his own. He began to consider Ben M'Hidi not as an enemy but as a worthy opponent, a warrior like himself.

In the next few days, the two men had conversations that went on into the night. There was no animosity between them. They discussed the war in a detached manner, like two chess masters analyzing game strategy. Bigeard felt that they had in common their modest origins. Ben M'Hidi was the son of peasants. "I was promoted from the ranks," Bigeard told him. "I'm not an imperialist. I want the Arabs to remain in the Western camp."

Ben M'Hidi said he understood the para methods and that they were "the only valid methods, since the French legal system allows terrorism to spread with impunity." They said *tu* (the French familiar form for "you") to each other, as if they were old friends. But there were limits to their mutual understanding. Bigeard asked, "Aren't you ashamed to place bombs in the baskets of your women?"

"Give me your planes," Ben M'Hidi replied. "I'll give you my baskets."

And so the apostle of peasant socialism, modest, stubborn, and incorruptible, conversed with the embodiment of French might, proud, stubborn, and incorruptible. Bigeard explained that he too had been a captive, of the Viets, and that despite the loss of Indochina, "I still believe in a greater France."

"You survived captivity," Ben M'Hidi responded. "I know that I will die, but when I am gone, someone will replace me, and one day Algeria will be free. You are above me and you can see beyond me, but I am beneath you and I can see under you. The sad thing is that those who have done the fighting will not be those who take power."

Bigeard and Ben M'Hidi spoke in the interrogation room of the 3rd RPC, but the usual methods were not employed, and for 10 days there existed something akin to the medieval Truce of God, and the rebel leader spoke voluntarily. But the situation could not last. Massu did not want a public trial with international repercussions. Ben M'Hidi had to disappear.

Aside from the regimental interrogation centers, Massu had a secret torture unit under the shadowy Major Paul Aussaresses, about which little was known until he published a book in 2001. Aussaresses, whose name and photograph never appeared in the newspaper, was a longtime secret service officer recruited by Massu for his willingness to torture and assassinate. Massu asked him to handle the Ben M'Hidi problem.

On the evening of March 4, Aussaresses arrived at Bigeard's headquarters in El-Biar with a dozen men, some jeeps, and a Dodge pickup. Ben M'Hidi was removed from Bigeard's benevolent supervision and pushed into the cab of the Dodge. They drove to an isolated dairy farm 20 kilometers south of Algiers. In the barn, Ben M'Hidi was hanged from a beam, and a milking stool was placed next to his body. Aussaresses called Massu and said: "Ben M'Hidi has committed suicide." Massu grunted and hung up. Aussaresses continued to use the farm for executions and dug a ditch to bury the bodies.

At *Réalités Algériennes* we printed the official version. We didn't learn the truth until later, but we had our doubts. I had never seen Bernard angry before. "Anyone who knew anything about Ben M'Hidi knows he would never kill himself," he said. "He was a devout Moslem and an example to his people. We're peddling more shit than Goebbels."

"We're not alone," I said. "Look at the headline in *l'Echo d'Alger* [the number-one daily]: 'Chief Terrorist Hangs Himself.' They could at least have said 'Found Hanged.' "

After the arrest of Ben M'Hidi on February 23, the four other rebel leaders fled Algiers. Ben Khedda, who wore dark glasses and had grown a mustache, had an ID card in the name of Albert Molina and a studio on Boulevard Saint-Saens. He went by rue Debussy and saw two paras standing outside. One of his aides drove him to Blida that day, with Saad Dahlab.

Dr. Pierre Chaulet, a Communist sympathizer, was recruited to drive Abane Ramdane and Krim Belkacem to Blida. On February 25, as he was having lunch with his pregnant wife Claudine in their apartment on the heights of Algiers, the paras burst in and arrested him. As he kissed his wife good-bye, he said, "Don't forget your rendezvous." The paras assumed she was seeing her gynecologist. Half an hour later, she picked up Krim and Abane on street corners and drove them to Blida. All four rebel leaders made their way to the mountain hideout of Colonel Sadek, the commander of *wilaya* 4.

In the Casbah, the departure of the leaders and the seizure of the bombs left the militants demoralized. Yacef Saadi was angry at the FLN leaders, who had fled without warning. He had to regroup his remaining forces. It was a miracle he was still at large, and when he went out, he dressed as a woman, with a veil hiding his mustache. The paras were under order not to search veiled women. His office was his briefcase, filled with false ID cards, seals, FLN documents, and half a million francs.

Yacef started over, practically from scratch. He had his two loyal aides Zohra Drif and Djamila Bouhired, and his number-one hit man, Ali-la-Pointe, and his girlfriend, Hassiba Ben Bouali. Slowly, he gathered the remnants of his former teams and there rose from the ashes a new political and military organization. But that took time, and in the wake of the January raids, morale in the Casbah was low. Every family had been affected, and people preferred to return to their normal activities. Men went to work, children to school, and long lines of women stood in front of Barberousse prison with hampers of food for relatives.

Outside the Casbah, Colonel Jeanpierre's 1st REP followed leads that ferreted out a network of French sympathizers of the FLN. They searched the apartment of a 35-year-old social worker from Besançon, Denise Walbert, and found hundreds of FLN flyers and a mimeograph machine. After a workout at the Villa Sesini, Walbert gave names: André Gallice, a member of the Algiers city council, whose apartment had been used for meetings of FLN leaders. Eliane Gautron, a schoolteacher from Annecy, who had come to Algiers in 1948 and found friends among the Algerian militants and French Communists at a student center. She married baker Jacques Gautron, and when her friends asked her to hide wanted men in their home, she agreed. When they were arrested, the reputation of the Villa Sesini made torture unnecessary. They gave more names, and on March 6 the green berets arrested a lycée professor, a trade union leader, a salesman, a stationer, several female social workers, and a priest, all French. Father Barthez was a worker priest in Hussein Dey who had been helping the rebels for years, particularly in supplying them with hard-to-get medication. When he arrived at Villa Sesini, a Catholic para officer objected that they should not arrest priests. Roger Faulques, the chief interrogator, said, "He's as guilty as the bomb-throwers." Faulques took him into a room, and when he came out, he said, "Father Barthez talked as if he was in a confessional."

There was consternation in Massu's entourage at the extensive networks of French "liberals" assisting the terrorists who blew up French women and children. Brissac came back from a Massu briefing and said, "Really, it is incredible." Bernard said, "The military cannot grasp that political loyalties cross national lines. A man like Gallice believes in a free Algeria as fervently as Massu believes in a French Algeria."

Brissac bristled and said Massu had been given some letters found among the social workers. "They're a gang of *gouines*" (lesbians).

The one Massu most wanted to find, Brissac said, was Raymonde Peschard, who was said to be a militant Communist deeply involved in bomb-making. Peschard, an uncommonly pretty girl, pink-cheeked and pigtailed, had vanished after the three bombs exploded in September 1956. The network had parked her in the convent of the Missionary Sisters of Our Lady of Africa. But when the mother superior saw an article on her activities, with her photograph, in *L'Echo d'Alger*, she decided to pass her on to a Carmelite order, where newspapers were not allowed.

Brissac was given the assignment to leak to the Algiers newspapers the false news that Peschard had been arrested, in an attempt to flush her out. When the item was published, the Carmelites heard about it, and Peschard left the convent and was evacuated to an FLN *maquis* (camp) in the Constantinois, near the Tunisian border. There, she worked as a nurse and was said to have married an FLN officer. On November 26, 1957, she was killed in a gun battle with French forces.

In France there was growing concern over the use of torture, not only among antiwar leftist elements but in government circles. The concern was fed by rumors that a renowned para general serving in Algeria had condemned Massu's tactics and asked for a transfer. Jacques Paris de Bollardière, a general at 48, had arrived in Algeria in July 1956, to command a sector southeast of Algiers. He was a Saint-Cyr classmate of Massu's, with whom he had served as a para officer in Indochina. But there the resemblance ended. In 1944, Bollardière had been parachuted into a *maquis* in France. In their battles with the Germans, some of his men were captured, tortured, killed, and thrown into ditches. When his men seized a Nazi prison camp, he found one of his officers hanging from a butcher's hook. From then on, he rejected torture as a dishonorable method used by totalitarian regimes.

In Indochina, where he had commanded a para brigade, one of his noncoms shot a coolie in the back of the head because he was too exhausted to carry a field radio. Bollardière had the noncom court-martialed. Most of the Indochina veterans who were in Algeria still dreamed of empire and French prestige, but it was a dream Bollardière did not share. The loss of Indochina had made him aware of the Third World and its destiny. He was a curiosity in the army, an anticolonial general. Algeria was another interminable and useless war, he thought, sapping French lives and resources.

In his sector, he had a great many unhappy reservists serving their second tour, who were thrown into operational units without proper training. He thought it was wrong to fight the war for the *colons* and against the Arabs. It would be better to lock up the ultras and negotiate with the FLN. He refused to carry out an order to search mosques for weapons. He wrote a directive on February 18 rejecting torture in his sector. All it did was increase the number of rebels. The anthem of the Resistance buzzed in his head: "Friend, if you fall, a friend will come out of the shadows and take your place."

Shortly after that, he came to Algiers in the midst of the para raids. He saw Massu, to whom he said, "Your methods disgust me." Massu said he was just following orders. He saw Lacoste, who told him: "Let Massu's men accomplish their task."

On March 7, Massu ordered Bollardière in writing to give priority to police actions over pacification, since he was getting reports that Bollardière's sector was overrun by the FLN, and that he was more interested in building roads and digging irrigation ditches than he was in fighting the rebels. On March 8, Bollardière resigned his command and asked General Salan for a transfer. Salan agreed, on condition that he keep his reasons to himself and refrain from writing articles.

News of the Bollardière resignation, however, leaked out and sent tremors through political circles in Algiers and Paris. Thus, on

March 10, Governor-General Lacoste wrote Premier Guy Mollet that Massu had done an effective job and that the situation had improved, "but I must admit that I am deeply apprehensive concerning the conduct of his troops. Max Lejeune [secretary of the army] shares my feelings. I would like to get rid of these [para] troops as quickly as possible, but I cannot let them leave until I have enough trained police and gendarmes to continue their work dismantling the FLN in Algiers."

Having encouraged Massu to use "all methods" to restore security in Algiers, Lacoste was now covering his ass, in case the Bollardière resignation should lead to a court of inquiry on the conduct of the war.

On March 11, Massu wrote his own CYA letter to Colonel Jeanpierre regarding the recent arrests and torture of French fellow travelers: "Certain European networks have interpreted charity in an abusive and unpatriotic manner, but you must employ tact in arresting them, since among them are genuinely disinterested social workers." The subtext was: "I'm getting complaints from Archbishop Duval and other influential figures." The sub-subtext was: "It's okay to arrest and torture Arabs but not native French."

On March 13, Massu told Bigeard his regiment must leave Algiers. Massu admired Bigeard, but he was too much of a lone ranger and glory-hound. He didn't want him around any longer than was strictly necessary, particularly with this firestorm of protests over torture, about which Bigeard had spoken too candidly. The 3rd RPC went back to the *bled*, and many of them were glad to go. As for Bigeard, who was in the habit of talking about himself in the third person, he wrote Massu: "I know Bigeard is a pain in the ass, and I know Bigeard will be a lieutenant colonel for life, but I wanted to show those who wanted Bigeard to stumble that he is still here."

Then, on March 21, General Salan was summoned to Paris for a meeting with several cabinet ministers. Bourgès-Maunoury, the minister of defense, told him that the brutality of para interrogations was unacceptable and that he was getting reports of thefts committed by the paras during searches. Salan replied, "My men would be happy to go back to fighting in the *bled* and not have to do this work."

As for Bollardière, upon his return to France, he self-destructed by breaking his word and writing a letter on March 27 that was published in the antiwar weekly *l'Express*. He underlined the "terrible danger, under the fallacious pretext of immediate results, of losing sight of the moral values that until now have guaranteed the greatness of our civilization and our army." His indiscretion resulted in his being placed under arrest and sentenced to 60 days' imprisonment in the fortress of La Courneuve, outside Paris. His career was over, and he left the army in 1961.

Bernard was practically in shock at the news of Bollardière's imprisonment. "If a general gets sixty days just for writing a letter, imagine what we would get," he said.

"He should have used a pseudonym," I said.

Massu, in the meantime, was on a small crusade of his own. He wanted us to bring out an issue on how to be polite to Arabs. "He's being pushed by his wife," said Brissac, who thought the topic was frivolous. "She has the heart and soul of a social worker."

Suzanne Massu was indeed sensitive to the misery of Arabs and was said to have saved her husband from falling completely into the *colon* camp. Having seen too many Arab families without a father and too many Arab children in rags, she launched her own charity, which included an orphanage and an employment office for young Arab women. The Massus had a daughter, Véronique, who soon had an Arab sister, Malika, adopted by Suzanne. One day Massu came home for lunch and found a small Arab boy sitting at the table. "He was picked up by some of your soldiers, wandering the streets," Suzanne told her husband. "He doesn't know his name, so they called him Rodolphe." Once Rodolphe had learned a little broken French, Suzanne asked him about his parents, and all the boy could say was, *"Yavait beaucoup de sang"* ("There was a lot of blood").

"Madame Massu does her own shopping," Brissac said, "and then tells the general about the vulgar *colon* housewife who insulted the

Arab vegetable merchant by accusing him of using crooked scales. Now she's become fixated on the *tu"* (the familiar form of address used in French with one's friends and family, as opposed to the more formal *vous*).

Suzanne Massu had noticed when she went to government offices that the ushers were elderly Arabs who wore spotless *gandouras* and their veterans' decorations. When they brought in the mail, the French officials at their desks spoke to them brusquely, using the *tu* form, like saying "boy." She felt that it was just another way to demean the Arabs.

On March 22, our issue came out, with an appeal from Massu to the European population to treat the Arabs as equals. "In particular," he said, "you must renounce the *tutoiement*, which was until now the habitual form of syntax. . . . Give up this form of language and reserve it, as we do in France, for our friends. May God help each one of you to find several Moslem friends."

"This doesn't sound like Massu," Bernard said.

Brissac agreed. "It's pure Suzanne."

"Well," I said, "the very fact that we can put out an issue on *tutoiement* shows that things have calmed down. Soon we'll be able to go to the beach."

"You go to the beach," Bernard said. "I've got better things to do."

After work, Bernard asked me to join him at the brasserie Aux Auvergnats, where he knew the owner, who sent over two beers. "I know it's an illness," Bernard said, "but I cannot bear not knowing what's going on."

"It's a professional deformation," I said. "In my case, I prefer to forget about the war in my off hours, so I go to the American library and read magazines."

"That's a fantasy world," Bernard said, "although I confess that I know nothing about America except what I've read of one of my favorite authors, E. M. Forster, whose *Passage to India*, by the way, is a brilliant dissection of British colonialism. In an essay on Sinclair Lewis, he wrote that America is 'a very large apron, covered with a pattern of lozenges, edged with a frill, and chastely suspended by a boundary tape round the ample waist of Canada.' "

"That describes its shape, not its content."

"In any case, right now, I'm fixated on finding out what the paras feel about the work they're doing," Bernard said. "The ones I talk to say, 'We were trained to jump out of planes, not to do police work.' Of course, they're not altar boys, and they like being admired by the locals, and some of them behave badly. So they say, 'We have no choice. It's a mission like any other.' "

"In wartime, there's a Hyde in every Jekyll," I said.

"I'm expecting a Foreign Legion officer who's agreed to talk about the Villa Sesini," Bernard said. "He says he knows you. That's why I asked you to come."

At that moment, a short but sturdy green beret second lieutenant walked in. It was Jean Berger, my dorm mate at Saint-Maixent, the only one among us who had asked to be a paratrooper in Algeria.

He gave me a hug and said, "So you ended up in this shit-hole after all, you species of *fainéant*" ("loafer").

"And you got what you wanted," I replied.

"Not exactly. I'm running one of the interrogation teams at the Villa Sesini. I saw Jeanpierre yesterday and told him I couldn't continue, that I'd come to Algeria to fight, not to torture. I'm obedient by nature, but even I have limits. So I'm being transferred to a regiment in the Aurès."

"When did it start?" Bernard asked.

"After the strike," Berger said. "We needed operational intelligence, and we started using the *gégène*. I'm here to tell you, you can't imagine what it's like. The guys are paid bonuses. We tell them they've got the toughest job, but they get used to it. They have no qualms."

"I hear they drink as an anesthetic," Bernard said.

"You're in the cellar. The suspect has electrodes attached to his ears and his cock. You notice the way his eyes are moving. The changes in his breathing. You lose all emotional reactions. You're like a surgeon who's whistling while he saws a body in half. You take a break, a cigarette, and a glass of wine, and you talk about the soccer matches this coming weekend."

"How do you justify it?" I asked.

"We're told that we're saving lives. It's always done at night. A guy is brought in. We make him take his clothes off. Being naked is a terrible humiliation for an Arab. We have various methods. Pouring water down their throats with a funnel, or using a soddering iron on the soles of their feet, or a lit cigarette on a nipple. The *gégène* works best, with one of our boys turning the handles faster to turn up the juice. There's no risk of electrocution. We call the *gégène* the *machine à faire parler*" ("the machine that makes people talk").

"Do you torture women?" Bernard asked.

"Of course," Berger said. "A few weeks ago a girl was caught with a message. She said someone she didn't know gave it to her and she forgot where she was supposed to leave it. She was brought to the cellar, sniffling like a child. The sergeant that day was Hans, one of the German legionnaires."

"There's been a lot of talk about your Germans using the same methods the Nazis used on the French Resistance in World War II," Bernard said.

"It's true that our regiment is thirty percent German," Berger said, "but they're not all alike. This one likes his work. 'If you're a virgin, you won't be for long,' he tells the girl. He tells her, *'À poil'* ['Get naked']. She removes her clothes, except for her bra and panties. 'I said, *'À poil,'*' Hans tells her. She pulls off her bra and raises her hands to cover her breasts. She's tied to the bed with her legs spread and a wire in her vagina. The juice is turned on, and she screams, and in less than a minute she shouts, 'Ask me questions.' Hans says, 'You could have talked before the striptease, you dumb cunt.' Her information led to the arrest of a dozen young women, most of them still in school—liaison and weapons carriers."

"But why didn't you do something to stop Hans?" Bernard asked.

"You don't get it. This is the Foreign Legion in wartime. There's a system, and you're either inside the system or outside the system, but you can't change the system. That's why I asked for a transfer to a combat zone."

I knew that Bernard wanted a tête-à-tête with Berger, so I excused myself, but I jotted down my address and phone number and told my Saint-Maixent classmate to look me up anytime. He had yearned to be a warrior and was now thoroughly disillusioned.

When I got home, Georgette told me I had a call from Jean Daridan, who was staying at the Aletti Hotel. He was a lawyer I knew in Paris, tall and distinguished, with long sandy hair swept back on a diagonal and a voice like one of the heralds in the *Iliad.* He told me that he belonged to a lawyers' collective that defended those Arabs who were brought to trial and that his first case in Algiers was two days away. I was surprised, since I knew him to be more to the right than to the left of center. Most of his clients were corporate types, and his apartment on the rue de Rivoli had one of the best views of Paris—the Jardin des Tuileries.

"What possessed you to get involved in this hornet's nest?" I asked him on the phone.

"I still believe in the Declaration of the Rights of Man," he said.

It occurred to me that the trial could make an article for Brissac. Bernard and I scratched our heads each week to find topics that weren't the obvious catechism and yet advanced the cause to fill our four pages. His refrain was "It's hard work being a whore," to which I responded, "But you get used to it." Brissac agreed and gave me credentials, and on the morning of the trial I walked over to the Aletti for breakfast with Daridan. Algiers was up early, the jeeps and trucks mingling with civilian traffic, the *fatmas* in their robes seeming to slide along the sidewalk, men with briefcases, children with their book bags. The light shimmered between the buildings, and I could hear the waves beating against the admiralty pier. The Aletti was an oasis; its terrace smelled of jasmine. I joined Daridan at an outdoor table.

"I saw my client yesterday at Barberousse," he said. "His name is Mohammed Slimane. He is accused of throwing a grenade into a café and wounding five persons. I asked him to lift his shirt, and it was evident that he had been tortured. I could see long brown lines on his back left by the flame of a soddering iron, other burn marks still unhealed, blisters, and black-and-blue marks."

"I hope you realize," I said, as I dipped my croissant into my coffee, "that these trials before a military tribunal are preordained, and that the death sentence is likely."

"We'll see," he said.

The military tribunal, consisting of three army officers, sat in a drab room in the Orléans barracks. Daridan conferred with his client, a weary-looking Arab, slight of build and stooped, who kept craning his neck as if he had on a tight collar.

One of the judges banged his gavel, read the charge, and asked the accused to give his name and age. The prosecutor, clad in a black robe and a white jabot, his hands clenched in the folds of his robe, then strode up to face the accused.

"You claimed before the examining magistrate," he said, "that someone you did not know handed you a grenade with the pin removed, wrapped in a newspaper, and that you had to get rid of it before it exploded, so you threw it away, and it landed in a café."

"It wasn't me," Slimane said in a barely audible voice.

"How can you say that?" the prosecutor asked. "You confessed. You gave all the details. And you waited until now to deny your confession?"

"I was beaten," Slimane said. "They would have killed me. But I had nothing to do with the bomb."

One of the judges said, "The tribunal takes note that you have retracted your confession."

"This," said the prosecutor, "is the final attempt of a guilty man clutching at straws while overwhelmed by indisputable evidence, and hopefully, by the horror of his act."

I knew that these trials were nothing if not expeditious. No witnesses were called. The prosecutor questioned the defendant, the defense lawyer stated his case, the tribunal retired to deliberate, and 20 minutes later the verdict was announced.

Daridan rose and addressed the tribunal. "How can we be sure when the defendant told the truth?" he asked. "Was it after his arrest or now? And yet to convict him, we must be sure beyond a doubt. Was there any evidence of guilt beyond his confession? There was not. As for the confession, it was obtained by violence."

Daridan described Slimane's condition when he had seen him in his cell. He said he was reminded of the Gestapo cells during the occupation.

The prosecutor rose in high dudgeon and shouted: "This is inadmissible! I protest! The defense is going beyond the bounds!"

"I will show you what is inadmissible," Daridan thundered. Turning to Slimane, he said, "Remove your shirt and show the tribunal what was done to you."

Slimane took off his stained tan T-shirt and turned his back to the judges. In the small courtroom, he was only a few feet away, and they tried to hide their revulsion when they saw the welts and burns.

"A French tribunal," Daridan went on, "cannot base its verdict on confessions extracted by torture, particularly when the judges are wearing the French uniform."

The judges retired and deliberated for half an hour, which was unusually long. When they returned, they pronounced the verdict of not guilty.

I told Daridan afterward that what he had accomplished was highly unusual. "Cases like this don't often come to trial," I said. "When an Arab is arrested by the paras, he's taken away by them and never enters the court system."

"I know," Daridan said, "but this one was arrested by the police before the paras took over, and there are still hundreds like him, rotting in Barberousse."

"I've seen the lines outside."

"*Entre nous*, I'm sure Slimane was guilty, but I'm pleased I got him off."

When I got back to the office, I described the trial to Brissac and said, "I don't think it's for us."

"Why not?" he asked. "It shows that an FLN terrorist can get a fair trial before a military tribunal."

"It also shows that torture was used to extract a confession."

Brissac grumbled under his breath, à la Massu, whom he liked to imitate, and that was the last I heard of it.

Between Battles

ARCH WAS A quiet month, without explosions in downtown Algiers and with fewer paras in the streets. People were breathing easier. I had time to idle away the hours at the American library. Don Davies told me attendance was up and he'd hired a *pied-noir* female receptionist. He took me over to her desk and said, "This is Geneviève Zimmer. As you can see, she alone would bring in customers." Geneviève smiled. Her upper and lower lips were the same size, which gave her a faintly fishlike look. She wore no makeup, and her blond hair was pulled back in a bun, framing a full, round face with a high brow, a straight nose, and shrewd, appraising blue eyes. There was something of the gendarme about her, but the kind of gendarme who pats school children on the head at street crossings.

"Don has spoken to me about you," she said. "You live in Massachusetts."

"I did until I came here."

"Can I get you some coffee?" She came back with two cups. "I spent a year in Massachusetts, at Smith College. They have a French house there and all the girls have to speak French. I had a scholar-ship to converse with them."

"Did you learn any English?"

"Yes, I learned 'Keep your hands off' for when I went out with a boy. These American college boys don't court you; they paw you."

"What did you think of Smith girls?"

"They were young for their age. They had very little knowledge of history. Some of them had never heard of Algeria."

"They study the history of their own country, just as the French do."

Geneviève sat at her desk, where she was filling out file cards by hand. She didn't want to be just chatting. Idle hands do the devil's work. "The paradox of their history," she said as she wrote, "is that they pretend to be a democracy while owning slaves and slaughter-ing Indians."

"Yes, but they freed their slaves," I replied.

Geneviève looked up at me and said with a radiant smile: "One thing I liked about Smith College—there were no Arabs." This open dislike of Arabs was such a common *pied-noir* reflex that I should not have been taken aback, but coming from this intelligent, urbane young woman, something must have shown on my face.

"Have you been outside Algiers?" she asked. "My father owns a farm in the Mitidja. It might be interesting for you to see it. Would you like to accompany me this weekend?"

I sensed that she had the missionary spirit and wanted to convert me to the *colon* cause. I began to think of Geneviève as a *pied-noir* Pasionaria, but I welcomed the opportunity to be introduced to a *colon* family. She said she went out every weekend because her father was a widower and needed company. We could drive out Saturday for lunch.

On Saturday morning, she picked me up in her Peugeot and we drove out of Algiers, encountering only one checkpoint. Geneviève chatted with the paras and flashed a big smile to let them know she admired them, and in her slacks and suede jacket she radiated *colon* vivacity. Then we came upon a group of Arab children playing in the street, and she said, "They multiply like rabbits. It's useless to teach the women birth control. The only thing we can count on is infant mortality."

The children were playing in front of a housing project that had been built by the liberal mayor of Algiers, Jacques Chevallier. Geneviève pointed out the whitewashed six-story buildings with balconies and said: "We build them apartments with electricity and running water, a kitchen with a refrigerator and a gas stove, and six months later they've brought in their chickens and goats."

I kept my mouth shut because I wanted to hear the full spiel. I felt like an ethnologist exploring the strange beliefs of a lost tribe. Geneviève found the main road heading south out of Algiers, and we crossed the long Mitidja plain, the masterpiece of *colon* enterprise, drained from malarial swamps and now transformed into farm after red-tiled farm and vineyard after manicured vineyard.

"I grew up believing that the Arabs were the ones who live in the slums," she said. "There's a hierarchy that can never be broken. Even among the shoeshine boys, there are those who pursue their customers with a rag and those who have a chair and pegs to put your feet on."

"There's also a hierarchy in prison," I said, "between the common-law and the politicals."

Geneviève snorted. "In prison, they're better fed than our poor tramps who've committed no crime. And our very adroit archbishop defends them in his sermons."

We reached Boufarik, capital of the Mitidja, one of the rare towns that had more *colons* than Arabs. Its streets were lined with majestic plane trees, and we passed the statue of Sergeant Blandon, who was killed in 1841 with 12 of his 17 men when he was surrounded by 300 Arab horsemen.

On a one-lane dirt road 10 kilometers out of town, we came to a high wooden gate that said Domaine Zimmer. The gate was locked, and Geneviève honked the horn.

"You love this land," I said. "I'm surprised you didn't stay on it."

"Oh," Geneviève said, flipping back a stray strand of spun gold, "I was engaged to a landowner my father approved of, but one day he told me, 'You don't have enough hectares.' "

I said that seemed like a coarse way of putting it.

"That's the way *pieds-noirs* are."

"Did you love him?"

"I never got the chance to find out. Unmarried women here don't give themselves easily. What we say is, 'Don't celebrate Easter before Palm Sunday.' "

An Arab worker unlocked the gate and doffed his hat as we drove by, up to the ochre farmhouse, where her father stood waiting in the doorway, wearing suspenders over a blue workshirt and denim trousers. He was a big, heavy man, with a belly that the *pieds-noirs* called *l'oeuf colonial* (the colonial egg). His curly hair had gone white, and over a boxer's broken nose he had the same appraising blue eyes as his daughter. His biceps bulged from the rolled-up sleeves of his shirt, and he gave me a bone-crushing handshake.

"So you've come to see how the horrid *colons* live," said François Zimmer.

"Papa, he's on Massu's staff," Geneviève said. "Don't start off on the wrong foot."

"I'm just joking," he said, clapping me on the back. "Come inside." He led us into a big room with a stone fireplace, a couple of couches, and a low table carved from the trunk of a tree. "Have a glass of rosé. It's the best in the Mitidja," he said, as he filled three glasses from a bottle on the table. "I drink a liter every morning for breakfast, but only in the summer."

I took a swallow and said: "It's rosé, but it's got a punch."

"I have nothing against Massu," Zimmer said. "It's his wife I don't like. She doesn't understand the Arabs. She gives the girls sewing machines, and the next day they sell them in the Casbah markets."

When we'd finished the bottle, he proposed to take me on a tour of his farm while Geneviève prepared lunch. "I've got a thousand hectares," he said, "half in wheat and half in vines." We jumped into his jeep and drove down a dirt road where the wooden, metal-rimmed wine vats stood, under a big shed. An elderly Arab was fixing some loose boards in the shed.

"There's no wine in the vats; it's not the season," Zimmer said. "See that Arab in the shed? He's been here for forty years, since he was a kid. Once he fell into a vat after harvest, and I pulled him out with a rope under his shoulders. I lay him on his stomach and stuck two fingers down his throat until he coughed up the wine and started breathing."

He pointed to a small whitewashed cottage and said, "After that, I built an infirmary for my workers. Some of them had never seen an aspirin."

He seemed to want to come across as a humanitarian who treated his Arab workers well.

"The smell of grapes fermenting in the vats—I live for that," he said. "We don't even bottle it. We send it to France in metal containers so they can mix it with their anemic vintages."

I couldn't resist asking, "What do you pay your men during the harvest?"

"Ten francs a day" (two 1957 dollars).

"In France that's the hourly wage," I said.

"If I paid them more, they'd disappear after a few days."

"You could give them a bonus after the harvest."

"I'd never see them again."

This was *colon* logic: The Arabs were so undependable that paying them a starvation wage was actually doing them a favor, in that it kept them steadily employed. It was the same kind of logic that Anatole France derided when he wrote: "The rich as well as the poor are forbidden from sleeping under bridges."

We drove on, past endless rows of vines and irrigation ditches, and came upon a grove of ancient olive trees. "My father planted those trees," François said. "My parents were Alsatians who had the choice of taking German nationality in 1870 or leaving behind all they had for the sole benefit of remaining French. You can understand how I feel when anyone dares to tell me I'm not really French."

"I wonder if the Spanish and Italians and Maltese who came after your parents feel the same way," I said.

"My father called them the sixty-*centime* French, because that was what it cost to get a naturalization application. To be frank, there's always been a pecking order, with the Arabs at the bottom. My wife used to say, when scolding the children, 'Even the *fatma* would understand.' "

The jeep bumped across a shallow, rocky stream, and on the other side lay fields of winter wheat. "My father cleared the ground and used the rocks to build walls," Zimmer said. "Arabs are poor farmers. They don't dig the rocks out. My father turned the earth at a depth of a foot to plant wheat and cotton. The Arabs scratch with their hoes at a depth of three inches. My father had great stands of wheat with thick clusters in tight rows. The Arabs have meager stands meandering around rocks they haven't bothered to remove. They don't even understand that if you plant on flat land you get a better return than on a rocky slope."

Maybe all that flat land was stolen from them, I thought, but there was no point in arguing with the classic sermon that one heard a dozen times a day: How can you say we stole their land when we were the ones who dried the swamps and planted the fields and brought in vines and fruit trees and irrigation, and now we have a country with fine harbors, good roads, sparkling cities, and sturdy bridges, so all I can say is long live colonialism.

Geneviève had prepared her father's favorite lunch, an Alsatian *choucroute* with four kinds of sausage. Since he had told me that at harvest time he had a couple hundred Arab workers, I asked him if he spoke any Arabic. François went into another room and came back gripping a MAT submachine gun. "This is my Franco-Arab dictionary," he said.

With the *choucroute* there were copious rounds of rosé, which went to my head, so that I ventured onto conversational ground that I should have avoided, as François continued to expound on the backwardness of Arabs.

"Why not at least give them the right to vote?" I asked.

François slammed his fist on the heavy oak dining table, shaking the glasses, and said, "You're proposing the death of French Algeria. They will use the vote the same way their grandfathers used their rifles, to throw us out."

"Can't you respect their beliefs and leave it at that?" I asked.

"But I don't respect their beliefs," François shouted, "and it's a mistake to tell them they can be good Frenchmen. A Frenchman can't have three wives. And what about the Moslem practice of sending their wives out to be prostitutes?"

That one really threw me. I wondered whether the rosé had gone to his head as well. But Geneviève didn't say anything, so I assumed she agreed with her father.

"I thought they sequestered their wives," I said.

"They do both," he said.

I realized that *colon* arguments were rational only up to a point and then erupted into grotesque diatribes that couldn't be rationally discussed, so I shut my mouth.

François had drunk more than a bottle of rosé, and his head dropped to his chin in a stupor. But then he raised it, opened his eyes, and said in a low voice: "If you want to know the truth, we're finished here. Have you heard the phrase *la valise ou le cercueil*" ("the coffin or the suitcase")?

I had heard it many times. It was the *colons'* worst-case scenario, the one they were desperately trying to avoid.

"We are being betrayed by our own government," François said. "They don't give a shit about Algeria. They're negotiating with the FLN behind our backs. As Maurras used to say, 'In order to love France today, it is necessary to hate what she has become.' " (Charles Maurras, the monarchist and profascist who founded the Action Française movement, was much admired by the *colons*).

François's rant was so off target, at a time when the paras had been given full powers in Algiers, that there was no more to be said. Even Geneviève realized that her father was over the edge, for she said, "It's time for your nap, Papa, and we'd better be going."

We drove back to Algiers, and Geneviève said, "You'll have to excuse my father. He gets a little overheated."

"He has strong convictions," I said, "and he's worked all his life on his farm. But I agree that France is not going to win the war."

"That's the rosé speaking," Geneviève said. "In his heart, he knows that he will never leave." She put her hand over mine and asked me if I wanted to go to Le Rowing, a chic *colon* club, where the men practiced sculling in the harbor. I begged off. I had had enough of the *colon* point of view for one day.

Sunday, March 30, was my birthday. I was 25 years old. Georgette said she was taking me to lunch at the Club des Pins, which had tennis courts, a swimming pool, a small beach, and a good restaurant. No Arabs allowed. She ordered champagne and gave me my family's ancient toast that I had taught her: "To our horses, to our women, and to those who mount them."

"By the way," she said, "Julien is coming home on leave next weekend. You'll have to move back to your apartment. But I'd like you to come to dinner with us."

I was surprised at how angry I was. After all, I was the interloper. But I tried not to show it and I said, "I'd rather not."

"He knows I gave you the apartment, and if I don't introduce you, he'll be suspicious."

"My problem is that I might like him, and I don't want to be sleeping with the wife of someone I like."

We left it at that and had a swim on the beach. I had thought since childhood that lying on the sand under a hot sun was barbaric, but Georgette was a sun worshiper. Her favorite saying was "The sun burns, but it also energizes." I lay down beside her with a towel over my face, dozing, and sometime later I felt the lower part of the towel being lifted and my mouth being kissed. "Let's go home," Georgette said.

Four days later I was in the office working on an article entitled "Calm Has Returned to Algiers." Governor-General Lacoste and his entire military and civilian staff had visited the Casbah to show that it was safe again. Spring brought back the street crowds and the traffic to the beaches. Because it was Ramadan, the curfew had been advanced to 1:00 in the morning to accommodate Moslems who had fasted during the day. I had asked Georgette never to call me at work, so when she did I thought, What's going on? Georgette said, "I'm holding a telegram in my hand. Julien has been killed *en service commandé* [in the line of duty]. But there's no explanation." She was sobbing. I told her I would try to find out.

Brissac was able to reach an officer in Julien's unit in Hassi-Messaoud, who told him that Julien had been killed in an ambush, but his driver got away. I spoke to the driver over the radio, and he gave me this account: He and Julien were taking a truck to a depot five kilometers outside Hassi-Messaoud to pick up some machinery. Halfway to the depot, the *piste* (unsurfaced road) was blocked by three uniformed Arabs with submachine guns. One of them told Julien, "Get down from the truck."

"Why should I get down?" Julien asked.

The *fel* fired a burst in the air, and Julien and the driver got down. "Why aren't you carrying anything in the truck?" the Arab asked.

"We are on our way to pick up some machinery," Julien said. "You could have asked me before. I would have told you that the truck was empty."

The *fel* whipped the barrel of his MAT across Julien's face. "I'm requisitioning this truck," he said. He got into the driver's seat, but he couldn't start it, which made him angry. He told the other two Arabs, "Tie their hands behind their backs with wire and throw them in the back of the truck." He finally got the truck started and followed the desert trails.

Julien told the driver, "They're taking us to a palm grove, and they will shoot us. Our only chance is to get them before they get us." They were able to get the wire off each other's wrists. Then the truck got stuck in the sand and they could hear the three *fels* cursing in the cab of the truck.

The *fels* got out of the truck, and the leader said, "Get down, you French dogs."

Julien and the driver looked out and saw that the *fels* were in a huddle about three feet away. Julien yelled, "Now," and they leaped from the back of the truck at the *fels*, who swerved and fired as they jumped. Julien was killed in the first burst, but the driver hit the ground without being shot and was able to kick the advancing *fel* in the stomach and make a run for it. He made it back to the base at Hassi-Messaoud, dehydrated but alive.

The driver told me: "I wanted my officer to live, but it happened the other way around."

When I got back to Square Bresson, Georgette had regained her composure, and I repeated the driver's account. "What a shame," she said. "Just as they were about to strike oil." (They did in fact strike oil a couple of months later.) "And in one more day, he was to come home on leave."

Georgette was already in mourning, in a pleated black skirt and cashmere cardigan. She asked me to move my things out of her bedroom. "I must respect his memory," she said, "so we can't continue in the same way. You can stay in the other apartment, and we'll remain friends."

I reflected on the ironies of life: not only that Julien had not lived long enough to see the gusher but also that Georgette had become posthumously faithful. I had come to appreciate the comfort she provided, but it would have been crude of me to try to change her mind. She would make a lovely, chaste widow.

On April 12, that excellent reporter Eugène Mannoni (who later became a friend) wrote in *Le Monde* that the Algérois were relieved, the patrols were less frequent, and there were fewer arrests. I knew that Massu's transit camps were full, for he did not trust civilian justice, with its laxity, paroles, and transfers. Those arrested, he felt, should be treated as prisoners of war, and assigned to a transit camp for interrogation. The civilian authorities, with the exception of Teitgen, said, "Let the paras handle it; we don't want to know about it." The paras had handled it so efficiently that by mid-April, there was only one of Massu's four regiments left inside the city. Jean-pierre's legionnaires (1st REP) were gone, as were Fossey-François's red berets (2nd RPC), who had handled the "suicide" of Boumendjel and arrested 200 suspects. There remained only the 1st RCP (blue berets) under Lieutenant Colonel Mayer, with headquarters on the

Boulevard de Verdun, above the Casbah. Inside the Casbah, Captain Sirvent's *zouaves* continued to patrol.

Word leaked out from Massu's office that there had been a bizarre incident in the Casbah on April 9, which we pieced together as the information came in.

Yacef Saadi had a hideout on rue du Nil, which was so narrow that from the fourth floor he could jump from the odd- to the even-numbered side. His bomb-maker, Mourad, was on rue Porte-Neuve. Yacef's team at the time consisted of Ali-la-Pointe and three young women: Hassiba Ben Bouali, 19, a pretty, blond Arab who advanced from social work to terrorism; Zohra Drif, 23, the daughter of an Arab judge, long-nosed and with close-set eyes, who had attended law school, where the *colon* boys called her "dumb Zohra," and who was already a veteran, for she had dropped off the Milk Bar bomb on September 30, 1956; and Djamila Bouhired, who had on the same day left the bomb at the Air France terminal that did not detonate. Djamila was 22, hot tempered and foul-mouthed, but she could look pretty when she wanted to, with a warm smile, liquid brown eyes, and curly chestnut hair. Her father Omar was a star soccer player, idolized by his fans; he wanted his daughter to get into couture.

Yacef, whose instinct for survival was well honed, felt there was too much traffic between rue du Nil and rue Porte-Neuve. He had to find a new hideout. There were still *zouave* patrols 24 out of 24. A place was found on the rue du Sphinx, offered by a supporter, Mafoud.

Yacef decided to move his office, which consisted of a single brown imitation leather briefcase, on April 9. The curfew lifted at 5 AM, and the Casbah quickly became animated as dockworkers walked down to their jobs in the harbor and dozens of *fatmas* went to work in the European quarter. Among those veiled *fatmas* that morning were Yacef and Ali-la-Pointe, who started out at 5:30 with the three women, a point man, Alilou, and Mafoud. Yacef gave his briefcase to Djamila Bouhired, for he had a MAT under his robe and wanted to keep both arms free.

They walked in single file at intervals of 60 feet. They had only a few blocks to go. Mafoud took the lead, to show them his place on rue du Sphinx. When he got to the intersection of rue du Sphinx and rue Porte-Neuve, he came upon a *zouave* patrol. Instead of walking calmly ahead, he abruptly about-faced and strode rapidly away. The *zouaves* cried, "Halt," and fired in the air. Djamila Bouhired, who was behind Mafoud, ran toward the *zouaves*, gesticulating wildly, in an attempt to draw their attention away from Yacef. Thinking that the *zouaves* had fired at his group, Yacef fired a burst in their direction, but hit Djamila Bouhired in the left shoulder. She fell in a heap, dropping the briefcase, which contained 800,000 francs, fake ID cards, FLN documents, and Yacef's address book. Intrigued by the briefcase, the *zouaves* let Yacef and the others escape.

The *zouaves* took Djamila to the Maillot Military Hospital, where the captain of surgery examined her. The bullet had gone through her left shoulder without breaking the collarbone, nicked a lung, and exited. He had to decide whether to operate to avoid a possible hemorrhage, which meant cutting open her chest and leaving a long scar. As he later put it to the officer who interrogated her, Captain Jean Graziani: "She had a chest like the Venus de Milo. I could not maim this marvel."

Normally, Djamila, who had a record as a placer of bombs, should have been transferred to an interrogation center, where she would have been tortured and probably killed. But Suzanne Massu intervened. She had a desire to help young Arab women, and she wanted to find out more about those who played an active part in the rebellion. In view of the traditional role of women in a Moslem society, hidden behind veils and relegated to household tasks, she wondered what drove these young women to take on dangerous assignments and risk arrests and worse.

Not only did Madame Massu visit Djamila in the hospital and engage her in long talks but she also asked her husband to have one of his staff officers question her rather than turn her over to the torture mills.

The officer chosen, Captain Graziani, was the assistant head of Massu's military intelligence bureau. He was a good-looking, charming man in his thirties, with a relaxed, nonthreatening manner. After four years in Viet captivity, he had reached the conclusion that there were better methods than torture to make suspects talk. He now had a chance to test his conviction.

Captain Graziani went to Djamila's beside at Maillot Hospital and introduced himself. She spat at him and called him a son of a whore. He gave her a hard slap *aller-retour.* She quieted down. He looked through the snapshots in her wallet, which included a particularly unflattering one on her ID card. "Tomorrow we'll release this photograph to every newspaper," he said. When she begged him not to, he saw that she had a coquettish side, and he agreed to use another photo.

On April 17, her lung having healed, Djamila was transferred to Massu's divisional headquarters, where Graziani proceeded to turn her interrogation into a courtship. He found her some new dresses and took her to the officer's mess for dinner. The other officers, who were in on the stratagem, came up to their table and asked to be introduced. Soon they were holding hands and kissing.

Brissac, back from Massu's briefing, said: "It's Héloïse and Abelard over there."

"But is she talking?" Bernard asked. "Sometimes it's hard to tell between the cat and mouse."

She talked on April 20, giving away the bomb cache on the rue Porte-Neuve, where the *zouaves* found 13 bombs and two FLN flags, though bomb-maker Mourad had fled. She also gave away her friend Djamila Bouazza, who had placed the January 26 bomb at the Coq Hardi and was arrested at the post office where she worked on April 25. One thing that had escaped Madame Massu's notice was that girls like Djamila Bouhired did not have the discipline of veteran rebels.

When Graziani had finished questioning her at the end of April, Djamila Bouhired was transferred to the womens' dorm in Barberousse Prison to await trial. There, she helped turn the ward into a hotbed of FLN propagandists. On days when the guillotine was busy, the women took up the cry "Assassins." When the guards, to punish them, took away their sewing baskets, Bouhired organized a hunger strike. As for Graziani, her romantic interrogator, he was killed in combat at the head of his company in Kabylie in 1959.

I N EARLY May, Georgette was still in mourning, but she was hardly a recluse, and she asked me to escort her to the opening of a show by a local painter, at the Libraire des Colonnes, which doubled as an art gallery. She knew the artist, Sauveur Galliero, one of the rare eccentrics in the polarized communities of Algiers, she said, who had been a boyhood friend of the writer Camus.

At the gallery, he was easy to spot, for he wore sandals, khaki shorts, and a short-sleeved open-necked shirt. "That's his uniform," Georgette said. Galliero's black curly hair and leathery face made him look like a gypsy, but a dispirited gypsy, for he had downward-cast eyes and the mournful expression of a basset hound, as well as a pronounced overbite. I liked his pointillist watercolors of the beaches and the Algiers street life, and I told him so when Georgette introduced us. "I think it's remarkable," I said, "that you can circulate with your watercolors as if there was no war on."

"But that is exactly my attitude," he said, "I continue to live as I did before these events. Today in Algiers, there are two categories, paras and suspects, and I refuse to belong to either one." He spoke slowly and deliberately, as if chewing his words, and he emanated a serenity that was completely at odds with the mood of the city. He was someone I wanted to get to know. In a city where people were shooting each other daily, he was painting them.

I asked him where he lived and he said Bab-el-Oued, the working-class neighborhood on the water's edge, known as the proletarian Riviera. "I used to live in the Casbah," he said, "but that's become impossible." I asked if I could come and see him, and he told me to meet him at 6 the next day at the Café de Provence on the Place des Trois Horloges.

Sauveur and I became friends. We saw a lot of each other during the rest of my stay in Algiers. He helped me keep my sanity, for when I was with him, I forgot about the war; he was easy-going, undemanding, and operated by the power of suggestion. Sauveur came from Sicilian and Spanish stock. His father was a coachman and his mother was a cook. Aside from French, he spoke Spanish, Italian, and Arabic. Born in 1914, he helped me understand the importance of the first war for the *colons*. "When I was a kid," he said, "there was a World War I veteran who'd been hit by shrapnel at the Chemin des Dames. He opened a furniture store on Avenue de la Marne called Au Mutilé. He sold dining room sets like *petits pains*. Don't forget that among the millions of dead, there were one hundred fifty-five thousand French and Moslem Algerians.

"When I grew up," he said, "we thought of Bab-el-Oued as a village outside the city, with its own customs and language. People still had oil lamps. They refused to have electricity because the nights were so short. But those who had electricity made fun of those who didn't. Everybody knew everybody, Francis the barber, Marcello the shoemaker, the Lopez grocery, the Perez bakery, Omar the coal merchant, all on one block, rue des Moulins—the fish on stone slabs, the chickens hanging from hooks, the fruit on wooden stands.

"Everyone lived in the street," he said. "I started playing soccer in the street with apricot pits. We didn't belong to any clubs, so, we swam in the harbor. The water was like warm piss. There was a lot of splashing and dunking to make you *boire la tasse* [drink a cupful of dirty seawater]. I went onto the rocks with gloves on to catch sea urchins."

When he went to school, he said, "there were boys of all backgrounds, even a few Arabs, the sons of the big tents. I still remember the history book, the *Malet-Isaac*: 'Before the arrival of the French, Algeria was prone to anarchy.' One day in class, a father barged in and asked for his son. The teacher said he wasn't there. The father said, 'When he comes in, I'm going to kill him.' The teacher said that would not be helpful, and the father said, 'I'll kill him, but I won't put out his eyes.' That tells you a lot about the Bab-el-Oued mentality. But the violence is mostly verbal, on the order of 'Hold me back before I do something I'll regret.' The Bab-el-Oued personality is all in exaggeration."

Venturing into Bab-el-Oued that first time to meet Sauveur, I had the impression of being in a stage set where hundreds of boisterous extras chattered furiously in a colorful argot. Families in chairs on sidewalks, the wives in bathrobes with floral designs, dogs foraging in garbage cans, the laundry drying on balconies. I found the Place des Trois Horloges, at the center of which stood an iron candelabra with three white globes that told the time. At the zinc counter of the Café de Provence, Sauveur was talking soccer to the owner, Marcel, who had a face like melting wax, all in folds and jowls. "Have a glass of anisette," he told me, pouring from the bottle. "Did you know that anisette cures malaria?"

Marcel brought *kemia*, saucers with olives, anchovies, little red mullets, grilled sardines, and snails in hot sauce, all lined up on the counter and free with your drink.

"My father sold wine from barrels with wooden faucets," he said, "twelve hours a day for twenty years. He said hello all day long. He knew everyone in the neighborhood, that was his life, and he left me enough so I could open this place."

Marcel interrupted our conversation to greet arriving customers with the usual banter: "Drunk again last night, Paul. Ashamed, you should be! Hey, Georges, how's your sister? Still spreading her legs?" No one took offense. If Marcel insulted you, it meant he liked you.

"They talk about the *colons* stealing the land," Marcel told us. "I don't own any land. I'm fighting for the sun and the sea; I'm fighting not to have to wear an overcoat ten months a year."

Sauveur said, "A friend of mine told me, 'Go to Paris. You're better off being the worst painter in Paris than the best painter in Algiers.' " I said, 'What about the sea, what about the light? Paris is dirty. It's full of pigeons and dark courtyards.' "

"And now they want to throw us out," Marcel said. "They talk about self-determination. What about us? We're people too. Can you imagine the people of Marseilles being thrown out of their city? If there'd been ten million of us, it would be different, but we didn't want to have eight or nine children."

"Have you had any bombs in the neighborhood?" I asked.

"There are no bombs here because we keep our eyes open," Marcel said, pouring another round of anisette. "But look at that young man, Grabagnati, murdered on his Vespa outside the hospital. He was apolitical, working class, he was a goalie for the Sporting Club. Can you tell me why?"

"There is no why," Sauveur said. "That's the method. To kill people at random."

"The Arabs are never satisfied," Marcel said. "The shoeshine boys Madame Massu sends to school complain they're being persecuted. What the Arabs really want is a fig tree with some shade to sit under."

Sauveur told Marcel he wanted to show me the sights, but when he pulled out his wallet Marcel wouldn't let him pay. We walked down the Avenue Bouzarea, and he said: "You can't change the way they think. But you know the proverb—and it applies to both sides—'When you want to kill a dog, you say he's got rabies.' "

"What they don't realize," he went on, "is that they're a lot like the Arabs. They want complete control over their wives and they wish they had more than one. When their daughters have jobs, they're supposed to turn over their salaries to their parents."

I asked him when he had met Camus. "In 1934, when he was working with a theater troupe and I was painting the sets," Sauveur said. "What you have to understand about Albert is that he never knew his father. He was born in 1913 and his father Lucien left for France a year later, wearing the blue vest and red trousers of a *zouave*, and got himself killed in October on the Marne. It didn't take much—a bit of shrapnel in the arm that turned to gangrene. Albert's mother was an illiterate cleaning woman. They lived in a stinking hole in Belcourt, without running water. Albert is self-made entirely."

Their friendship was partly based on having broken out of their familial poverty. "In 1934," Sauveur recalled, "Albert made two disastrous decisions. He got married at the age of twenty-one—I was a year younger—and he joined the Communist Party."

"Was his wife a Communist?"

"Worse. She was a drug addict, in and out of rehab, and she cheated on him. She finally left him, and he got fed up with the party. 'They live on proclamations,' he said. Of course he never sold *The Class Struggle* in the streets."

"I think Camus liked me because I didn't talk all the time," Sauveur said. "There were long silences between us. Later on, he pretended to the world that he was somber and ascetic, but he loved dirty jokes and the low life, card games and anisette. The trouble was, he didn't have the stamina. He was already spitting blood."

We were walking along and came up to a long wooden one-story building painted blue, right on the water. "That's the Padovani bathhouse," Sauveur said, "the poor man's Cannes. There's a narrow band of yellow sand, a row of dressing rooms on stilts, a dance floor, and a café that sells fried fish. It has a certain Belle Époque style."

"So where did you and Camus hang out?" I asked.

"Oh, we played poker dice at the Provence, we played *boules* on the esplanade, we played a little soccer, we went to the beach and checked out the girls, and when you saw a pretty one you'd shout, '*mouette*' [seagull]. At night, we went to the Bas-Fonds, a bar in the harbor with whores and pimps. The owner was a crazy dwarf who liked to put on a clerical collar and 'baptize' his customers by sprinkling them with wine. He had a cigar-cutter that was a miniature guillotine."

We were on Avenue Durando, and Sauveur said, "See those trolley rails? They're a frontier. On the left you have Spanish Bab-el-Oued, and on the right Italian Bab-el-Oued."

"So when did Camus leave Algeria?" I asked.

"Let's see. In 1939, he was the editor of *Le Soir Républicain*, and the war seemed absurd to him, and the paper was shut down in January 1940. He was turned down by the army, because of his tuberculosis, and he didn't have a job, so he left for Paris in March and got hired on a paper there."

"Did he stay in France?"

"Well, in 1942, *The Stranger* came out, and that changed everything. He didn't come back until after the war, and by then he'd gotten too big for his britches. You had to wait in line to see him. He did tell me that the main character, Meursault, was based partly on me. Meursault had a bad attitude. He was indifferent to the conventions of society and insensitive to his mother's death. He didn't throw himself on her grave, sobbing. Neither did I. I suppose it was a mixture of hedonism and low-level nihilism that he saw, although I've never killed an Arab. I remember that I owed him money, but he didn't want to be paid back. 'I owe you a lot,' he said."

"Was that the last time you saw him?"

"No, I saw him when he was here last year. By then he'd written *The Plague*, and he said, 'they want masterpieces out of me like loaves from the oven,' which I thought was a mite self-glorifying. He was weighed down by the question of Algeria, as if only he had the answer. He was torn between his *pied-noir* upbringing and his sympathy for the underdog. He told me, 'I can't accept an independent Algeria. Can you imagine me needing a passport to come to the land of my birth?' I said, 'There's a shadow on the sun. We've begun to realize that we can't win.' "

It was through Sauveur that I discovered Algiers, for I had deliberately limited myself to the area between Square Bresson and my office on the rue d'Isly. With Sauveur I got to know other neighborhoods, Climat de France, Saint Saëns Park, Belcourt, Notre Dame d'Afrique. He was a walker in the city, so detached (although acutely observant) that he attracted no attention. And everywhere he went, he knew people, both *pieds-noirs* and Arabs. He taught me to see the Casbah in other than military terms. From the rue d'Isly we climbed up the Rampe Bugeaud, where a florist was arranging a galaxy of roses and lilies on wooden shelves. Rue de Tanger, parallel to the rue d'Isly, still had its share of cafés and bistros. Sauveur pointed to an alley and said, "There used to be a place there called Bitouche, with eight stools, where you ate the best kidneys in Algiers. I can still smell the brochettes, washed down with a bottle of Tanqui rosé and an onion salad with virgin olive oil. The last virgin in Algiers, Bitouche said. Europeans and Arabs still mixed then."

Once we took the streetcar to the Barberousse Prison above the

Casbah, with its corner watchtowers and tile fringe on the outer walls, and walked down through the tangle of iron-banistered staircases and blind alleys, the houses almost touching. The Casbah seemed to me not picturesque but decayed, the crumbling walls of the houses shored up with wooden supports, the smell of urine and garbage piled in the streets waiting for the donkeys. Sauveur pointed out street names that evoked a more alluring past: Man with the Pearl, Red Sea, Lion's Bath, Street of Honey. He took me into the Café du Sport, where he knew the owner, Ahmed, a former soccer goalie. A few elderly Arabs sat drinking mint tea. Ahmed greeted Sauveur warmly: "Come in. What a pleasure. Why don't we see you more often?" He said business was terrible. "And I have to pay taxes to you know who," he whispered. He sat down to talk about the old days. "I got a bonus for every save," he said. Sauveur lit a Gitane with a little tilt of the head and hands and lost his hangdog look. He seemed content. "You know," he said, "when I lived in the Casbah, everybody pitched in if there was a fire or a woman giving birth or a dispute between neighbors." When we left the Café du Sport, I noticed a line of children, waiting to fill buckets from a spigot in the wall. Most of the houses still didn't have running water.

Sauveur loved the beaches outside Algiers but had no way to get to them, since he didn't drive, and the tram service out of Algiers had been interrupted for security reasons. Since I had been lucky enough to find a guide who was also a friend, I bought a beat-up 11CV Citroën, the black model used in French movies by both the police and the gangsters. It belonged to a Jewish garage owner I knew named Jian, who was selling everything and leaving for France. I paid $300 of the money I'd saved from my *Telegram* articles, and despite Jian's pushing a car on me that I only half wanted, I felt I'd taken advantage, as had many others, of the distress of those who were leaving and had to sell at rock-bottom prices.

Sauveur had a fisherman friend at Pointe Pescade, a steep cliff jutting into the sea, with sandy beaches between its indentations. From Bab-el-Oued, you continued west along the shore road to

Saint-Eugène, and another six kilometers to Pointe Pescade. Farther on was the Bainem Forest of eucalyptus, Aleppo pines, and casuarina trees.

We drove out there on the third Sunday in May. Sauveur's friends had a cottage at the top of the cliff, with a fine view of the Mediterranean, a deeper blue there, thrashing and less welcoming than on the city beaches. Sauveur had warned me that his friends, Jules and Dolores, both of Spanish stock, were an animated couple. "They've been married a long time and they've fallen into a routine," he said. "She's very experienced."

"Experienced at what?"

"Household disputes," he said.

We came to a wooden cottage with a scalloped sign over the door that said *Notre Port* (Our Harbor) and a porch overlooking the sea. As we walked in, we could hear Dolores shouting, "You good-for-nothing, you walking calamity. *Madre de Dio*, throw him into the harbor with forty pounds of lead around his neck." But when she saw us, her tone changed and she said, "Sauveur, we've missed you, you mule-headed *calamar*" (squid).

"How can I be a mule and a *calamar*?" Sauveur asked.

"And who's the big asparagus you brought with you?" she asked.

"That's my pal. He's in the army."

"Why isn't he in uniform?"

"It's his day off."

"The army," Dolores said. "Fat lot they're doing."

Dolores was a stout woman in her forties with a small but wide nose, intense dark eyes, a single heavy eyebrow straight across her forehead, and black hair tied in a braid around her head. She wore a dark blue apron over a cotton dress with a floral print. Jules was a short, brawny man with a big bald head, deep lines in his forehead, blotches on his cheeks from the sun, and crow's-feet around his remarkably bright green eyes. He kept wiping his brow with his handkerchief and saying, "*Que calor*," although it wasn't that hot.

Dolores was at the oven, preparing her famous fish soup with saffron. Jules sat by the window with a needle and thread, repairing one of his nets. Sauveur told him he looked preoccupied.

"It's our son, Raymond," he explained.

"A son should do what his father does," Dolores interrupted. "But this one, since he came back from France, he's turned his back on us, *la mort de ses os*" (death to his bones).

"Be quiet for one instant," Jules said. "He wanted to run a farm, so I sent him to an agronomic college in France for two years. On the boat coming back, he met a twenty-two-year-old woman, the same age as him, married to a dentist in Oran. But when the boat landed, she didn't go to Oran; she stayed with him. And here's what's hard to believe. The girl is half Arab on her mother's side."

"We've never met her," Dolores said. "I wonder if she wears a veil." Addressing me, she said, "You're about the same age; what do you think?"

"The woman must have been desperate to leave her husband like that," I said.

"Desperate!" Dolores shouted. "May Allah give her eczema and shorten her arms so she can't scratch. She got her hooks into my son, and he's running up debts, spending his money on clothes like a zebra."

"I never expected him to be a fisherman," Jules said. "But now he wants to go back to France with the girl. Sauveur, what do you think?"

"You've got to give the grass a chance to grow," Sauveur said.

"He's got a stone where his heart should be," Dolores said, as she brought the steaming cauldron of fish soup to the table.

Jules opened a couple of bottles of rosé. "I disapprove of disorderly lives," he said, "and sometimes I wonder if his disorder is connected to the disorder of the country as a whole. There's something wrong with our way of life. I've been a working man all my life, but there's never been a real working class here, since the Arabs aren't citizens. The usual class struggle that we've seen in Europe never took hold—it erupted as a full-blown revolution. How did we arrive at such an imperfect society?"

"All colonizers are bound to be oppressive," Sauveur said, "but here, I think it's already too late, and that partition is the answer."

"You mean give them the desert and keep the coast?" Jules said.

"No, split it down the middle," Sauveur said.

"This soup is really marvelous," I said, tired of listening to theories of what to do about Algeria.

"Finally—someone who appreciates my cooking," Dolores said.

"Good God, this woman exasperates me," Jules said.

Dolores raised her thumb to her lips and pretended to be biting off her nail, then flung out her arm. This was the ultimate gesture of contempt in Bab-el-Oued.

I N EARLY May there had been an incident that could be called appalling even by the standards of the Battle of Algiers. On chemin Polignac in the eastern suburb of Le Ruisseau, two paras were killed, and their bodies were found in the street by men of their unit. The enraged paras raided a Moorish bath nearby that served in the evening as a homeless shelter. They barged in, lined up the Arabs, and fired bursts from their MATs, leaving 80 dead. Governor-General Lacoste was incredulous: "Eighty dead to avenge two paras? These paras are assassins. And yet they are essential to the security of the city."

There had been no FLN bombs since February, but the Ruisseau massacre opened a new chapter. The Casbah population was up in arms. Yacef Saadi was asked: "They massacre eighty of our men and you do nothing? Where is the FLN?" He had to respond. He was, in fact, reconstituting his bomb network for the third time. The head of his bomb team, Hattab Reda, made a proposal. He knew a sympathizer who worked for the EGA (Electricity and Gas of Algiers) and who could supply them with four of the company's blue uniforms and one of the special keys that opened the bases of the streetlights when they needed repairs. If bombs were placed inside those hollow, cast-iron bases, they would explode like artillery shells.

All this took time to arrange, and it was not until June 3 that four men in EGA uniforms, carrying three small bombs timed to explode at 6:30 PM, appeared in downtown Algiers at 3:00 in the afternoon. No one paid any attention when they saw EGA repairmen squatting at the base of the streetlights that were also trolley stops. They seemed to be tightening a few bolts: One light was on rue Alfred-Lelluch, near the Grande Poste; one on rue Hoche, near the Air France terminal; and the third on rue Sadi Carnot, in the heart of downtown.

At 6:30, when crowds were lined up at the trolley stops to go home from work, the bombs exploded, and the shrapnel flew in all directions, hitting Europeans and Arabs alike, workers going home to Bab-el-Oued, schoolchildren, shoppers, and strollers. On the rue Lelluch, a Moslem woman sat on the sidewalk holding her dead child in her arms. Georgette, who was out shopping, told me she was on a ramp above rue Hoche and looked down and saw bodies lined up covered with blankets in front of the Cote pharmacy. The total casualties were 8 dead and 84 wounded. Once again, the *colon* population was badly shaken. But because there were Moslem casualties, Yacef Saadi was scolded for his choice of targets. He was already planning another spectacular bombing, but this time he had to make sure that no Arabs would be hit.

In the meantime, there was no government in France, for on May 21, Guy Mollet was overthrown. It took the politicians until June 12 to play out musical chairs and invest Maurice Bourgès-Maunoury as prime minister. General Salan took advantage of the vacuum to bring back a regiment of paras from the *bled*.

June 9 was Pentecost Sunday, a major holiday in Algiers, ushering in the summer. Sauveur proposed a day at Casino de la Corniche, a popular establishment on a rocky spur between Saint-Eugène and Pointe Pescade. We could go to the beach, one of the finest in the area, have a swim, and then walk up to the casino, where there was a garden with stands that sold food. Then we could look in at the casino, where from 4:00 to 8:00 there was a *matinée dansante*, featuring the band of Bab-el-Oued's own Lucky Starway. He was a friend of Sauveur's, and his real name was Lucien Seror. "He was in the rag trade, and he sold everything to start the band," Sauveur said.

When we got to the beach around 2 PM, it was crowded and the sun was high. Sauveur took out his sketchbook and said: "Is there anything better than this? The deep blue of the Mediterranean, the cloudless sky, the honey-colored sand, the intense light, the gulls circling, the young men preening, and the girls pretending not to notice—it's all there for the rich and the poor."

I didn't particularly like sitting on the sand, so for me it was a mixed blessing, with radios blaring, the occasional beach ball landing on us, and the elaborateness of their picnics; folding tables and parasols and tablecloths and silver and glassware. One man reading a paper lost a page that the breeze sent tumbling along the beach. A small boy retrieved it, and when he returned it, smiling, the man didn't bother to thank him. Girls walked by, giggling and whispering, and casting side glances to see if they were being noticed.

"In Bab-el-Oued," Sauveur said, "a girl isn't beautiful or ugly, she's *mettable*" ("doable").

When I told him I was going for a swim, he said, "I'm not one of those who jump into the water. It takes me fifteen or twenty minutes, centimeter by centimeter, hands and feet, then legs and shoulders, until I'm up to my neck. And never more than ten minutes. The true lover of the sea prefers brief and repeated immersions."

In the late afternoon, we ambled up to the casino garden and sat under acacia trees at a picnic table eating *mergues* (spicy sausage) and drinking Oranginas. We could hear the strains of the tango inside the casino. "Why do we remain in this turbulent land?" Sauveur asked. "Because of its beauty. On the catastrophe scale, this war is not the worst. There was a time when the plague knocked off half the population. Hopefully, now that it's summer, everyone will go to the beach and things will calm down."

As he spoke, there was an explosion inside the casino that blew out the windows. We ran inside, down a long hall with a red carpet covered with splinters from the broken mirrors, and up the steps leading on one side to the gaming room, where croupiers had just been calling out roulette numbers, and on the other side to the dance floor. The bomb had gone off under the bandstand, which had been torn to pieces. The dance floor was littered with body parts, dancers lying in their blood, piano keys, mangled saxophones. Some dancers, those farthest from the bandstand, were still standing and trying to hold each other up, as in some grotesque marathon. Instead of music for fox-trots and tangos, the dance hall was filled with the screams of the wounded. Sauveur picked up a woman's shoe and the foot was still in it. "I can't take this," he said. "I'm going to be sick." "Maybe we can do something to help," I said, thinking that the last time with Georgette, I had walked away.

A call went out for those with cars to line them up in front of the casino and take the wounded to the Mustapha Hospital, which was on the shore road. I ran to the parking lot to get my Citroën and joined the line. Sauveur helped a young couple into the backseat. The girl, in a skimpy beach outfit, was bleeding from the back and shoulders, and her boyfriend had deep cuts on his neck and face. Sauveur took off his shirt and tore it into strips to staunch the blood. As we took Route Moutonnière to Mustapha, the boy kept repeating, "Filthy Arabs, filthy Arabs," while the girl wept.

We learned the next day that the casino bomb had killed 9 and wounded 85. There was not a single Moslem casualty, for the *matinée dansante* was barred to Arabs. Most of the casualties were under the age of 25. Lucien Seror, who was 38, was killed. His singer, Josy Ley, lost both feet, and his dancer, Paul Perez, lost both legs. The four-pound bomb had been placed under the bandstand by a 17-year-old dishwasher, Imaklal Lounes, who left the casino after placing it and escaped into the *bled*. Sauveur gave me a pen-and-ink drawing of a young girl dancing with a skeleton: *Sex and Death*.

Two days later, on June 11, came the funeral procession for the casino dead. It started solemnly, with a crowd of mourners walking slowly behind black hearses. Soon they were joined by a phalanx of 200 students, marching 10 abreast and singing the *Marseillaise*. They were flanked by young men on scooters. From our office off rue d'Isly, Bernard and I heard the noise and went down to take a look. The mood quickly turned from grief to anger, and students broke away from the cortege to overturn cars that had ID stickers with Arab names on the windshields. Others, as the procession progressed toward the church in Bab-el-Oued where the funeral service was to be held, broke into Arab-owned shops. As the decibel level rose, Bernard said: "Don't you see how stupid these *pieds-noirs* are? They think with their lungs. Don't they know they're doing the work of the FLN for them?"

Policemen stood at every street corner but did not intervene. We asked one what was going on, and he said, "They're overexcited. They're getting it out of their system." When the procession passed an open-air market, young men carrying gasoline-filled water cans doused the stalls, starting fires. A couple of ringleaders accosted us and said, "Don't just stand there; join us," but we left. Finally the paras were brought in and arrested 200 demonstrators, but not before 5 Arabs had been killed, 45 wounded, 20 cars set on fire, and 100 shops looted.

To his credit, Massu drafted a note to the troops: "Certain European elements behaved in a foul manner and should have been arrested on the spot. The forces of order must protect all elements of the population, including the Moslems."

The Second Battle of Algiers

B Y THE BEGINNING of June, General Massu was feeling the strain. He had not had one day off in five months. He rented a villa on the ocean in Bains-Romain, near Pointe Pescade. Every morning he rose at dawn and listened to the cries of the gulls and the deep sea swell, as he breakfasted on the terrace, then had a quick swim before the drive to his office in Hydra. In the late afternoon on June 9, he was on the terrace of his villa having an aperitif when he heard the casino explosion. After being debriefed, Massu decided something had to be done. He brought back to Algiers a regiment of red berets and a regiment of green berets. The blue berets had already returned, so he had three out of the four regiments in his 10th Division. He restored the 9 PM curfew. And finally, he named a paratroop colonel, Yves Godard, the head of the Algiers sector. With his square jaw, husky build, and gruff manner, Godard resembled an intelligent bulldog. Massu worried that he wasn't decisive, that he was a ruminant, chewing his cud for days and even weeks before he made up his mind, but at the same time obstinate and smart. He was also intensely competitive and resolved that if Bigeard had won the first Battle of Algiers, he would win the second. By mid-

June he was installed in the Bruce Palace near the Casbah, with his arm in a cast, the result of a bad landing in a training jump.

Just when Godard had moved into the sumptuous Bruce Palace with its white marble staircase, I happened to run into him in unusual circumstances. Since I no longer saw Georgette in the evenings, I sometimes went to a private officers' club, the Léopard. Instead of a sign on the laquered black door, there was a small bronze vaulting leopard. Located on the top floor of a downtown office building, with a panoramic view of the bay, it reminded me of the Crillon Bar in Paris, with its long mahogany bar, high mirrors, wooden barstools with leather seats, and small tables scattered around the room. Most of the members were para colonels, majors, and captains, but Brissac had gotten me in, and in any case, no one could tell my rank, although my age gave me away, for there weren't any 25-year-old captains in the French army.

The drinks were expensive; this was a scotch rather than an anisette clientele, and the French hostesses were friendly and also expensive. Most of them were wives of noncoms stationed in the *bled* who needed to upholster their bare-bones monthly allotment, but it was rumored that there were also a few officers' wives. The rule was that you could not approach a woman; she had to approach you— though the rule was broken if eye contact was made. The women were attractive without being vulgar, and conservatively dressed. They were women you might meet at a party. If one sat down at your table and you weren't in the mood, you might chat with her and offer her a glass of champagne. Only first names were used. Another rule was that the barstools were reserved for men. Some officers came to the club only to drink and talk shop. The half-dozen rooms in the back had modern, Scandinavian-type furniture and the indispensable bidet. I could not afford going there more than once or twice a month.

One evening around June 22, I was at the bar of the Léopard having a drink with a green beret captain I knew when I heard loud voices at the other end. It was Godard, who was rumored to be a heavy drinker and was obviously in his cups. "This can't continue," he shouted. "The man's become a killing machine. All the Catholics, lefties, and fairies, are raising a hue and cry." His friends quieted him down and sat him at a table, and he looked around bleary-eyed.

I wondered who he was talking about, and I did not get the whole story until a year later, when I was out of the army, although I was told parts of the story as it developed. The paras were still looking for the leaders of the Algerian Communist Party's Action Service, who were suspected of having a hand in the terrorism. On June 10, a police sergeant did a routine check on a big sedan driven by Dr. Georges Hadjadj, who was found to be listed in police files as a high-ranking Communist militant. He was turned over to the paras, who tortured him until he admitted that he was in charge of the antiwar underground newspaper *La Voix du Soldat*, which was printed on a press in the basement of his villa and clandestinely distributed to the troops.

The name of Maurice Audin, a 25-year-old assistant math professor at the University of Algiers, was found in the doctor's papers. Again, under torture, Hadjadj said that Audin was also a Communist and that his home was used as a safe house for wanted militants. Audin lived in the sector of the 1st RCP (blue berets), who arrested him on June 11 at midnight at his home on rue Gustave Flaubert. Wakened from his sleep, he mumbled, "At this time of night?" and barely had time to kiss his wife Josette and his three sleeping children before being trundled off to the triage center in El-Biar, where Boumendjel "jumped or fell." Teitgen signed Audin's "assignation to residence."

When a suspect was arrested at home, the procedure was to leave behind a police inspector in case anyone turned up looking for him. On June 12, Audin did have a visitor. He was one of the most prominent underground Communists, Henri Alleg, editor of the defunct party newspaper, *Alger Républicain*. Unable to get Audin on his office phone at the university, Alleg had foolishly come to see him, since Audin lived in a housing project and did not have a home phone, and was arrested on the spot. He too was taken to the triage center, a two-winged building still under construction, with iron rods sticking out of the masonry and a courtyard crowded with jeeps and trucks.

What happened to Alleg was not known until he published his book, *La Question*, in 1958. He was taken to a big living room in an unfinished apartment, furnished with a folding table and a *gégène*. A torture team of blue berets, headed by the bearlike Lieutenant Charbonnier, welcomed him, saying, "Ah, here is our client." Pointing to the *gégène*, Charbonnier told Alleg, "You've heard about it, you've written articles about it; now you're going to experience it." A para applied the pincers, known as "crocodiles" because of their teeth, one to a finger and one to the lobe of an ear. They turned on the juice, and he jumped and screamed. "He sure is noisy," Charbonnier said. "Gag him."

Alleg found that biting the gag helped him bear the pain. He was tied down to a plank on the floor with leather straps on his wrists and ankles. When they applied the pincer to his penis, he shook like an epileptic, as paras sat around watching and drinking beer.

Charbonnier said, "Go get Audin. He's in the other building." Audin, unable to walk, was carried in between two paras. He had been so badly beaten that he was unrecognizable. Charbonnier said, "Tell him what it's like."

Through swollen and bleeding lips, Audin mumbled, "It's hard, Henri." They took him away.

"You're going to talk, you son of a whore," Charbonnier told Alleg.

On the second day, there was another session with a bigger *gégène*. Alleg got to the point where he couldn't stop shaking, but he didn't talk. One of the paras said, "Do you know how to swim? We'll teach you." They dragged him to a big sink, wound a cloth around his head, and pushed a rubber hose that extended from the faucet under the cloth and down his throat. When they turned on the water, he couldn't swallow it. It went into his nose and all over his face, and he felt he was drowning.

"If you decide to talk, move your fingers," Charbonnier said. Alleg was suffocating. He twitched his fingers. The water was turned off and the paras slapped his stomach so he would throw it up. But he still refused to talk. This annoyed the paras and they gave him the water again until he lost consciousness. When he came to, Charbonnier said: "You almost bought it that time."

The next morning, he realized that he was in the building where Boumendjel had been held before being led out to the passageway and pushed off. He was taken to the office of a blue beret captain, who said, "You're a journalist—you must understand that we need to be informed." When he remained silent, they gave him the *gégène* again and burned his hands with matches, as the captain sat at his desk, calmly smoking. "You're thirty-six," the captain said, "too young to die."

Since Charbonnier was getting nowhere, the paras brought in the master interrogator, Captain Roger Faulques of the green berets, the chief torturer of Villa Sesini. Faulques said he simply wanted to chat; and Alleg obliged him, since he would be spared the *gégène*. He talked at length about his newspaper, and without knowing it, he gave away the identity of an important Communist militant, about whom the paras knew only that he walked with a limp. Faulques asked about the man with the limp. Alleg said, "Don't insist. I will never discuss my comrades at the paper." Faulques thus knew that the man with the limp had worked on the paper, making him easy to identify. In their wide-ranging discussion, they talked about Suez, and Faulques said, "You know, during Suez, I kept wishing an American submarine would sink a French ship so we could go to war with the Americans and clear things up." The French military still blamed America for botching Suez.

In the meantime, the arrests of Audin and Alleg had had repercussions in France, where committees were formed and articles were written. On June 29, two members of a commission of inquiry, General André Zeller and Professor Richet, visited the blue beret triage center where Audin and Alleg were being held. But they were evacuated in time for the visit.

Alleg was sent to the Lodi Camp near Médéa. It was a former summer camp for the children of railway workers, with showers and a basketball court. There Alleg drew up a criminal complaint for the prosecutor of the Algiers Court of Appeals, which was smuggled out and released to the Paris papers. This way his case went to the courts instead of to the paras. In August, he was transferred to Barberousse Prison, where he wrote his book, which sold 66,000 copies in less than a month when it was published in 1958, before being seized by the government. In June 1960, he went to trial and was sentenced to 10 years for "prejudice to the security of the state and reorganization of a dissolved party." He had already served three and was transferred to the French city of Rennes to serve the rest of his sentence.

As for Audin, it was announced that he had been killed while trying to escape during a transfer by jumping out of a jeep. And this is where the comments of Godard that I overheard at the Léopard Club could be explained. For Brissac, who received his information from Massu's headquarters, was told what had really happened to Audin. He was turned over to Major Aussaresses, the head of the killing teams, and taken out to a burial ground west of Algiers, near Zeralda. Before he was shot, he said, "It's a mistake. I'm French."

One of those who agreed with Audin was Colonel Godard, who blamed Aussaresses for his indiscriminate assassinations and had him transferred back to France. "Godard and Aussaresses have never gotten along," Brissac said. "It goes back to 1948, when Aussaresses was commander of the 11th *Choc* and Godard pulled strings to take his place. He added insult to injury by offering him the number-two job. Godard doesn't mind if Aussaresses kills Arabs, but he doesn't want him killing Frenchmen, which makes a stink in France, and Audin was the proverbial last straw."

ON JULY 2, 1957, at a meeting of Republican leaders, President Eisenhower was warned that 40-year-old Senator John F. Kennedy was about to make a speech on the Senate floor in support of Algerian independence. The text of the speech had been sent to news outlets on the previous day. Kennedy had beaten Ike's friend, Henry Cabot Lodge, in Massachusetts in 1952, and after four years in the

Senate, he was a member of the Committee on Foreign Relations and chairman of the subcommittee on United Nations affairs.

Although he believed that the answer for all colonial peoples, including Algeria, was independence, Ike did not want to disrupt relations with France, a key NATO member. And yet he felt that Republicans should not argue against the Algerian cause, "even though the people of Algeria still lack sufficient education and training to run their own government in the most efficient way."

"Perhaps," Ike said, "Republicans might best just chide Mr. Kennedy for pretending to have all the answers."

Later that day, Kennedy delivered his 5,000-word speech, entitled "Imperialism—The Enemy of Freedom," before a meager audience of 14 senators. It was an impressive effort, blending historical background and political perceptiveness, far above the usual windy Senate speech. It must have taken several weeks of research and many hands, including those of Jay Lovestone, the éminence grise of the AFL-CIO, who was a passionate advocate of Algerian independence and sometimes advised Kennedy.

Kennedy opened by stating that Algeria was no longer a French internal matter but "a matter of international, and consequently American, concern." Reasons for concern, he said, were that the war "has stripped the continental forces of NATO to the bone. It has affected our standing in the eyes of the free world, our prestige, our security, as well as our moral leadership in the fight against Soviet imperialism in the countries behind the Iron Curtain. It has furnished powerful ammunition to anti-Western propagandists throughout Asia and the Middle East.

"Algeria is no longer a problem for the French alone," he said, "nor will it ever be again. [This was one of the lines that infuriated the French.] American military equipment—particularly helicopters, which the natives fear and hate—has been used against the rebels."

At this point, Senator Jacob Javits, a Republican senator from New York, felt the need to question Kennedy's motives: "One would get the feeling . . . that there are overtones of criticism of the administration implied."

"My criticisms are not meant to be partisan," Kennedy replied.

"The essential first step," he continued, "is the independence of Algeria along the lines of Morocco and Tunisia." This line also infuriated the French, as did the next line that "each identifiable rebel has behind him the silent or half-articulated support of many other Algerians." This was contrary to the *colon* precept that the Arab masses supported France.

On the nature of guerrilla warfare, Kennedy quoted General Orde Wingate, who in 1943 ran a unit of guerrillas in Japanese-held Burma: " 'Given a population favorable to penetration, a thousand resolute and well-armed men can parlay for an indefinite period the operations of a hundred thousand.' "

Another, more arcane quotation came from Anne Robert Jacques Turgot, the minister of finance under Louis XVI, from 1774 to 1776, for Kennedy wanted to use the words of an admired eighteenth-century French statesman against the French: " 'Colonies are like fruit, which cling to the tree only until they ripen.' "

Kennedy concluded by submitting a resolution urging "that the President and the Secretary of State be strongly encouraged to place the influence of the United States behind the effort . . . to achieve a solution which will recognize the independent personality of Algeria and establish the basis for a settlement interdependent with France and the neighboring nations."

At a press conference on July 3, Ike said: "We are trying to remain neutral between the two camps. . . . This situation could lead to a catastrophe if we let it get out of control." Suez was still fresh in Ike's mind, and he preferred to consider Algeria a French internal matter. But the unspoken question was "Why is freedom fine for us but not for others?"

The French response to Kennedy's speech was not temperate. Governor-General Lacoste said: "This young senator should stop talking like someone who is deaf and blind." The French, he said, were no more ready to give up Algeria than the Northern states were ready to give up the Southern states during the Civil War. The speech fanned anti-American embers, and the usual shibboleths were trotted out: America had designs on Saharan oil. If the Americans had let us handle Nasser, the Algerian war would be over. Massu told a visiting American journalist: "Why don't you take care of your Negroes instead of worrying about our Moslems?"

On July 8, Kennedy returned to the Senate floor. "Nothing can obscure the fact," he said, "that Algerians will someday be free. To whom will they turn, to the Americans, whom they may feel have rejected the issue as none of our affair, while at the same time furnishing arms that help crush them—or to Moscow, to Cairo, to Peking? . . . The Algerian situation is a deadly time bomb."

Although Kennedy's resolution was bottled up in the Senate, his July 8 remarks further infuriated the French. Even the doddering 75-year-old figurehead president, René Coty, awoke from his torpor to respond to the senator who was little more than half his age: "I ask the people of civilized nations," he responded on July 9, "if you had a million of your compatriots established in Algeria, would you be so cowardly as to abandon them? Do not count on us to sacrifice a new Alsace-Lorraine on the other side of the Mediterranean! . . . We all know who would profit from the chaos and misery that would follow French abdication."

In our office at *Réalités Algériénnes*, Brissac decided to write the editorial himself. It began: "Algeria had become a pawn on the American chessboard."

A T 2 PM on July 4, a Frenchwoman in her fifties, whose mousy appearance concealed her strength of character, left her room in the Saint-Georges, a luxury hotel in the hills above the suburb of Mustapha, with a fragrant garden and tennis courts. She was Germaine Tillion, the respected ethnologist who had done fieldwork in Algeria and written extensively on the plight of the Arabs. She walked down an alley to the trolley stop, where she waited. It was so hot that the tar on the road had started to melt and was imprinted with the tracks of tires that drove over it. When the trolley came, she got on. A young Arab stepped out of the shadows and got on with her.

Tillion was back in Algeria as a member of an international commission investigating prisons and camps. The commission included a Dutch lawyer, a Belgian doctor, and a Norwegian World War II heroine. Tillion was shocked by what she found. The Algerian elite, those very men who could have formed the nucleus of a Franco-Moslem understanding, were either in jail or dead. The period of colonialism had ended and the period of extermination had begun. The commission's work was done, and Tillion was in despair, about to return to France, when an Algerian female friend gave her a verbal message: "They want to see you. You should take the trolley and follow the young man when he gets off." She went, not knowing whom she was going to meet.

The young man changed trolleys and buses three times before entering the Casbah on rue Randon. At the outdoor market, they took rue Caton. She was led into a house at 3 rue Caton and told to wait in an empty room, its shutters closed against the heat. After about 10 minutes, a dark-haired man with a mustache and unusually large eyes appeared. It was Yacef Saadi, who had read one of her books, and wanted to meet her, saying, "She's a woman who understands our problems." Yacef, who was carrying a MAT, was with Ali-la-Pointe, armed to the teeth, and Zohra Drif.

As they talked over glasses of mint tea, Yacef became more relaxed. He said he was sick of ordering bombings that struck innocent civilians. A *pied-noir* friend he had once played soccer with was a casualty of the casino bombing, and he was deeply sorry that his friend had lost both his legs. The first bombs in 1956, he said, had been reprisals against the executions at Barberousse. "The guillotine revolted us," he said. "I'm willing to stop the bombs if the French stop the guillotine."

Tillion was taken aback. Instead of a heartless terrorist, she found a man who seemed disturbed over the violence of his methods. She told Yacef Saadi that if he meant what he said, she would pass his message on to the cabinet ministers she knew in Paris. That very evening, she flew back to the capital. One of her childhood friends was Louis Mangin, who was on the staff of Premier Bourgès-Maunoury.

Mangin was interested in what she had to say and promised to relay it to his boss. On a second visit, he asked her to return to Algiers and act as a liaison between Lacoste and the FLN. Tillion said: "I am willing to do that, but I don't want any dirty tricks. If I promise Yacef Saadi that there won't be any more executions, it can't be an empty promise."

Tillion felt that she might actually be able to accomplish something, and reserved a seat for Algiers on a July 20 evening flight. That morning, Mangin called her and said he needed to see her urgently. She went to his office, where he told her, "On July 25, there will be two executions." Tillion had been through other ordeals. During the war, she had been deported by the Nazis. She rarely cried. But when she left Mangin's office, she was crying. What was the true nature of this hateful war, she wondered, but a series of lost opportunities? In Paris, the government might prefer to ask President Coty to exercise his right of pardon, but in Algiers the military would object that they were not allowed to do their jobs: "We catch them and you free them. How can we maintain order when you undermine us?" Still, she went back to Algiers and left a note for Yacef Saadi at a post office box, to warn him that executions were coming, and that their pact was broken.

On July 25, there were not two, but three executions: Badeche Ben Hamdi, who had confessed under torture to the December 1956 murder of Amédée Froger. It was later learned that he was not involved. The two others had also admitted under torture that they took part in the Froger murder, although they too were innocent. Ben Hamdi's last words were "If they can melt iron, imagine what pain they can inflict on a man."

In our office, we heard that morning that the executions had taken place at dawn. Bernard said, "When you've seen a head fall in a basket, it makes an impression." He had never actually seen one, but he had heard about it.

Brissac said, "I'm going to form the Association for the Friends of the Guillotine, which is getting a bad name. After all, it's painless. We'll invite members to attend executions and give them little flags to wave, and we'll have a band playing Strauss waltzes. Afterward, we'll give them a good breakfast."

"Strauss also wrote a funeral march," Bernard said.

"Don't be so macabre," Brissac said. "Haven't you heard of the murderer who had a beer at the gallows and blew off the foam because he believed it was unhealthy?"

P RIOR TO the executions, I had been sent to cover an important trial on July 11, in one of the courtrooms of the military tribunal building on rue Cavaignac. Ten terrorists were on trial, each with his or her own lawyer, but the three star defendants were Djamila Bouhired, Djamila Bouazza (whom Bouhired had turned in, and who had planted the January bomb at the Coq Hardi), and Taleb Abderrahmane, the chemist who made Yacef Saadi's bombs.

I was surprised to see how uncrowded the courtroom was. The defendants sat in the dock, with their black-robed lawyers facing them across the room, and the three judges presiding on a dais. There were a few reporters from the Algiers dailies, and relatives of the accused, including Bouazza's mother in the front row.

As it turned out, the real star of the trial was Bouhired's lawyer, Jacques Vergès, whom I would get to know rather well 30 years later when I covered the trial of Nazi war criminal Klaus Barbie, whom he also defended.

Vergès was a man of small stature and oversized ego, with yellowish skin and slanted eyes behind thick glasses. His father Raymond came from an old French colonial family on the volcanic island of Réunion, in the Indian Ocean. Besides being a medical doctor, Raymond Vergès served as a consular official in Southeast Asia. He married a Vietnamese woman, and in 1925 Jacques Vergès and his twin brother Paul were born in the kingdom of Siam. Marrying an Asian woman brought an end to Raymond's diplomatic career, and the family moved back to Réunion. In the thirties, Raymond became a Marxist and founded the Communist Party of Réunion, which won enough votes in 1946 to send him as overseas deputy to the National Assembly in Paris.

Jacques Vergès grew up an outcast as the half-Vietnamese son of a Communist in the stratified and racist colonial power structure of Réunion. He saw forced labor in the sugar cane fields and native coolies pulling French passengers in rickshaws. When they wanted to stop, they slapped the coolie on the back with a cane. Jacques's childhood and adolescence taught him to loathe colonialism, and he became convinced that the only solution for the pariahs of Africa and Asia was rebellion.

In 1942, at the age of 17, Vergès left the oppressive latitude of Réunion and joined the Free French in London. As a law student in Paris after the war, he formed a militant Association for Colonial Students, which was under Communist control. Vergès embraced the Communists as the only openly anticolonial party in France, then in the midst of the Indochina War. He held a meeting in the courtyard of the Sorbonne, decorated with Vietminh flags. In 1950, the party sent him to Prague to be the director of the International Union of Students. He later recalled what a jolly time he had during those years of the final Stalinist purges.

In 1955, he passed his bar exam in Paris and joined the lawyers' collective that took on FLN defendants. The Bouhired trial was his first big case, the case that launched his career. Vergès knew that he had no defense, since Bouhired had confessed without being tortured. The evidence against her included the documents found in Yacef Saadi's briefcase after she was shot and arrested on April 9. His only chance was to employ a deliberate "strategy of disruption" in the hope of moving the venue from the military tribunal to the court of international opinion. He used the courtroom as a soapbox to attack the colonial system and the army. During a recess, he told me that all methods were permissible under a crooked system where the courts, the military, the press, and the *colon* public all conspired together. Self-assured to the point of arrogance, he saw himself as being in a no-lose situation. "Either I will get my client off," he said, "or I will say, 'What did you expect from this corrupt system?' "

Vergès told Bouhired that when she took the stand she should claim that she had talked under torture, which caused a commotion in the courtroom. Vergès had not anticipated that Bouazza was furious with Bouhired for turning her in. Bouazza rose up in the defendant's dock and shouted, "Don't deny what you did, you whore. If I go to the guillotine, I want you to go too."

When Bouazza testified and one of the judges asked her if she had been tortured, she said, "Not at all. I was not tortured." Then, addressing Bouhired, she added, "Neither were you, you piece of garbage."

These histrionics, although sincere, were not spontaneous. Bouazza's lawyer, Maître Talbi, had advised her while she was awaiting trial in Barberousse prison that her best shot was to act like a madwoman; she might get a mistrial. Not realizing that her mail was being opened, Bouazza wrote a friend, Rachid Hattab, from prison, "You'll see what a drama the day of sentencing will be. I'm supposed to laugh and start dancing the samba. When the audience starts laughing, I'll start singing and the judge will have to clear the courtroom."

The second day of the trial was worse than the first. Bouazza kept up her Ophelia act, laughing inappropriately and singing incoherently, while Vergès constantly interrupted the defendant's testimony with points of order. Vergès figured that if Bouazza was declared incompetent to stand trial, her testimony would be invalidated, which would help his case with Bouhired. He asked for a psychiatric evaluation of Bouazza, which the judges granted, and when the trial was suspended that day she was taken to the Saint-Eugène Psychiatric Clinic. Its director, Dr. Valience, examined her and concluded that she was entirely sane and responsible.

On the third day, July 13, Vergès asked for a psychiatric examination by an expert of his own choosing. When this was denied, he flew into a tantrum and removed his robe, saying that the trial was a charade and there was no reason for him to stay any longer. He walked out and went directly to the post office, where he sent Bouhired a telegram informing her that he was still her lawyer. Then he went to the airport and flew to Paris to try to win the support of the French order of barristers, who told him to settle the matter in Algiers.

The trial opened on its last day, July 14, without the provocative Vergès, and the summations had already begun when he walked in and stated that he was ready to proceed. The judges ruled that he could sum up for Bouhired on condition that she confirm that he was still her lawyer. Vergès flew into another tantrum, shouting, "The judges are not doing their duty" and "You will see blood on the floor." The chief judge pounded his gavel and ordered the courtroom evacuated. The trial was declared closed. Vergès was kept from pleading for Bouhired. After more than four hours of deliberation, the judges announced death sentences for the two Djamilas and for Taleb the chemist. When her sentence was pronounced, Bouhired laughed raucously. The chief judge told her, "Don't laugh. This is serious."

Vergès's guerrilla tactics did not help his clients. He rarely seemed to be acting in their interest; more often, he was working toward a larger cause, which could be called either a political ideal or self-promotion. He lost so many cases that he became known as "Maître Guillotine." He made a point of attending executions. In the case of Bouhired, he did manage to get her death sentence commuted in 1958 to life imprisonment. When Algeria became independent in June 1962, she was freed. Vergès moved to Algeria to work for the foreign office and became romantically involved with Bouhired. She married her mouthpiece in 1963. Since Vergès already had a wife and child in France, he converted to Islam so that he could have more than one wife and took the name Mansour (meaning "the triumphant one"). Vergès and Bouhired had two children, and when they were divorced a few years later, he left Algeria and she opened a couture shop.

When I saw him again in Lyon in 1987 and took him to one of the fine restaurants he favored, Vergès told me that his "strategy for disruption" had not changed. "I am alone against fifty," he said, for the families of Barbie's victims were also represented by lawyers at the trial. True to his word, he claimed that the crimes of the French in Algeria were as bad as the crimes against humanity Barbie was charged with when he was the head of the Lyon Gestapo. Barbie was sentenced to life and died in prison.

As for my reportage on the trial for *Réalités Algériennes*, I felt that for once I was not writing propaganda. The Vergès defense was a tissue of lies. He was playing to that part of public opinion in France that had turned against the war because of torture and was programmed to believe his falsifications. In this case, however, the tribunal convicted two terrorists who had planted bombs that had killed and wounded civilians. Vergès had as little concern for the truth as those government officials who denied the existence of torture.

Fearing a reprisal of terrorism, Massu took the precaution of bringing back from the *bled* Bigeard and his 3rd RPC (red berets). They had left Algiers on March 15, and upon his return on July 20, Bigeard declared that nothing had been accomplished since his departure. The only thing that had changed was public opinion in France, which was increasingly antiwar. "I've just about had it with police work," he told his company commanders.

Bigeard was angry at being summoned back to Algiers, after all the commissions of inquiry, the press campaigns, and the rest. Now he would have to do the same dirty job over again, and he set up shop in a school near the Casbah with his charts of empty rectangles. In addition, he was not keen to take orders from Godard, a colonel like himself, and so he went his own way, ignoring directives from above. He remained in Algiers less than two months but accomplished a great deal. As Brissac put it, "Bigeard wants to be the lone horseman, and he does a good job, but that's not the army way."

To his men, Bigeard said: "I can't give you written orders. I can only tell you—do what you did in January. Interrogate the guilty and use the well-known methods, which we find odious. Whatever you do, I take full responsibility."

On July 27, in reprisal for the July 25 executions, Yacef Saadi sent out a team of nine bombers, but there were patrols on every Casbah street and they could not find open exits. Of the nine, only three were able to get their bombs out via the public baths on rue d'Anfreville. Since the timers were already set, the others hurriedly got rid of their bombs anywhere they could, in doorways or on windowsills. Two of the bombers were blown up with their bombs, and in all they did little damage. After this fiasco, Yacef had trouble finding volunteers to carry bombs. The bomb network, with many of its members killed or captured, was in disarray. Actions in the ZAA (Autonomous Zone of Algiers, divided into three sectors, the Casbah, Algiers center, and Algiers east) had come to a standstill. Yacef found himself cut off from the FLN leadership in Tunis. Most of the taxes collected in the Casbah were sent to Tunis to buy weapons, but when he urgently asked for help, he got only blather: "May Allah protect you" and "We are all waiting for the great day of independence." It was as though the leaders had given up on him, and he carried on his shoulders the weight of impending doom.

By early August, Bigeard was on the warpath again. The red berets were back in the Casbah, patrolling alleys and staircases, positioned on terraces and rooftops, making arrests, and using intelligence gleaned from those arrested. On the night of August 6, his men searched a villa in El-Biar and found a man asleep. The only thing unusual about him was that the paras found a loaded .45 under his pillow. He was taken to Bigeard's headquarters, to be questioned by the OR (intelligence officer), Captain Chabanne. The suspect was a skinny young Kabyle with an angular face and light hair. Handcuffed, he sat on a stool in Chabanne's office. When Chabanne walked in, he already knew from the files that the man was Gandriche Hacène, head of the Algiers east sector, code-named Zerrouk. Chabanne chatted amiably with the man, whom he found articulate and well educated. In the course of the conversation, he called the man Zerrouk, and the man blanched. Chabanne could see his inner resistance leak out of him.

Chabanne asked Zerrouk how long he had known Yacef Saadi.

"Since we were both eighteen-year-old soccer players on the same team," Zerrouk said.

He pointed out that Zerrouk could avoid capital punishment by cooperating. "Let's work together," Chabanne said. Zerrouk caved in, reinforcing General Massu's conviction that the more evolved and intelligent a man was, the easier it was to get him to talk.

"How do you get your messages to Yacef?" Chabanne asked.

"Via my wife Latifa," Zerrouk said. "She sings and dances at weddings, and she's always on the move."

Chabanne told Bigeard: "We're holding Zerrouk, the chief of Algiers east. He's the link with Yacef. Let's keep his arrest secret so that he can continue to communicate with Yacef, under our control."

Bigeard liked the idea so much that he called a press conference to declare that they had caught Zerrouk but that he had escaped. He also decided to keep the Zerrouk operation from his superiors and did not inform Massu or anyone else at divisional headquarters.

Zerrouk was moved to a studio on rue Tanger, which runs parallel above rue d'Isly in downtown Algiers, under the guard of two paras. Chabanne visited him on August 8 and dictated Zerrouk's first letter to Yacef since his capture: "Last night in El-Biar, I was captured by the paras, but I jumped off the jeep and hid behind a bush until I got a ride on a milk truck. I'm in hiding and can be reached through Latifa." The letter was signed with Zerrouk's code words, "patriotic salutations." His wife's suspicions were not aroused, because of the personal details in the letters.

On August 9, Colonel Godard scolded Bigeard for letting Zerrouk escape. Massu wrote Bigeard that "Colonel Godard called to tell me that in spite of his patience, you are not acting like a subordinate and that he has had enough, since he is not accustomed to swallowing squid [a French expression, *avaler des couleuvres*," meaning "to have to swallow unpalatable substances"]. I haven't got the time to solve your problems; I have enough to do. I would like you to know that if you cannot rein in your excessive pride, you will never be the leader you have it in you to be."

Bigeard was laughing up his sleeve, for he was hot on Yacef's trail. But even in the midst of approaching victory, he worried that "it's not up to us to play Sherlock Holmes." He felt that his paras were poisoning their souls by doing dirty work for which they received the adulation of the Algiers *colons*, and he hoped for a quick return to the *djebel*, the mountains.

On August 11, Zerrouk received a reply from Yacef that said: "We are moving to the second stage. Until August 16, armed actions in the three sectors of the ZAA. From August 16 to 31, bombs and armed actions until September 15."

Captain Chabanne was gratified. They had the messages going, setting the trap for Yacef. Another message from Zerrouk said he needed clothes and money. Soon it got to the point where they exchanged messages daily. Yacef said in a letter that he was down with a bad case of the flu.

I N THE meantime, during the dog days of August, I went to the beach with Sauveur as often as possible. On August 15, I was invited to a cocktail party at Hans Imhof's for a visiting Massachusetts state legislator, Barclay H. Warburton III. A big man with a full face, a ruddy complexion, tousled reddish hair, and the weather-beaten blue eyes of a yachtsman, he wore a double-breasted blue blazer with brass buttons. His stepfather, William K. Vanderbilt, had circumnavigated the globe in his yacht *Alva* in 1930. After serving in the navy in World War II and graduating from Harvard in 1948, Warburton married Margaret McKean Read, who was a descendant of John Quincy Adams.

Warburton bought an 18-acre farm in Ipswich that had belonged to actor Raymond Massey but spent most of his time aboard his brig, the *Black Pearl*. He was also elected to the lower house of the Massachusetts legislature, where his pet issues were the patronage corruption in Boston and the waste in federal programs. When he arrived in Algiers that August, he was in his third term. He had come to see how and what the French were doing, since he was thinking of running on the Republican ticket against John F. Kennedy, who was up for reelection in the Senate in 1958.

Warburton was friendly and jocular, and we hit it off. I hadn't been following Massachusetts politics, but he assured me that the Kennedys and the Fitzgeralds were "a bunch of crooks" who ran the Boston Democratic machine, and that Jack Kennedy was "an empty-headed cunt-hound" whose speech on Algeria verged on treason.

I asked him what he planned to see in Algiers, and he said, "I love that movie *Pépé Le Moko,* and I've always wanted to see the Casbah, but they tell me it's too dangerous." I assured him it was as safe as any street in Boston if you knew your way around (I was showing off after a few scotches), and I offered to take him on a guided tour the next morning. Warburton could already see the lead sentence in his local paper: "I walked safely through the Casbah with a young French lieutenant in civilian clothes as my only escort."

The next morning at nine, I met him on Square Bresson, under the ficus trees with big waxen leaves and swarms of squalling sparrows. Algiers that day was gray, with an August drizzle pushed by sea winds. "Are you sure it's all right?" he asked. "You know, I've got five children."

I assured him it was fine and took him up rue Randon to the open market, where melons were in season and he could see the bustle of the shoppers and the occasional para patrol. We stayed on rue Randon, the Casbah's widest street, just in case. Sauveur had taken me to the café Le Babar up the street, whose owner, Dédé, he had introduced me to. "Let's try this Arab café," I suggested to Warburton. "It's run by a former pimp who in his day was known as the Napoleon of the mattress." I explained that the FLN, as part of their campaign to control the Casbah, had gotten rid of the gangsters and the pimps, some of whom now ran cafés.

"Do you think I can get a gin and tonic?" Warburton asked. "It's hotter than hell."

"Only mint tea, I'm afraid," I said. "The FLN does not allow alcohol or smoking in public."

"Goddam Puritans," Warburton said.

Dédé, who wore a blue-and-white-striped sailor's shirt and a red bandana around his neck, greeted us effusively. When I told him I was with a visitor from America, he said, "I like very much America, where prostitution is legal and the whores marry millionaires."

"I wonder where he got that?" Warburton said.

"Must be a movie he saw."*

"In a way, he's right. In Boston, the madams pay off the cops."

"Two years ago, I was running a string of twenty girls," Dédé said, "and now I'm reduced to serving mint tea."

"What a humiliation," I said.

I told Warburton the little I knew about the Casbah. How the architecture was a response not only to the demands of the climate, by letting in scant sun, but also to those of Arab society in terms of the multiple bedrooms around a courtyard required by polygamy and the sequestration of women.

"I never understood this business of having more than one wife," he said. "One is quite enough."

I told him about the Mozabites, a Berber sect from the Sahara whose commercial skills had turned them into a close-knit tribe of shopkeepers in all of Algeria's cities and towns. Among other things, they sold trinkets for tourists. Warburton asked me if I knew one. "I promised to bring Maggie a *fatma*'s hand for luck." I did know one, again through Sauveur, who had impressed me by saying that each week he made the trip back to the Mozabite capital of Gardhaia, a 20-hour bus ride, to see his wife and children. He had built a prodigious inventory of curios and bric-a-brac over the years, and he once showed me a first edition of *Madame Bovary*.

We strolled up a quiet street, a cat dozing in a doorway, kids playing, veiled women chatting—postcard scenes. The shop smelled of incense, and there were piles of rugs on the floor, rows of babouches, and display cases of Berber necklaces and bracelets. Short and round, wearing a fez, the shopkeeper said, "Come in, my friends—not to buy but for the pleasure of the eyes." He brought mint tea and suggested

---

*Although I did not know it at the time, there was a 1933 Gregory La Cava film, *Bed of Roses*, with exactly that theme, starring Constance Bennett as one of the whores.

that Warburton purchase the brass table that the tea set was on. After a certain amount of palavering, Warburton bought his *fatma*'s hand, and the shopkeeper saw us out, telling us, "You are *kif-kif* [same as] my brothers."

Warburton had seen a peaceful Casbah, where commerce, although not thriving, was still in evidence. When he went home, he did not get far in challenging Kennedy for his Senate seat. In the 1958 election, the now-forgotten Vincente J. Celeste was the Republican candidate who lost by 26.2% of the vote against 73.2% for Kennedy.

I was glad I had met Barclay. We stayed in touch, and I kept up with his deeds and misdeeds. Early in 1959, he was hospitalized after a fall in his Ipswich home. I suspected that anyone who wanted a gin and tonic at 9 AM was a round-the-clock drinker. Shortly afterward, he resigned from the legislature. Later that year, on September 14, a warrant was issued for his arrest after his wife charged him with assault and battery. But since he was outside territorial waters, sailing the *Black Pearl*, the warrant could not be served. They were divorced after 14 years of marriage.

Sailing was his passion, and in 1972 he took the *Black Pearl* to England for the training races for the Munich Olympics. He ran a popular restaurant in Newport also called the Black Pearl. His moment of glory came in 1976, when he hosted the "tall ships" that visited New York for the bicentennial, as founder of the American Sail Training Association. In 1981, at the age of 61, he died of a brain tumor.

THE PLACID Casbah I had shown Warburton was a Potemkin village, for Bigeard was busily mopping up the FLN. On August 20, his men arrested Hattab Reda, who under questioning admitted making the streetlight bombs and gave away the names of four other bombers. The leader was a mailman named Nourredine. All four were sentenced to death and executed. In Bigeard's office, Hattab Reda wrote his name in the empty rectangle on the wall chart. Bigeard held a press conference to announce his capture, which annoyed Massu and Godard, who saw him as a glory-hound.

Apart from the red berets, a new and highly original intelligence-gathering unit had started operating in the Casbah. It was the brain-child of Captain Alain Léger, who formed an infiltration group made up of Arabs. Some were unemployed veterans of the French army, such as his bodyguard, nicknamed Surcouf, a large, violent man with a tiny Vietnamese wife. Others were low-level FLN that Léger found in the Beni-Messous triage camp, after asking them: "Do you want to go to Barberousse, or do you want to work for me?" Among his recruits was Alilou, who had been dismissed as one of Yacef Saadi's liaison agents because he was a drug addict. Another was Farès Said, a schoolteacher who had lost faith in the FLN.

Léger's method was the opposite of Aussaresses', who questioned suspects and then killed them. Léger questioned them and then re-cruited them. In July, he took his plan directly to Colonel Godard, explaining that he intended to use his recruits inside the Casbah like hunting dogs, as spotters and retrievers. Godard gave him the green light, and he set up shop in a house in the upper Casbah at 21 rue Émile Maupas, with a big courtyard bordered by arcaded columns, near the *zouaves'* Klein Palace. His men, all armed but dressed in working clothes, were known as the *bleus de chauffe* (blue overalls).

On August 26 at 9 AM, Léger was on patrol on rue Abencérages, with Surcouf and Alilou, who recognized a young man coming out of a café as the leader of an armed group. They grabbed him and took him to their headquarters, where they searched him and found a let-ter for Ramel, who with Mourad was one of the two most wanted bomb-makers.

"Where were you taking this letter?" Léger asked.

"To a *crèmerie* [dairy store] on rue de la Grenade. At noon, I'm supposed to give it to a guy wearing a brown leather jacket. I don't know his name."

The *crèmerie* was shuttered when Léger and his men arrived at noon. Slowly the shutter lifted, and out of the shadows came a man in a leather jacket. Surcouf searched him and said, "He's got mail for

Ramel and lists of those who paid their taxes and those who haven't. He lives at 5 impasse Saint-Vincent-de-Paul. It's not far from here, and we've got the keys."

The liaison agent was taken to an interrogation room at the *zouave* headquarters where Captain Chabanne happened to be. Fearing torture, he fell to his knees and said to Léger, "Swear that you will protect me if I talk."

"Okay, but make it *fissa*" ("quick"), Léger said.

"Ramel and Mourad are staying at my place. They've got weapons and bombs."

This was an important catch. Chabanne notified Bigeard, who rounded up some paras and headed to the Saint-Vincent-de-Paul dead end with his aide, Major Lenoir. Chabanne and Léger also hurried there, down the rue de l'Intendance, past the Lavigerie Cathedral, and into the dead-end alley, which was six feet across. They came to a heavy oak door decorated with metal arabesques and the number 5 above it.

Léger and Chabanne, who had picked up a couple of *zouaves* along the way, got there first. The two *zouaves* recklessly hopped up the stairs and were met with a stream of automatic fire that wounded both of them. Soon the paras arrived and took up positions in the building across the street, holding the terraces. Léger left the scene to get some of his men, while Bigeard, Lenoir, Chabanne, and four or five paras entered the courtyard.

Ramel and Mourad were on the second floor. Chabanne grabbed a loudspeaker and called out: "Ramel, Mourad, we know you're up there. If you surrender, you have my word that you will be treated as prisoners of war." From a window, Ramel replied, "We want it in writing. We'll lower a basket on a rope." Bigeard wrote the note, and Ramel lowered the basket. It contained a bomb the size of a cigarette pack, which the FLN called a Gauloise, with a two-minute timer, covered by a newspaper. Chabanne and Lenoir moved under the window with a couple of paras. The basket was lowered so slowly that Bigeard sensed something was wrong and instinctively pulled back into a doorway. A noncom yelled, "Hit the ground!" and five seconds later, the bomb exploded, wounding Captain Chabanne, Major Lenoir, and two other paras. They were evacuated to the Maillot Hospital.

Sergeant Lepigeon asked, "What if we try an antitank grenade?" Lepigeon fired the grenade into the window from which the basket had been dropped. Moments later, two men carrying bombs ran down the stairs and were riddled with automatic gunfire and killed. The paras found 17 bombs in their refuge. Massu arrived a few minutes later to congratulate Bigeard and his men. "Getting armed men out of a Casbah alley is a little like getting them out of a cave in the *djebel*," he said.

Back in his office, Bigeard crossed out the names of Ramel and Mourad from the rectangles on his chart. There were three names left. Ali-la-Pointe, Ben Hamida, the head of finance, and Yacef Saadi.

Yacef and Zerrouk were still exchanging messages, under the auspices of Captain Chabanne. An August 28 message from Yacef named Zerrouk military chief of the entire ZAA, which showed how shorthanded he was. Captain Chabanne congratulated him on his promotion. Zerrouk wrote back that he would avenge the murders of Ramel and Mourad by ordering the assassination of the traitor Al-ilou, who had been spotted with the paras.

Just at that time, Bigeard and his 3rd RPC were pulled out of Algiers, robbing him of his final victory. Massu felt that in the siege of Ramel and Mourad, much of the credit should have gone to Captain Léger, whereas once again, Bigeard hogged the limelight with another press conference. Godard too found him impossible to work with. So they sent him back to the *bled* and brought in Colonel Jean-pierre and his 1st REP (Foreign Legion green berets) to replace him. What they did not realize was that Bigeard was just as relieved to be leaving Algiers as they were to be rid of him. I admired Bigeard's courage and independent spirit, and I attended most of his press conferences in the line of duty. I always found him blunt to the point of rashness, but I liked that about him. I went to his office on September 2, the day before he left, to tell him I was sorry to see him go.

"For me, it's a stroke of luck," he said. "I was on the front page every day. I was the hero of Algiers, and I admit it went to my head."

During the transition period, Jeanpierre took over the Zerrouk mousetrap. Captain Chabanne turned Zerrouk over to the OR of the 1st REP, Captain "La Boulaya" Allaire, a big burly man with a bushy black beard (not to be confused with the Jacques Allaire who had earlier been Bigeard's OR). La Boulaya (a nickname alluding to his full beard) soon realized that no one at 10th Division headquarters knew about Zerrouk, so he informed Massu and Godard, the latter of whom turned livid with rage and threw one of his famous fits.

Captain Allaire was now dictating Zerrouk's daily letters. One announced that his wife Latifa was pregnant and that if it was a boy, Zerrouk would name him Mourad. This fine sentiment touched Yacef, who sent Zerrouk funds to cover the pregnancy and birth. Colonel Godard, however, now that he had been filled in, worried that the correspondence was dragging on too long. Surely, the day would come when Yacef would ask Zerrouk to meet him in the Casbah, and then all bets would be off. They still hadn't been able to follow the epistolary trail back to Yacef.

On September 7, Colonel Godard summoned Captain Léger to a strategy meeting with Colonel Jeanpierre and Captain Allaire. "This Zerrouk situation can't last," Godard said. "We must find a way to have him lead us to Yacef." He asked Léger, who patrolled the Casbah daily with his *bleus de chauffe*, if he had any ideas.

"We should go up the chain of transmission until we find out where Yacef's letters originate," Léger offered.

Godard got up from his desk and shouted, "Don't you think we've already figured that out? I didn't bring you here to tell us what stands out a mile to everybody."

Léger, who later wrote a memoir, had to think of something fast. There was a blackboard in Godard's office with three names connected by arrows: Zerrouk → Latifa → Yacef.

Léger said: "We know that Latifa gets Zerrouk's letters at a drop, and that she never sees him. But we don't know how Yacef's letters atifa. Why don't we insert one of my female agents in the chain mission? Zerrouk can vouch for her and say she is needed as ed security measure. My agent may be able to identify the person who comes to Latifa from Yacef, whom we can tail."

"Don't forget that Latifa works for the other side," Godard said.

"We can give my agent a letter from Zerrouk telling Yacef he needs to bring another link into the chain."

Captain Allaire was frowning and stroking his beard. "You're going to blow the whole system," he said. "Your agents are too well known by now in the Casbah."

"Not this one," Léger said. "And not those I'll use to tail Yacef's messenger. In any case, it's worth trying, instead of watching the correspondence grow."

Godard agreed, saying, "We don't have any time to lose."

Up until then, the FLN had used young Arab women effectively to move around the Casbah and central Algiers and deposit bombs. Captain Léger was the first to recruit Arab women in the service of the French. The one he had in mind, 17-year-old Ouria, had been thrown out by her FLN husband. Léger had established her reliability.

A few days later, Ouria, wearing a veil, a hood, and a gray robe called a *cachabiah*, arrived at Latifa's Casbah home on rue Kléber and gave her Zerrouk's letter. They chatted, and a few minutes later a teenager in a blue serge suit came in, holding a little girl by the hand. He read the letter, folded it, raised the little girl's dress, and pinned it to her underpants with a safety pin.

Léger had three agents in the street, tailing the young man and the girl at intervals. The young man was soon identified as 17-year-old Mahmoud, who lived at 4 rue Caton, a house belonging to Fahira Bouhired, the aunt of Djamila. The little girl went back and forth between number 4 and number 3 across the street. After observing the routine for several days, it seemed obvious to Léger that Yacef was hiding at number 3 and getting his mail from the little girl at number 4.

He was back in Godard's office on September 15 and announced his results. "Yacef Saadi is hiding at number 3 rue Caton," he declared.

Godard was incredulous. The whole thing was too pat. Yacef Saadi was known to change his hiding place every few days. What neither Léger nor Godard knew was that Yacef was still down with the flu and a bad case of angina, and was running a fever of 104, which restricted his movements. Godard insisted on some sort of confirmation before he sent the paras in.

Léger was a touchy fellow, proud of himself for the success of the *bleus de chauffe*, and he didn't appreciate Godard's caustic put-downs. He was miffed, but he couldn't show it, so he said to himself, "The hell with it," and asked for a leave in France. "I haven't seen my kids in nine months," he said. Godard reluctantly gave him two weeks.

On September 22, in a routine ID check in downtown Algiers, the gendarmes picked up a man in a raincoat. In one pocket, he had a receipt from an optician in Tunis for a pair of glasses, and in the other pocket he had a plane ticket showing that he had just flown in from Paris. The man was Hadj Smain, a high-ranking FLN emissary who was involved in back-door talks with French cabinet ministers in Paris and who shuttled regularly from Tunis to Paris and Algiers.

The gendarmes turned Smain over to Colonel Jeanpierre, who decided to question him personally, given his high station. Smain was taken to an improvised interrogation room in a bathhouse on rue Scipion. They sat in a disused steam room facing each other, the blond, lean, incisive para colonel, a veteran of 20 years in the Foreign Legion, and the self-possessed, equally lean, almost haughty FLN leader, who thought of himself as an important diplomat, and talked without hesitation.

"Have you seen Yacef recently?" Jeanpierre asked?

"I saw him this morning," Smain said.

"At 3 rue Caton?"

"No, at 4."

Yacef had apparently moved across the street to Fahira Bouhired's house.

This was the confirmation that Godard sought. An operation was mounted by the 2nd company of the 1st REP, the *zouaves*, and the gendarmes. After midnight on the morning of September 24, these troops surrounded the rue Caton area and blocked off the street. At 3 AM, Colonel Jeanpierre led his men into number 4, a courtyard with rooms around it, and a staircase leading up to a room with a trap door. Yacef, who once had more than 100 men under his control, was now down to his last companion, Zohra Drif, who was with him behind the trap door. A legionnaire with a pickaxe started banging on the wall of the room at the top of the stairs. Yacef opened the trap door and flung out a grenade that rolled down the stairs. Jeanpierre was hit with shrapnel and had to be evacuated.*

Godard arrived and took command, saying he wanted Yacef alive. He asked Yacef to surrender. Yacef said he wanted to talk to General Massu. "We don't have time for that," Godard said. "I promise that you will be treated as a prisoner of war." Smoke was escaping from under the door. Yacef was burning his archives. Godard ordered an explosive charge to be placed near the trap door. An explosive expert prepared the plastic charge. "We've placed a charge with a long fuse," Godard said. "You have ten minutes." Yacef threw out his MAT and came out with Zohra Drif, their hands raised in surrender. He didn't need ten minutes.

Yacef said he was running a fever and needed medical care. He and Zohra were taken to the headquarters of the 1st REP, a Moorish villa in El-Biar where a doctor gave him some shots. In the Casbah, the word spread that he had been captured without resisting, in marked contrast with Ramel and Mourad, who fought to the end.

Later that same morning, the press was summoned to para headquarters for a news conference, and I saw the 29-year-old Yacef for the first time. He was a short man with slicked-back hair, wearing a brown sweater, khaki pants, and an expensive watch, striking a defiant pose and half smiling behind his mustache. Zohra, pale and sul-

---

*Jeanpierre, the father of five girls, was killed in combat in May 1958 on the Tunisian border.

len, her head bowed, wore a red velvet skirt and a white blouse with red pinstripes, and was abundantly bejeweled—earrings, a necklace, a ring, and a bracelet. "She must think this is a fashion show," one of the Algiers reporters said.

Yacef and Zohra did not take questions and were led away. A para spokesman described the operation that had led to their capture. When I got back to the office, Brissac said: "Lacoste wants to send the message that the FLN in the Casbah has been wiped out and the Battle of Algiers is over. Our headline will be 'The End of the Battle of Algiers.' "

"It's not quite the end," I said. "There's still Ali-la-Pointe and a couple of others."

"If Lacoste wants 'The End,' we'll give him 'The End,' " Brissac said.

Yacef and Zohra spent 22 days at para headquarters, giving depositions that added up to hundreds of pages. No one laid a hand on them. The French high command came to look, as if Yacef were a rare panda in a zoo. General Salan came and stared at him but did not say a word. General Massu told him that he would not be treated as a terrorist but as a combatant. Massu left with the impression that Yacef looked more like a movie actor than a hardened terrorist. He was no Ben M'Hidi. He seemed soft. There was nothing heroic about him. He had let himself be captured, and in his deposition, he gave away the location of bombs and the hiding place of a cache of gold coins.

In her deposition, Zohra described the role of young women like herself in the uprising. With the patrols in place, only women could wander with ease in the Casbah. It was the Moslem world upside down, where the men were cloistered and the women moved freely. During the January strike, she and her friends Djamila and Hassiba had gone from terrace to terrace to organize a silent march of veiled women in support of the strikers. Zohra confirmed Yacef's meeting with Germaine Tillion on July 4. She found the French ethnologist extremely annoying. They were holed up in constant fear of capture, and Tillion was lecturing them, and saying, "The bombs, they are wrong." Zohra finally lost her temper and told Tillion, "Shut up, you big baby." Zohra admitted drafting a leaflet saying that after every execution, bombs would go off. One of the para officers showed her a copy of the FLN newspaper *El Moujahid*, in which she had written a signed report on torture. "Look what you are saying about France," he said, shaking the paper at her. She said she thought it was amazing that they had held out so long against the massed forces of France.

On October 6, while still in the custody of the 1st REP, Yacef received a visit from his mother, the grandmother of little Omar, Yacef's 12-year-old nephew, who was hiding out with Ali-la-Pointe and his girlfriend Hassiba, and acting with Mahmoud as their liaison. Ali was doomed, she said, but could Yacef do something to save her grandson? Yacef could, and gave away Ali's hiding place, 5 rue des Abdérames. In mid-October, Yacef and Zohra were transferred to Barberousse Prison to await trial. After being tried and sentenced to death, Yacef was placed on death row, and he later claimed that the guards often woke him up at dawn as if it was the day of his execution. Both Yacef and Zohra were eventually pardoned.

Ali-la-Pointe, the illiterate one-time pimp and hoodlum, was now the leader of nonexistent combat groups, holed up in a small hideout from which he did not dare emerge. The only other leader still at liberty (or so Ali thought) was Zerrouk, with whom he continued to correspond, using Mahmoud to carry his letters to Latifa. Mahmoud was under surveillance by the *bleus de chauffe* and led them to Ali's den, confirming Yacef's disclosure that he was at 5 rue des Abdérames.

On the evening of October 7, men of the 1st REP surrounded the Porte-Neuve neighborhood. At midnight, paras were deployed into unlit alleys and from terrace to terrace. At 5 AM, neighboring houses were evacuated. At 6, a dozen paras entered number 5. Yacef Saadi was with them, wrapped in a spacious hooded *gandoura* and handcuffed to one of Captain Léger's aides (Léger was still on leave), Lieutenant Joseph Estoup. They climbed the stairs in step to the second floor, and went into an apartment, where Yacef pointed behind a couch, to a hidden door on hinges in a brick wall.

The paras knew that unlike Yacef, Ali was not going to surrender, even though he had with him, cramped in a space of 15 square feet, Hassiba, Mahmoud, and little Omar. Ali was more like Ramel and Mourad, ready to fight to the end. He was impulsively violent and knew he was facing the guillotine. He'd spent time in jail and didn't want to go back.

The bushy-bearded Captain Allaire called through a megaphone: "Give up, Ali. It's over. Yacef is here. We promise you will not be harmed." There was no reply. Major Guiraud, commanding the para detachment in the absence of the wounded Colonel Jeanpierre, decided to place an explosive charge against the hidden door. They used a couple of antitank mines in case the door was steel-jacketed. Those inside might be shaken up, but they would come out alive.

At 6:15, the mines exploded, setting off a chain reaction that destroyed surrounding buildings as well as number 5, as if they had been bombed from the air. The walls of the building collapsed, and the beams followed them down. The paras on the second floor found themselves on the ground floor, covered with debris and dust. Screaming inhabitants, some of whom had quietly returned after the paras had moved them out, were trapped under the rubble. Evidently, the two mines, upon exploding, had set off the bombs in Ali's hideout.

It was crucial that they find Ali's body, or the FLN would announce that he had escaped. It took three days to remove the debris from the buildings and take it away by donkey. Eight teams of 30 legionnaires each rotated in three-hour shifts. In the first two days they found 17 bodies of bystanders, including 2 girls, 4 and 5 years old. On October 10 they found the bodies they were looking for. Hassiba, 12-year-old Omar, and 18-year-old Mahmoud were horribly disfigured. Ali-la-Pointe had literally been blown to bits but was identifiable from the tattoos that covered his body, even the soles of his feet, where he reprised his favorite motto, the Foreign Legion's own *Marche ou crève.*

When we got the news at the office, Brissac drafted a leaflet that was dropped by chopper over the Casbah: "Crime does not pay.

Ali-la-Pointe is dead! He was killed in an explosion on October 8 in the Casbah. His crimes have already been punished. The FLN has lost the battle. Inform yourselves, and put an end to the terror that has been imposed on you."

I went to look at the damage, and I thought that this must have been what Dresden looked like after the fire bombing. I spoke to a couple of Arabs in the street who blamed the paras for blowing up an entire block.

I was assigned to write the lead article on the operation. "We have to destroy the myth of Ali-la-Pointe as some sort of Robin Hood," Brissac said. "He was essentially a gangster." I summed up the career of this 27-year-old revolutionary who, before joining the FLN, had been arrested for larceny, rape, assault and battery, and attempted murder. He had been fingered by the man who recruited him, Yacef Saadi. As for Hassiba Ben Bouali, she was an educated 19-year-old social worker, sentenced to death in absentia for placing one of the January bombs. It was sad that a child like Omar was lost as well.

Ben Hamida, in charge of finances and propaganda, was still at large. His only remaining contact was with Zerrouk. Captain Allaire, Zerrouk's handler, warned that they had to act fast, for the turncoat's long internment in the rue Tanger studio was starting to tell. He had become overly fond of anisette and was drunk much of the time.

Shortly after the explosion on rue des Abdérames, Hamida wrote Zerrouk via Latifa: "I am alone and I don't know the Casbah that well. We must meet and draw up a plan."

Zerrouk promptly replied: "I have a safe house in the European quarter. You are now in charge after Ali's death. I can put you up."

They arranged to meet on October 15 at 3 PM on Rampe Valée, one of those uphill streets that connected downtown Algiers with the Casbah. Zerrouk wrote: "A black 203 Peugeot driven by a brother, with a sister in the backseat, will pick you up." The "sister" was Captain Léger's agent Ouria, and the driver was a *bleu de chauffe*.

The 1st REP ran the operation, with jeeps on side streets leading into the Rampe Valée, ready to block the Peugeot as soon as it came in. Ben Hamida was right on time. Ouria opened the car door, and he stepped in. Two para jeeps mounted with machine guns roared out and blocked Rampe Valée. Ben Hamida, who was unarmed, stepped out of the car and gave himself up.

The Battle of Algiers was over. The paras had won. The men of the 1st REP went back to their base in Zeralda. A few FLN remained, cut off from each other, demoralized and without leadership. The city was calm again. The people of Algiers could once again come to the Sunday soccer matches, sit in the outdoor cafés, and frolic on the beaches and in the casinos without fear.

9

My End Game

ON OCTOBER 8, 1957, Paul Teitgen resigned as secretary-general of the Algiers police. He was the man who signed the *assignations à résidence* that allowed the paras to detain suspects instead of turning them over to the courts. A survivor of the Nazi concentration camps, Teitgen was deeply disturbed by the para tactics, but when he tried to resign in March, in the middle of the Battle of Algiers, Mollet would not let him, and so he soldiered on. Now, with the battle abating, he resigned again. His careful day-by-day files showed that he had signed 24,000 *assignations*, and that 3,024 of those suspects had "disappeared." Except for a handful of clerical errors, or other circumstances, many of them had been murdered by Aussaresses or the para torture teams.

The Algerian experience was a stain on Teitgen's conscience, but he resigned quietly, without expressing his misgivings. Three years later, however, in September 1960, he appeared as a witness at the trial of members of the Jeanson network, a band of couriers who transported FLN funds from France to Algiers and were known as "the carriers of suitcases." Francis Jeanson was a 38-year-old disciple of writer Jean-Paul Sartre and a passionate champion of the Algerian revolution. He contributed to Sartre's review, *Les Temps Modernes*, but deciding that words were not enough, he began providing material assistance to the FLN. On February 24, 1960, 18 French and 6 Arab members of his group were arrested (but not Jeanson who was in hiding), for "endangering the external security of the state." Their trial opened on September 6, presided over by Judge Curvelier, and with as many lawyers as there were defendants, one of whom was Jacques Vergès.

This was another trial that became a stage for the antiwar movement, in which the lawyers appealed to French and international opinion. Judge Curvelier would not let the word *war* be used, since Algeria was part of France, which could not be at war with itself. The FLN were "terrorists," while the French military were engaged in the maintenance of order.

My principal interest in the trial, although I was long since out of Algeria and working for the *New York Herald Tribune* as a rewrite man, was Teitgen's deposition. He said that while a high official in Algiers in 1957, he had harbored at his home three Moslem nurses who were pursued by both the FLN, who had tried to grab them so they could help the wounded in the Casbah, and by the *colons*, who wanted them arrested. For Teitgen, the three nurses represented that gray zone where those who were not emphatically on one side or the other were in trouble with both sides. He took them in for a month and a half, although their presence created a serious problem for him.

Teitgen declared that although he had kept quiet while in office, the moral questions that the war raised were critical. To have an army perform police work, he said, was to rob it of its reason for being. And what about the conscripts? he asked. What were they doing in Algeria but committing some of the same excesses as the professional army? They began to ask themselves why they were there, some of them turned against this undeclared war, and a few deserted. "In my soul and conscience," Teitgen said, "I must forgive them."

Judge Curvelier asked Teitgen: "Did you have any personal knowledge of torture?"

"Torture was the reason I resigned," Teitgen said.

Jacques Vergès asked Teitgen if he knew that some of the detained men had been killed while being interrogated.

"I am under oath, and I must admit that I knew of certain disappearances," Teitgen said.

He went on: "When I was deported, there was a billboard in the concentration camp that said 'My country, right or wrong.' I hope that the justice system of France will not choose between a right or a wrong country but will act with the certainty that they are on the side of justice." This was not a friend of the rebels talking but an esteemed French statesman who seemed to be saying that Jeanson and his group were on the side of justice. The right-wing press predictably deplored that "the spirit of the [World War II] Resistance has been converted into a camp of French *fellaghas*." But Teitgen's testimony made headlines and helped turn the trial into a triumph for the antiwar movement.

ON OCTOBER 16, 1957, Sauveur, who rarely used the phone, called to tell me that Camus had been awarded the Nobel Prize for literature. "Did you hear it from him?" I asked.

"No, the *salaud* [filthy bum]. I heard it secondhand. They say he's the youngest writer to win it. He's not quite forty-four." That turned out to be off the mark. Rudyard Kipling had won it in 1907 at the age of 42.

"His twelve-year-old daughter asked him if there was a Nobel Prize for acrobats," Sauveur said.

"He should have told her that novelists are acrobats."

While he was in Stockholm to receive his award, Camus spoke to a group of university students and said the following about Algeria: "I have always condemned terrorism. I condemn the blind terrorism that strikes in the streets of Algiers, which could strike my mother or my family. I believe in justice, but I will defend my mother first."

With the end of the Battle of Algiers in mid-October, our little team at *Réalités Algériennes* stopped writing about bombs and shootouts. Brissac's instructions were that we should sell the *loi-cadre* ("framework law") to the Algerian masses. This law, promoted by Lacoste, called for a single electoral college, with a bit of autonomy here and a relaxation of strictures there. The single college, however, was anathema to the *colons*, who lobbied against it in Paris and who saw it as an open door to Arab parity. When it came to a vote in the National Assembly, on September 30, under the government of Bourgès-Maunoury, it was defeated by 279 to 253.

Bourgès-Maunoury resigned, which led to a five-week political crisis, during which France once again had no government. Finally, on November 6, the 38-year-old finance minister, Félix Gaillard, was named prime minister and eventually managed to get the *loi-cadre* passed, but only at the price of its emasculation. Promises to the Arabs were balanced by assurances to the *colons*, in addition to the stipulation that the *loi-cadre* would not become law until calm and order were restored.

During the time of no government, Brissac assigned me to research the *loi-cadre* and write about its positive aspects for the Arabs. One late afternoon in mid-October, I drove over to the massive masonry building that housed the Government-General (GG) offices, which featured the famous balcony looking out on a vast esplanade, where a succession of high-ranking speakers had and would address the crowd and make history. Lacoste's offices, where I went to collect the data I needed, were on the top floor. I found three secretaries at their desks. One was reading the paper, the second was buffing her nails, and the third, a striking Arab woman, was looking out the window. Lacoste had hired a few Arabs in an ecumenical spirit.

"I've come for the data on the *loi-cadre*," I said to the Arab woman. I'm with *Réalités Algériennes*."

"That crummy rag," she said. "It's not even good propaganda."

"Somebody's got to write it," I said. "It's better than being in the *bled*. What's your name?"

"Aisha," she said, "if it's any of your business." Aisha's clear-skinned oval face was framed by lustrous black hair gathered behind her head, leaving her ears and silver-and-coral earrings uncovered. Her coal-like eyes were set a little too closely to a nose that hooked down slightly above a pretty mouth, and her voice had an appealing hoarseness that was due to chain-smoking, as I learned. Aisha had a quick, nervous manner, disdainful, as if I was wasting her time. When she spoke, her head darted like a bird's.

My mother had warned me to stay away from high-strung women, but today I wasn't heeding that advice. I asked Aisha to have a drink with me.

"I don't drink," she said.

"I meant mint tea."

"I don't drink mint tea."

"Then we can look at each other across the table."

She smiled. It was 5 PM, and I asked when she got off work.

"Anytime I like," she said. "I'm the token Arab, and they can't fire me. But I don't want to be seen with you in a café."

"I've got my car downstairs," I said. "We can drive to the Bainem Forest."

We drove through downtown Algiers and its lazily swarming evening crowd. The cafés were packed, the *yaouleds* with their shoe-shine boxes roamed from table to table, and young couples arm in arm jostled one another on rue d'Isly. We passed Square Bugeaud, the fountain, and the palm trees, and at café tables on the pavement sat the voluble young men with constricted minds behind their sunglasses. It was all getting stale, and I longed to leave. Two more months! There was a pinpoint of light at the end of the tunnel.

On Route Moutonnière, Aisha asked what had prompted me to take her out.

"I find you intriguing," I said.

"What do you find intriguing?"

"Your feet."

"What about my feet?"

"The way you put one foot in front of the other."

"Do you think that emotions are more important than ideas?" she asked.

"What a question. They both have their place, and they interact.

Let's say you're committed to a cause. Is that an idea or an emotion, or is it part of a collective mentality?"

"Independence is an idea," Aisha said. "Hatred of the French is an emotion, and the movement is a collective mentality."

"So you hate all French, without exception?"

"Yes, including you. The French language has become so hateful to me that it makes me physically ill to hear it."

"But you hear it all day at the office."

"I know, but what to you is the language of Montaigne and Descartes is transformed for me into electric current, racist insults, and mass murder."

I tried to explain that I had come to Algeria as a conscript and that I was against the war, even though I plugged the French line. "I don't have the guts to desert," I said, "so I chose an easy way out."

"You're nothing but a coward," Aisha sneered as we reached the edge of the Bainem Forest and parked on the cliff overlooking the bay. It was time to begin the period of discovery and findings of fact, as the lawyers put it. Aisha told me she had grown up in a village outside Sétif, the city in eastern Algeria where the rebellion erupted in 1954. She lit a Gauloise and blew the smoke out through her nose.

"It was one of the few villages that had a Koranic school for girls. My father was the village *caïd* [Koranic judge]. He was blind from birth, but he knew the Koran by heart. He had nine children from three wives, and I was the youngest. At school, we had no desks; we sat on the ground and used pens made of reeds to write on clay tablets. In the summer we picked olives and cherries, and we offered the first fruit to pregnant women."

In 1944, when she was 12, she passed her *certificat d'études* and was admitted to the lycée in Sétif. A year later, "when I was thirteen, we marched with banners calling for independence on V-E Day, and the French opened fire. A few days later, when the minister of education came to visit our class of Arab girls, we refused to sing the *Marseillaise*. Instead we sang the scout song, 'From Our Mountains Hear the Call of Freedom.' "

In 1950, her family moved to Algiers, where her father taught in a Koranic school. Her brothers and sisters were grown, but she continued to live at home, an apartment in the harbor area. She went to secretarial school and worked in offices, but she was recruited by the FLN in 1956 and swore *Lil Fida* ("ready for the sacrifice"). At first, she was a lookout for a team that cut telephone lines in the suburbs. A few months later, "they told me I'd be more useful working for the GG, and here I am."

I figured that if she was confiding in me, she must like me, so I put my arm around her as we sat in the car watching the sun set over the western end of the bay.

"Down with your paws," she shouted in her salt-and-pepper voice. "You're the enemy. You're killing my people."

"I don't want to kill you—I want to kiss you," I said.

"I would feel like a traitor kissing a Frenchman," she said. She was so emphatic that I sensed a trace of playacting in her behavior, so I asked her, "Do you go out with men?"

"Yes, Arab men."

"Do you sleep with them?"

"None of your business."

After that evening, I started to see Aisha fairly often. I didn't want to ask her to my apartment, first because I didn't think she'd accept, and second because I was concerned that the concierge would report back to Georgette. But she agreed to meet me in a café near Square Bresson. She was not the typical Arab woman. For one thing, she drank Pernods and smoked Gauloises, both of which had been banned by the FLN. For another she wore chic Paris dresses rather than a veil and a djellaba. For a third, she used Arpège perfume. Nor was she as much of an extremist as she had first seemed. She hoped there would be a negotiated solution to the war and that liberal Europeans would remain in an independent Algeria.

In one area, she was inflexible. When I tried to kiss her in the car, saying that although I didn't smoke, I would like to taste the tobacco on her mouth, she pushed me away, saying, "Why are men so stupid?" Since I found our meetings of the variable but skeptical French mind and stubbornly committed Arab mind stimulating, I stopped trying.

One day at the end of October, she asked me if I would like to meet her father. "He isn't as anti-French as I am," she said. "He's a religious man who likes to argue points of Koranic law."

On the following afternoon, we drove over to her sixth-floor apartment above the docks and overlooking the bay, as I reflected that this was the first time I had been invited to an Arab home. As if reading my mind, Aisha said, "You won't meet my mother. She stays out of sight when there are guests."

The living room was furnished with upholstered ottomans and brass tables. Aisha's father, Abdullah, sat in a carved mahogany armchair inlaid with mother-of-pearl, near a window, for although blind, he could sense the light. He wore a turban and a white robe, so that the beard on his chest made a white-on-white pattern, and his eyes were like oysters on the half-shell. He shook my hand warmly, and Aisha introduced me as one of her colleagues from the GG, "an expert on Algeria."

"Welcome," he said, his upper body rocking as he spoke. "You are my brother in the family of Allah. Are you a believer?"

As I sat down next to Aisha on a couch, I pondered the question. I had been raised a practicing Catholic during the war years in Washington, and the year I went to school with the nuns at St. Matthew's, I was an altar boy. On Sunday mornings, my mother stayed in bed and I took my two younger brothers to the cathedral and served Mass and held the tray for Communion, and after Mass George and Pat played hide-and-seek, knowing that I could not go home without them. But after my father's death in 1943, the idea of an all-knowing and benevolent deity eluded me. Human nature, like the planet, was a blend of order and chaos, replete with catastrophies, droughts and floods due to disturbances in the climate, and human-made disturbances, such as religious wars (the Crusades) and religious persecutions (the Spanish Inquisition). In terms of cruelty and violence, the history of religion matched and coincided with the history of war-fare. My experiences in Algeria did nothing to reinforce any faith I might once have had in a watchful deity. I thought of the Swiss Guards' song: "We seek our way in the winter and the night, in a sky where no stars shine." Humans seemed left to their own devices, and religion was one of those devices.

But I did not want to argue with a blind old man who knew the Koran by heart. I wanted, for Aisha's sake, to make a good impression, so I said: "I believe in the natural piety of man."

"Ah, that's a beginning," he said, as Aisha served mint tea and cookies covered with powdered sugar, "and Allah is forgiving and compassionate. But never forget that his word, as revealed by the prophet Mohammed, is infallible in all respects."

"That is what we say about our Bible," I replied, while thinking, I've never liked the promises, the table spread, the harps playing, the loved ones restored . . . and I don't like the old man's random proselytizing.

"There is a fount of wisdom in the Koran," Abdullah said.

I thought, One man's religion is another man's heresy, but I said, "As there is in the Bible." It occurred to me that the Koran condemned alcohol, and I wondered what Aisha's father would say if he saw her knocking back Pernods.

As Abdullah and I talked, Aisha snuggled up to me as she never had done when we were alone. She lay her head on my shoulder, raised it, and kissed my neck. I was puzzled, and I concentrated on maintaining a normal conversational tone.

Abdullah was explaining that the outcome of the jihad was written in the Koran. But as he did, Aisha kissed me on the mouth. "Here is the proof of our victory," Abdullah said, rocking in his chair, as he recited, "How often a sparse company has overcome a numerous company. Allah is with those who endure."

I was finding it difficult to pay strict attention to what he said, since Aisha was now fondling me through my pants, with predictable results. I had lost my train of thought, but I managed to ask, "Shouldn't the state hold all religions equally in favor?"

"That is a grave fault, my friend," Abdullah said. "Equal toleration of all religions is as bad as atheism."

I felt I had to leave, and I moved away from Aisha, who was smiling an enigmatic half-smile. I wanted to ask her father why the Koran permitted four wives, and why a husband could unilaterally repudiate his wife, but that too would have been out of place. I said I must excuse myself but that it had been a great honor to meet him. I felt completely out of my depth.

"We will meet again," he said, "when the dead are resurrected, as the rain revives the grass."

Why not let him believe what he wanted, I thought. It's just as healthy to have competition in religions as it is in business. I gave a hand signal to Aisha, who said she was staying home, and when I shook the old man's hand, he took it in both hands and said, "There are those who think that you and I have just enough religion to hate each other, but we both know that isn't true."

When I got home, I reflected on Aisha's strange behavior. She had felt compelled to act out taboo scenarios in front of her sightless father, and I was simply a bit player in some secret drama between the two of them. When I saw her the next day at the café, I asked for an explanation. She told me she didn't quite understand it herself, as it had never happened before. But as she spoke, her face clouded. "Maybe it's got to do with something that's never spoken of outside the family," she said. I could see she wanted to tell me, and I waited until she blurted it out: "When I was fourteen in Sétif, I was raped by my uncle, my father's brother. When I told my father, he said I was making it up." She spoke in an oddly high-pitched voice, as if she had reverted to the time of the incident.

I reached across the table for her hand, but she snarled in her normal guttural tone, "Don't touch me." I paid the bill, got up, and went home.

That evening, I was reading Stendhal's *The Charterhouse of Parma* when there was a knock at my door. I knew it could not be Aisha, but it might be Georgette, who sometimes dropped by to chat. I opened the door and saw Jean Berger standing there in a beat-up raincoat and a slouch hat, disheveled and emaciated. "Can I come in?" he asked. "I snuck past the concierge. I need help."

When I had last seen him with Bernard, he had asked for a transfer out of the Villa Sesini and had been sent to a regiment of legionnaire paras in the Nemencha Mountains, a land of high plateaus and heavy combat near the Tunisia border. At the time, I had given him my address. Berger, who had badly wanted to be a para when we were dorm mates at officers' school, now seemed utterly disheartened. I remembered that when we assembled in the *amphi* (lecture hall) at Saint-Maixent to choose our regiments, the gung-ho blue beret captain on the stage had said as part of his spiel: "It was enough to say, 'I was at Verdun' to be told 'There goes a hero.' It was enough to say, 'I was at Dien Bien Phu' to be told 'There goes a hero.' It will be enough to say, 'I fought in Algeria' to be told . . ." and then I heard a muffled voice in the row behind me say, "There goes a fucking fool."

"Come in," I said. "Let me fix you a drink." I went into the kitchen to get the scotch I obtained from Hans Imhof at the consular PX. "What happened to you?"

"I deserted," he said.

"You of all people," I exclaimed. "You who were all fire and flame." He looked so downcast I wished I had kept my mouth shut.

I gave him his drink and told him to take a bath and shave.

Half an hour later, wearing my bathrobe, which hung down to the feet of his short frame, he looked a bit better. He sat on a couch with his elbows on his spread knees and his head bent, staring at the floor.

"I kept repeating to myself the reasons not to," he said in a voice without intonation. "I believed in the nation at arms, the citizen soldier. The conscientious objector doesn't exist in French law. A deserter sets a bad example and leaves a hole in the ranks. It makes you a wanted man for the rest of your life. If I'm caught, I could get the death sentence. And yet I did it."

"What drove you to it?"

"When I was a kid, my father locked me in the cellar when I was bad. I didn't mind it; I liked it down there. I went after the rats. But Arabs aren't rats."

Then it came out like water gushing from a crack in a dam, a torrent that lasted more than an hour, with digressions, parentheses, backpedaling, and long pauses. His mind wasn't focused; it wandered all over the place. What I render here is a feeble synopsis.

Berger was a platoon leader in a battalion that was in daily combat with well-armed *fellagha* units. One day his platoon was ambushed as it approached a densely populated Arab village, and he lost 12 of his 30 men. "My men were enraged," he said. "When their friends die, the sheep become wolves."

His company commander ordered him by radio to invade the village, which was said to be providing a base for the rebels, make house-to-house searches, and liquidate the able-bodied men. Berger refused and returned to the para base. "I was being ordered to commit murder," he said, "and I couldn't do it."

That evening at the officers' mess, a plate was placed in front of him with offal on it. "It's the brain of a dead *fel,*" one of his fellow officers told him. "Since you are so fond of them, eat it." Another officer, standing behind him, pushed the muzzle of a MAT 49 into his back. He ate it and threw up.

The following day, Berger was broken in rank in a time-honored ceremony before the entire battalion in formation. As he stood at attention in the center of the courtyard, the colonel in command ripped the second lieutenant's bars off his epaulets with a bayonet and announced that he was now a private for "refusing to obey an order and endangering the lives of his men."

In the battalion, he was a pariah, kept at the base because he was deemed unreliable, in charge of loading water into the flying water wagons, the two Sikorskys that brought it to the men in the field and flew back the wounded.

"You should have seen the kind of battalion this was—the scum of Europe." He'd once been shown the register where the infractions and sentences were listed, including his own, and recalled a few:

"Eight days of prison for firing, without a valid reason, a burst from a submachine gun out a window.

"Fifteen days of prison for refusing to pay a taxi driver while in a state of inebriety and for violently striking a gendarme who interfered.

"Fifteen days of prison for throwing a grenade into a café in the town of Tebessa on the grounds that the prices were exorbitant, and for removing the refrigerator from the bar and trying to sell it to the manager of the officers' mess.

"Eight days of prison for a private who wore lieutenant's bars while on leave in Algiers in order to facilitate his approaches to young women.

"And I had my lieutenant's bars ripped off me," Berger said, "for refusing to commit murder." As a one-time Communist militant, he particularly liked the crime committed by one of the German legionnaires, sentenced to eight days for singing the *Internationale* instead of the *Marseillaise.*

"I don't know whether you've ever read the French Constitution," Berger said. " 'The Republic will never undertake any war of conquest and will never employ its forces against the freedom of another people.' "

"Very well put," I said.

The breaking point came when he saw two FLN captives with their hands tied behind their backs with telephone wire, in the prisoners' corral, and gave them water. He heard a noncom say, "At midnight, they're going on the *corvée de bois*" ("wood-gathering detail"). The *corvée de bois* consisted of taking prisoners out to pick up firewood and shooting them in the back for "trying to escape."

"I had to do something," Berger said, "even though they'd been captured with weapons in hand." That evening at seven, when it got dark, he approached the two Arabs and said, "I'm going to help you. I'll be back at ten." He knew that the sentry shift was over at 10, and he planned to get there 10 minutes early and tell the sentry he was taking the shift in order to question the prisoners, after clearing it with his replacement. But then he thought, If the prisoners escape on my watch, my bacon is cooked. I might as well go with them.

In the dark, he untied their hands and told them, "It's time. We have a three-hour start." They hurried down a path into the valley, Berger said, "and after a while I stopped in my tracks. I realized what I had done. I remembered a friend telling me, 'Desertion is a form of suicide.' But it was too late. I couldn't go back, and we walked for two days, without food or water, until the barking of dogs announced a village, where we were given couscous and oranges and some tea. In the village, I burned my uniform and my green beret, and they gave me a turban and a djellaba and said, "Now you are one of us."

"I was passed from one FLN unit to the next," Berger went on, "trying to get back to Algiers. I came across a few violent fanatics, a few stunted Dantons, a political commissar who was a hair-splitting dialectician, and more than one apostle of Koranic morality. The same mix of well-defined types that one finds in our army. I even found one who was drawn to Communism; he said that Moslem believers were camels—when they walk, they nod their heads. As a former Communist, I had to agree; there's no real proletariat in the Arab masses, no notion of a class war, merely a generic hatred of *colons*."

"Well, that might not be so bad," I said. "Remember what Carlyle said? 'The French Revolution was made by writers who thought they were thinkers.' "

"But they were only a few, standing on balconies and throwing out meaningless words like *equality* and *fraternity*, when the words that counted were *employment* and *wages*." Berger seemed to be picking up.

I found some cold chicken and opened a bottle of Medea red.

He lit a Gauloise, nervously striking the match several times before it lit, for his hands shook. "These people don't need theories. They know what they want."

"And when they get their independence," I said, "there will be the usual rush for ministerial chairs."

"I was taught in the party to believe in the international working class," Berger said, "but what I've learned in Algeria is that a new idea has to be adopted by one particular nation—the Bastille for the French, the Winter Palace for the Russians, and the end of colonialism in French Africa for the Algerians. It's nation by nation that revolutions succeed."

Berger was like an engine that was idling too fast. White spittle was collecting at the corners of his mouth. To calm him down, I asked how he had finally made it to Algiers.

"It was simple," he said. "The FLN in Sétif gave me some clothes and put me aboard an Algiers-bound truck loaded with potatoes. There was a hidden compartment where I could barely fit when we got to checkpoints. The truck let me off at the rue Randon market, and I came straight here."

"What now?"

"You know, I was never the victim of recruiting posters. I wanted to test my courage. I wanted to belong to an elite branch of the army. I wanted to be the best. And now, where am I? I'm in a no-man's-land, wanted by the French, and the Arabs think I'm crazy. My only saving grace is that I saved two guys from being shot. At least now I hate the military shit, the marching in step, the medals."

"As for the medals, you don't have to worry."

"I don't want to be a burden to you. I must get back to France as quickly as possible. But I need some *flouss* [cash] and an ID card."

"I have a friend who may be able to help," I said. "We'll find out tomorrow." I hoped that Berger's story would strike a chord of sympathy with Aisha.

"But first, I have to get you some clothes that fit so I can introduce you to my landlady, Georgette. I'll tell her you're on leave, staying with me for a few days. You'll see, she's a great gal. Her husband was in the Corps of Engineers in the Sahara and got killed." Berger was not listening. He had fallen asleep on the couch.

The next morning, after doing my shopping, I went back to Square Bresson and called Aisha, who was in a foul mood.

"Why should I talk to you?" she said. "You walked out on me at the café."

"This is an emergency that has nothing to do with you and me. I have a friend who's in trouble. I need your advice."

"Civilian or military?"

"Military."

"I'll meet you at the café at noon."

"At our table in the back."

Aisha was chronically tardy, and I read the *colon* mouthpiece, *l'Echo d'Alger*, as I waited for her. There was a campaign in France against the cost of the war. Gaston Deferre, the Socialist mayor of Marseilles, said the war was costing 700 billion francs a year. Lacoste denied that figure "with energy," while pointing out that Marseille was one of the war's principal beneficiaries because of the increase in its maritime traffic.

Aisha pushed the newspaper in my face to signal her arrival. Still standoffish, she asked, "So what's eating you?"

"In a nutshell, a friend of mine deserted while helping two FLN prisoners escape, and he's staying with me at Square Bresson. He needs an ID card."

"Oh sure," she said. "I'll just ask my boss at the GG, 'Could I have an ID card for a French deserter?' And why not a plane ticket to Paris as well?"

"Good idea," I said. She was exasperating, but I had no one else to turn to, and I had to get Berger off my hands. "Let's be friends. You know how fond I am of you. If you want to, I'll take a few days off and drive you to Oran" (she had a sister she liked in Oran, married to an Arab lawyer who had only one wife, which was becoming the rule among educated Arabs).

"Now you want to drive me to Oran, and you've never even shown me your apartment at Square Bresson."

"I'd be glad to take you there right now so you can meet Berger."

"I don't want to meet him. I don't want anything to do with him."

"You have a chance to help someone who saved the lives of two

FLN combatants. I know you have connections. I can't understand why you don't use them."

With her customary turning on a dime, she said, "Very well, but it will cost you." I had no idea whether she was responding to my plea or whether she thought she had pushed me too far.

"I have some savings," I said. "What are we talking about?"

"A hundred thousand francs [$200] for the ID card and two hundred thousand francs to take him to Tunisia." I wasn't going to argue, though it was all I had. I knew there was an underground railroad to and from Tunisia for the passage of men and weapons. It was Berger's best bet.

While Aisha made the arrangements, I told Berger to shave his mustache and dye his sandy hair black. I took him to an instant-photo shop, and a couple of days later he had his ID card, the eyes in the picture looking severely at the camera. The card was made out to Jean Dulac, 14 rue des Thermopyles, Paris 14ème, *voyageur de commerce* (traveling salesman).

"It's funny," he said. "When we were at Saint-Maixent, I thought you were a layabout. But you're really not a bad guy, and I'll pay you back."

"You're not so bad yourself," I said, "for a deserter."

That evening, he had a rendezvous at the Randon market. I never saw him again, but Aisha told me two weeks later that he had made it to Tunisia. I breathed a sigh of relief.

W E WERE in early November, an Arabian summer, with winds off the sea and foglike drizzles but no turning of the leaves. There was still no government in Paris, which drew the ire of the *colons*, who felt abandoned.

On November 11, a horde of right-wing students threw tomatoes at Lacoste, who was marching at the head of the World War I armistice parade. He was a partisan of the *loi-cadre* and had been kept in office under the newly invested government of Félix Gaillard. Lacoste had the leaders arrested and revoked their student deferments. They were posted to combat regiments, where they could throw grenades instead of fruits and vegetables.

The rumor mill ground out plots to overthrow the government in Paris. The name of de Gaulle was bruited about. Men said to be his emissaries shuttled between Algiers and Paris. The Gaillard government's minister of defense, Jacques Chaban-Delmas, was an ardent Gaullist who had set up an Algiers office and was in close contact with right-wing *colon* elements. There was nothing you could pin down; it was still at the level of commedia dell'arte. Or like a sky where the clouds take strange shapes, changing from sheep to alligators. "Massu says he knows nothing," Brissac said. "No one tells him anything. Apparently, in *colon* circles, the new slogan is 'No more coffins, no more suitcases.' " Mixed commissions of *colons* and Arabs were formed in a dozen cities in preparation for the *loi-cadre*, which was to be submitted to the National Assembly. The Arabs who took these jobs were brave men. Some of them were assassinated.

The Algiers press (including our "crummy rag") insisted that the military situation was improving, which was true in Algiers but not the rest of the country. General Salan announced that the balance sheet for the year was positive: From January to September, 10,000 rebels were killed, while the number of French troops had risen to 425,000. And yet . . . in all Algeria, there were no safe zones. The rebellion seemed to be everywhere. Bigeard was sent to the Sahara to exterminate rebel bands that were ambushing the oil trucks from Hassi-Messaoud. Lacoste claimed that "the FLN front in the Sahara is backed by international companies that want the spoils from our departure." By the end of November, however, oil was flowing freely through the first pipeline, from Hassi-Messaoud to the port of Bougie.

Despite the *beni oui-ouis* who volunteered for the mixed commissions, there was a catastrophic loss of Moslem support for the French—the result of torture, unwarranted killings, the use of forced labor to repair the sabotage of the FLN, and the vast and oppressive system of searches, ID controls, and the unwritten code that every Arab was a suspect: Raise your arms, drop your packages, let go of your donkey, women and children pushed around and worse, when often they couldn't speak French and didn't respond to orders quickly enough. Or else their foot-dragging and ignorance were deliberate, the weapons of the weak. What made every situation worse was a seething combat fatigue among the troops, so that they were more jittery than usual. The war had gone on too long.

Brissac came in one day in a state of uncommon agitation, after attending a military intelligence briefing at Massu's headquarters. "Those who think Algeria is an internal French affair are deluding themselves," he said. "Algeria has become a pawn on the Cold War chessboard. The American choppers we're using that were intended for NATO are matched by the weapons the *fels* are getting from the Warsaw Pact nations. The arsenals of Eastern Europe are being shipped to the rebels via Cairo. They no longer use World War II surplus, but Skoda machine guns."

He proceeded to relate a remarkable tale of espionage. Our military intelligence had an Egyptian agent code-named Soliman, who had studied law in France, flirted with Marxism, and learned Russian. Upon his return to Egypt, he found himself on the wrong side when Nasser came to power in 1952. He was jailed but got out by joining the Volunteers of Death during the Suez crisis, where he performed well enough to be rehabilitated. Thanks to his knowledge of Russian, he was recruited by General Goleb, the head of the Egyptian mission that purchased weapons in Eastern Europe. He was introduced to the Algerian rebel mission in Cairo and put in charge of obtaining Czech weapons for the Algerians. Soliman shuttled from Cairo to Prague to Geneva to Paris.

It happened that Soliman spent more money than he earned. He gambled and kept mistresses. He had maintained his contacts with French friends from his student days, and in early 1957, during a trip to Paris, he agreed to work for French military intelligence. He began coming to Algiers to see the colonel who handled him, though his passport was not stamped. On November 12, he turned over a list of FLN "probationers" in Eastern European training camps: 9 in a flight school near Rostov, 22 in a tank school in East Germany, 21 in

Poland, 21 in Romania, 24 in Bulgaria, all in infantry schools. The trainees traveled on Syrian passports, delivered to them by the Syrian ambassador in Cairo.

"The entire ALN [National Army of Liberation] officer corps is trained in the Eastern bloc," Brissac said. "There are three hundred *fels* in Cairo right now, waiting to leave."

Soliman also provided information on the weapons recently obtained by the FLN from the Soviet Union—20,000 rifles and 1,700 machine guns, donated under the Warsaw Pact. Soviet cargo planes flew those weapons to Cairo. From there, they were trucked across Libya and Tunisia into Algeria.

"In war, fraud and deceit are virtues," Bernard said.

O N NOVEMBER 15, I came home as usual from the office around 6:00. Georgette had let herself into my apartment and was waiting for me. "Two men came looking for you today," she said. "They were policemen in plainclothes. I didn't tell them anything. They said they'd be back tomorrow morning."

I figured it might have something to do with the articles I'd been sending to the *Telegram*. I never used the military franking system but sent them air mail from the main post office with no return address. Although I signed them with a pseudonym, perhaps they had found a way to identify me, perhaps through my return mail, the clips and checks the *Telegram* sent back. My first reaction was to take the clips I had collected in a drawer and flush them down the toilet.

"It's nothing," I told Georgette. "Just a few articles I wrote for an American newspaper." Then I thought I'd better call Bernard at his boardinghouse, in case they were after him too. He said no one had come calling, but just in case, he was getting rid of his clips. I told him that whatever happened to me, I would not mention him.

"I've got one month left before I'm released," I told Georgette, "and this has to happen."

"I know how you feel," she said. "I'm waiting to sell this building, and then I'm off to Paris." I did not doubt that she would quickly find another husband.

The next morning at 8:00, the concierge buzzed to tell me two gentlemen were waiting downstairs. They wore belted raincoats and felt hats and asked me my name. They took out cards to show they were not ordinary cops but DST (Direction et Surveillance du Territoire, the French FBI).

"How can I help you?" I asked.

"You're under arrest," the short one with the trimmed beard said.

"You must be joking," I said.

"We've been tailing you since August," the tall one said, "since you met Warburton in the square we are now on and took him to the Casbah. We were tailing him as a visiting foreign dignitary, and we started tailing you."

It occurred to me that since I was dark-haired and olive-skinned, they might have taken me for an Arab. It also occurred to me how inattentive and naïve I was, for I had never for a moment suspected that I was being followed. Finally it occurred to me how slowly the DST moved, since it had been more than two months since my meeting with Warburton.

"We have a list of your meetings with American diplomats, and also of your meetings with Aisha Chachoune, an Arab woman who works at the Government-General and who is known to be in contact with the FLN."

"I saw her in connection with my work," I said. "I'm an officer in the French army and an editor on the newspaper *Réalités Algériennes*, under the command of Major de Brissac."

Though they tried not to show it, they were taken aback. After all this time, they still didn't know I was a soldier in civilian clothes. That was the style of their investigation, plodding and hesitant, stop-and-start. They must have followed me to the office and seen the nameplate, Compagnie Atlantique, but hadn't bothered to find out what that was. Also, it often happened that the cooperation between the DST and the military was tenuous at best. Also, they hadn't mentioned Berger, which meant they hadn't seen me with him when I took him to the photo shop, which was a blessing.

They drove me down to DST headquarters, though they didn't handcuff me, and they processed me, which took half an hour. I suggested they call Brissac, who could clear the whole matter up. After another long wait, while the tall one called out of my hearing, he returned and said: "Since you're an officer, you're out of our jurisdiction and you're being turned over to military intelligence. But first, Major de Brissac asked to see you, and we're taking you to him."

Brissac, with whom I had been in close quarters daily for nearly a year, had become a friend. He was protective of his team, but at the same time he was concerned that the reputation of his office would be tarnished. He ushered me in, lit a Gauloise, and said: "If you tell me everything just as it happened, without holding anything back, I can help you. But if you play games, you could be in serious trouble."

"I've got nothing to hold back," I said. "It was through the American consul, Lewis Clark [who had been replaced not long after my arrival], that I met Massu and got this job. That's how I met some of the others, whom I saw socially. I thought America was our ally. Anyway, how could I be a spy when I don't have any access to classified information?"

"What about the Arab girl?"

"She worked at the GG and gave me reports. Once, she took me home to meet her father."

Brissac grilled me for a while, then said: "I have to turn you over to military intelligence for questioning. I'm going to stick my neck out and give you absolution. But if you're trying to trick me, you'll get me in trouble too!"

"I swear to you on my father's grave that these were banal social contacts, as far as you can get from espionage."

"I realize," Brissac said, "that these guys in the DST have one-dimensional minds, and once they fasten on someone they're like dogs with a bone. You'll find that the Deuxième Bureau [military intelligence] captain I'm turning you over to has more finesse. He's a friend of mine."

That afternoon, Brissac drove me to divisional headquarters in Hydra, up in the hills above Algiers. Across the courtyard, where dozens of military vehicles were parked, and behind the main building where Massu's offices were, there was a separate two-story building with a flat roof and shuttered windows—military intelligence headquarters. He turned me over to a sentry and wished me luck. I was led into the office of Captain Pierre Mérillon, a young man of about 30 with light curly hair and a boyish face, in uniform, wearing his campaign ribbons. He was too young for World War II but had served in Indochina, and had a silver-dollar-sized scar stamped on his forehead like a vaccination mark. He stood to greet me. The holster at his waist had that new-leather smell.

"I have your DST dossier," he said. "It's quite voluminous. I've been going through it."

"They say they tailed me for several months, but I was never conscious of it."

"We're going to have to place you in isolation for a few days so that I can question you. Please understand that it's only a formality."

I was escorted to the upper floor, to a windowless room with bare whitewashed walls, a cot, a table, two chairs, a washbasin, and a toilet. From the ceiling hung a lightbulb that remained on, for there was no light switch in the room. "I have to lock you in and ask for your watch," the soldier who had led me there said. It was all very polite, the polite way to break down someone's resistance. Without a watch, I had no sense of time, and with the light always on, I had no sense of day or night. I tried to doze, but I was too worked up. I thought to myself, I'll pretend I'm in a doctor's waiting room.

But in a doctor's waiting room, I could read newspapers and magazines. I craved a newspaper the way a smoker craves a cigarette. Then I thought, I have to treat this as a game and figure out a game plan. I had nothing to hide. My only sin would be the sin of omission.

I wouldn't mention Berger. I realized that part of the game was to make me wait, to increase my anxiety level.

Finally, after what seemed like hours, the door opened and Mérillon came in and sat at one of the chairs, and beckoned me to sit on the other. He placed the DST dossier on the table, pulled a silver cigarette case from a jacket pocket, opened it, and said, "Will you have a cigarette? It's Virginia tobacco."

I told him I didn't smoke, realizing that he was making an allusion to my American connections.

"You seem to have spent quite a lot of time with American diplomats," he said.

Is that a crime? I thought, but I said, "Mainly Imhof. You have to understand—I grew up in America. My father was stationed at the French embassy in Washington. I was in America when I was conscripted, and I came back to serve."

"When you had lunch on October twelfth with Imhof at the Aletti, what did you talk about?"

I began to see what Mérillon's game plan was. He was calm and deliberate. He didn't pace, he didn't gesticulate, he didn't try to intimidate, which I would have actually preferred, for it would have allowed me to remain absolutely calm by contrast. Mérillon was going to go down every date in the DST dossier and ask me to recall conversations that had been forgotten with the end of lunch or drinks. If I said I didn't remember, or if I was vague, that would be an indication of my guilt, of what was left unsaid. But if I had total recall, I would show that I had nothing to hide.

I actually did remember something Imhof and I had talked about on October 12, because it was a coincidence about where we had grown up. We had both spent years in the Yorkville neighborhood of Manhattan, and he had explained to me that around the German core of Yorkville the other ethnic groups were arranged very much as they were on the map of Europe, with the Poles and Czechs and Hungarians to the east and the Austrians to the south. But if I repeated that to Mérillon, he would think it was an evasion. I had to invent more pertinent conversations that could form the basis of his report.

So I said, "We talked about the *loi-cadre*, which had just been voted down in Paris. Imhof said it was due to the lobbying of the *gros colons*. I said it was more of an attempt to bring down the premier, Bourgès-Maunoury."

He pressed me for more details, which I made up as I went along, knowing they would never question Imhof. When it came to cocktail parties, I described my chats with half a dozen guests, always on the topic of Algeria. And so it went for four hours, until I was exhausted and he probably needed a rest as well.

"I'll be back tonight," he said. "In the meantime, you'll be given the usual rations."

The usual rations were two slices of bread, a bit of *saucisson* (sausage), and a glass of water from the tap.

I took off my clothes and tried to sleep, but I couldn't under the stale warmth of the blanket, which smelled of previous occupants of the cell, so I threw it off, but I still couldn't sleep because of the light. I tried to think of pleasant things, dinner with Georgette, the beach with Sauveur. I was dozing off from exhaustion when Mérillon returned and said, "Get dressed."

I asked him what time it was. "That is information I am not permitted to give you," he said.

He was flipping through the pages of the dossier. "Let me see. Did you say, at some point, 'France cannot win this war'?"

That one threw me. I remembered quite clearly that I had used those words more or less when I was driving back with Geneviève Zimmer from her father's. The only way that could have gotten into the dossier was that Geneviève was an informant for the DST. Damned *pied-noir* snitch, I thought. She was taking down every word I said to use against me. I'll have to warn Don Davies when I get out of this hole.

"Yes, I did say that France would lose the war," I told Mérillon. "But I didn't mean it in a military sense. Massu won the Battle of Algiers. Other battles will be won. But the war will be lost politically. The Fourth Republic cannot absorb the cost and does not have the will to win. The government, when there is a government, trembles every time *Le Monde* publishes an antiwar editorial."

My answer seemed to satisfy him, since it was an article of faith among career officers that the politicians had lost the colonial wars the military were winning.

All the things I couldn't tell Mérillon were racing through my mind. Who was right and who was wrong? In terms of the forces of history, colonialism was in decline. Look at the Dutch in Indonesia and the British in India. Look at the French all over the map. Why should Algeria be any different, particularly when it was getting a leg up from the Arab world and the Eastern bloc? The momentum was on Algeria's side, propelled by the thriving antiwar movement in France. And while no one yet knew who was right, since the only certainty was that the winner would be right, both sides were frozen into their positions like Paleolithic corpses found intact in the ice a million years later. In Algeria, France had jettisoned its liberal values, adopting the hardball tactics of the terrorists. As that noncom of mine in Champlain had put it, "You can't fight this war according to the Marquis de Queensberry." But history doesn't have many breathing spaces, and those on the wrong side always suffer. It's fine to believe that the ends justify the means, but only if you win. If you lose, you suffer. Wars are fought on moral credit, and the loser must declare bankruptcy. Both sides are in good faith—that has nothing to do with it—but the victor takes possession, and the vanquished are dispossessed. The victor's crimes remain unpunished, but the vanquished are severely dealt with. The victors then spawn inquisitors, who denounce the heretics in their midst.

I wanted to have faith, but in what? Not in a French victory. Not even in an Algerian victory. "The coffin or the suitcase" was the wrong way to put it. The right way to put it was "coffins all around, on the house." I wanted out. I needed to quiet my nerves. I found myself waiting expectantly for the rattling of the key in the lock. How strange it was to lose track of time, the pervasive regulator of our daily lives. It was like losing the force of gravity, like floating.

Mérillon came and went, hoping to catch me off guard. He must get as little sleep as I do, I thought, although he always looked dapper and freshly shaven, smelling faintly of cologne and smoking his Virginia tobacco. On his fourth visit, he asked, "What about Aisha?"

"She works in Lacoste's office," I said. "I assume she was vetted by his people."

"His people didn't invent gunpowder," he said. "They slip up."

"I liked Aisha," I said, "but she wanted nothing to do with me."

"Didn't you visit her socially, at her home?"

"She wanted me to meet her father, who's some sort of cleric. He lectured me about the Koran. I think he was trying to convert me. I couldn't get out fast enough."

"Don't you know she has FLN contacts?"

"I'm the last person she would tell. She can't stand me."

"I think I should tell you we've opened a field investigation. She could be arrested."

"It will be no trouble at all for me to stay away from her."

"That wraps it up for me," Mérillon said briskly. "Shower and shave and come to my office when you're ready to leave."

I had trouble adjusting to the idea that my interrogation was over. It was a mental habit of mine to visualize the worst-case scenario, and I had imagined myself locked up with Aisha in the same cell.

Back in Mérillon's office, he gave me my watch and some coffee. I asked him how long I'd been held. "Three days," he said. "That's the usual time it takes." He was relaxed now, and smiling. "Brissac told me you were all right, though a bit naïve, and that your American friends were probably pumping you. Taking Warburton to the Casbah was not a clever move."

"But Warburton was pro-French," I said. "I wanted to show him that the Casbah was calm."

"Perhaps," Mérillon said, "but there are some American agents who are persona non grata in Algeria for trying to subvert our labor union, so we have to be on our guard."

"Maybe I was gullible," I said, "but I don't have a suspicious nature. I take people for what they seem to be."

"I take them for what their dossiers say they are," Mérillon replied. "But let me ask you: You've been in Algeria more than a year. Did you get your two weeks' leave in France?"

"I didn't even know I was entitled to it."

"Well, look. We don't want any problems with the Americans. If it gets out that you were arrested for seeing them, it might be embarrassing. But if you agree not to mention it to them, I could arrange for you to take your two weeks in December. You're due to be released from service on December 15, so you could leave the first of the month."

That sounded good to me, and I agreed. I reported back to Brissac, who said, "I knew it was just a formality."

Some formality, I thought.

"I'm sorry to lose you," he said, "in spite of your love for the Americans and other drawbacks."

I told Bernard he didn't have to worry about his articles. It hadn't come up. When I said I was leaving the first of December, he shook his head. "I'll have to write the entire lousy sheet," he said. He wasn't getting out until January 1958.

I spent my last days in Algiers tying up loose ends. I went to the American Library and told Don Davies that I had heard Geneviève was a possible "patriotic informant" for the DST. "Oh, I got rid of her a month ago," he said. "She was lecturing everybody, and since attendance was down, she was expendable."

Although I was pretty sure I was no longer being tailed, events had made me more cautious, and I avoided seeing Aisha. I called her, using a different name and voice, and warned her that she was on a list.

I saw Sauveur and told him I knew we'd meet again, and he said, "*Mektoub*" ("It is written"), but that was the last time I saw him. When I said good-bye to Georgette, she said "I'll miss you," and my eyes misted over, for I had made a few friends I would miss. I told her she could have my battered Citroën. She said she'd give it to one of her young cousins.

Back in 1951, when I was at the Sorbonne, one of my professors, philosopher Maurice Merleau-Ponty, told me: "You have something of Rousseau's noble savage." I figured he meant that I reminded him of man in his primal state, a hopelessly rudimentary but amiable dolt. Algeria had rubbed all that off me. I now had a master sergeant in my brain ordering me to be suspicious and watchful.

The Algerian experience did not enrich me; it diminished me. Young men are sent out to fight wars and are placed in situations they are not prepared to deal with. I was deeply ashamed of what I had done in Champlain, but at the same time I did not recognize the right to be criticized by those who had not been put in harm's way. It's a little too easy to sit in one's living room and watch TV and be horrified by the reprehensible acts committed by men in combat. Only those who have been there have the right to do that, and I have been horrified at myself, and I have known myself to be morally compromised.

I wanted to put Algeria behind me, get on with my life, and never think about it again. When I left in December 1957, I felt that I was fleeing a burning building. I had been scorched, but I was still alive. Back in New York, I got a job with the Associated Press. A year later, I was hired by the *Herald Tribune,* and in 1961 I was back in Algiers as a foreign correspondent. But that's another story.

As for those I have written about in the preceding pages, Georgette moved to France and married a titled Parisian who was a member of the French Olympic Committee. After independence, Aisha worked in the cabinet of Prime Minister Ahmed Ben Bella and was one of my sources when I covered Algeria in 1962. Bernard Brodin became an art critic and remained friends with Major de Brissac, who eventually retired as a general. Sauveur Galliero died in the 1970s. Jean Berger vanished. There's no statute of limitations for deserters, and he may well have changed his name. My two friends from basic training are in America. After a distinguished career at Cornell, Alain Seznec has retired to Las Vegas (for the climate, not the gambling). He and Janet recently celebrated their fifty-fifth anniversary.

Upon leaving the army, Jean Aslanian decided to go to America and try his luck. He married a fellow Armenian in California, got into the rag trade, and made lots of money selling American bowling shirts to the French. Today, he lives in a gated community in Palm Desert, California, where he hits the golf links and tennis courts daily.

In the rebel ranks, Yacef Saadi and Zohra Drif were freed in June 1962 after the liberation of their country. Zohra studied law in prison and passed her bar exam when she got out. She practiced family law and married one of the top FLN leaders, Rabah Bitat. They had three children. Yacef went into the movie business and produced Gillo Pontecorvo's 1965 classic, *The Battle of Algiers.* Thanks to Yacef, Pontecorvo was able to shoot in the actual Algiers locations, which gave the film its gritty sense of place. The film struck a balance, showing the torture of the paras, as well as a *pied-noir* child eating an ice cream cone who is killed by a bomb. The para colonel Matthieu, based on Bigeard, is depicted as a rational military technician, rather than a sadist. But there is a serious flaw in the cinéma vérité style. Yacef Saadi starred as himself, and he embellished and distorted the facts of his capture. In the movie, a tortured informer gives away Ali-la-Pointe. In reality, it was Yacef who led the paras to his colleague, and the girl and two boys with him. Once captured, Yacef and Zohra talked freely, without being tortured.

In January 2004, *The Battle of Algiers* was shown at the Film Forum in New York. I went to the premiere, never having seen it before, and Yacef was there to present the film, looking spry and fit at 76. When it was over, he made some brief remarks, translated from the French. I went up to him and introduced myself as having been on Massu's staff in 1957. I was surprised that he had bowdlerized his true role, but since this was almost half a century after the events, I decided not to mention it.

Instead I said, "If I had met you then, I would have had to shoot you."

"Not if I shot you first," he replied.

Epilogue

A NATION AT WAR is a nation in peril, not only of losing the war but also of internal cataclysms. The havoc in Vietnam unseated Lyndon Johnson. The war in Algeria toppled the shuffling Fourth Republic. In Algiers on May 13, 1958, there was a reprise of the oft-seen scenario—a crowd at the war memorial, rioters scrambling up the stairs and across the broad esplanade to invade the Government-General building. Lacoste was in Paris, but Massu agreed to head a committee of public safety, "to keep hotheads from spilling blood."

Two days later, Salan spoke from the famed balcony overlooking the Forum and said, *"Vive de Gaulle."* In France, the general released a statement: "I am ready to assume the powers of the Republic." France was seen as being on the brink of civil war. Or would the army seize power with a banana republic–type junta? The situation was whirling out of control, and the newly named government under Prime Minister Pierre Pflimlin could only watch in a state of hopeless befuddlement. Army units were in open insubordination, and on May 24, paratroopers seized the island of Corsica as a staging area to invade France. Facing a putsch, Pflimlin resigned on May 28.

On June 1, the undertaker of the Fourth Republic came before the National Assembly and was named prime minister by a vote of 329 to 224. After 12 years in the wilderness, de Gaulle returned to usher in the Fifth Republic. The vox populi said, "This can't be worse than what we had before."

These events were like a series of train wrecks caused by faulty track signals. The *colons* firmly believed that de Gaulle would keep Algeria French. The army took credit for bringing him back to power and saw him as one of their own. De Gaulle, however, privately thought that a French Algeria was a "lamentable stupidity." He deeply respected the rule of law, which is why he refused to take power by a coup d'état, à la Napoleon III. His bedrock certitude was that the army must serve the republic and not vice versa.

And so he wasted no time reducing the power of the army in Algeria, by transferring praetorian officers by the hundreds back to France from the top down. Massu was transferred, as was Salan. In October 1958, de Gaulle called for a negotiated peace, the "Peace of the Brave." But the FLN refused. De Gaulle realized that the situation was hopeless, because of the dilemma of the draw. The French might be winning the war on the ground, with its highly effective barriers on the Tunisia and Morocco borders, and its 1959 offensive that broke up large rebel bands. But they were incapable of wiping out the rebellion, and the best they could hope for was a draw. But in a draw, the FLN were the winners, as long as they refused to negotiate and could keep fighting.

For the French, the war was quicksand, and after a visit to Algeria in August 1959, de Gaulle began to prepare public opinion for the end game, craftily. In a television and radio speech that reached an audience of millions on September 16, he outlined the choices: independence, which he called "secession," would lead to pauperism and the installation of a Communist dictatorship; "Frenchification" was no good either—the two communities were like oil and water; but "association," a "government of Algerians by Algerians," could be achieved within four years after a peace was signed.

In Algiers, the ultras responded with barricades on January 24,

1960, and the army temporized. The gendarmes closed in and shots were fired. It was a bloody confrontation, with 14 gendarmes killed and 123 wounded, while among the ultras, 6 died and 26 were wounded. The stalemate lasted a week, until de Gaulle called on the army to do its duty. The barricades were dismantled and the militants were interned. The ultra leadership was on the run, but only temporarily, for the diehards, both among the *colons* and in the army, were propelled by the conviction that they had brought de Gaulle to power and he owed them a pound of flesh.

In a referendum in January 1961 on self-determination for Algeria, de Gaulle won two thirds of the vote, but to placate the diehards, he had to rob Peter to pay Paul. Pursuing his zigzag course, he was back in Algeria in March, on a *tournée des popotes* ("mess-hall tour"), telling the army to press the offensive.

When he spoke of "an Algerian Algeria" that summer, however, the army felt that, once again, victory was being snapped from their grasp by corrupt politics, by the very man they had installed on the throne. The putsch of April 1961 was an act of desperation on the part of the superior officers who were willing to throw away their careers and a lifetime of service to their country and become renegades, so strongly did they feel they had been betrayed. Among the four generals who led the putsch were Salan, who had shouted, *"Vive de Gaulle"* in May 1958, and Maurice Challe, the general who succeeded him and was the mastermind of the 1959 offensive. Challe had felt he had the rebels on the run, and then he'd been recalled when he was on the verge of winning. The prestige of Salan and Challe drew other officers into the putsch, such as Colonel Godard. The putsch lasted all of three days, foiled by the refusal of the conscripts to follow. On April 22, the 1st REP (green berets), led by putschist officers, moved into Algiers and took over government buildings. But in almost every other regiment, the conscripts stayed put, particularly when they heard, on their transistor radios, de Gaulle condemn the putsch. On April 25, Challe and his followers surrendered. Challe was tried before a military court and sentenced to 15 years. Salan and Godard went underground and became leaders of the OAS

(Organisation de l'Armée Secrète), a terrorist mix of renegade officers and ultras that hammered, through their lunatic violence, the final nails in the *colons'* coffins.

I happened to be in Algiers covering the putsch for the *Herald Tribune*, and I saw the men of the 1st REP leave their barracks in Zeralda, outside Algiers, under arrest in trucks, singing at the top of their lungs Edith Piaf's *"Non, Je ne Regrette Rien."* In this tragedy of the lost soldiers, as the rebellious military became known, 200 French officers were jailed.

Having put down the putsch, de Gaulle was now the undisputed leader of France, above parties and factions. Even so, the end game took more than a year. Once begun, negotiations with the FLN dragged out. The trigger-happy terrorists of the OAS hoped to subvert the talks. Algiers and Oran were dangerous places to be. In Algiers, I was sitting at a café terrace across from the Aletti Hotel with Henry Tanner of the *New York Times* when an Arab was gunned down in the street three feet away and a pool of blood collected around his body before the ambulance arrived. We were on our way to a briefing at the GG, but Henry said he didn't feel well and asked me to fill him in—he was going back to the hotel.

A week later in Oran, where the OAS was targeting journalists, a friend of mine who was a photographer for *Paris-Match* showed me that he had ingeniously hidden two cameras inside his raincoat. He was shot and killed the next day. I was having lunch in an oceanside bistro with Eric Pace of *Life*, and when I asked for the bill, it came with a note in an envelope with my name on it. The note said: "Leave Oran by tomorrow or die. OAS." I went back to my hotel, paid the bill, and drove back to Algiers with a British reporter who'd also been threatened, Alan Williams, son of actor Emlyn Williams.

At least there was now a clear division between the officers loyal to de Gaulle and the renegades who had joined the OAS. The OAS were nihilists whose slogan was *"Vive la mort."* They murdered French soldiers and veiled Moslem women and blew up the library of the University of Algiers. Their scorched-earth tactics were counterproductive, in that they sped up the negotiations in Evian and other locations, making both sides more accommodating: to the FLN, because the OAS was blowing up buildings and harbor facilities in Algiers; to de Gaulle, because the *colons* backed the OAS, who murdered French soldiers and police, which made him feel they deserved their fate.

On March 18, 1962, came the agreement to end the war, in a 98-page document, followed by a cease-fire the next day. To his chagrin, de Gaulle had to give up the oil-rich Sahara, which he had hoped would become a French enclave. Settlers who decided to stay would be given a special legal status, but the actions of the OAS had poisoned all hopes of the two communities coexisting.

The French and the FLN respected the cease-fire, but the OAS kept up its senseless killing, lobbing mortar rounds into the Casbah to provoke a massacre of *colons*. The Arab masses, knowing what was at stake, showed great restraint. Bab-el-Oued, the last stronghold of the OAS, was where the poor-white *colons* were entrenched, those without properties in France or fallback positions. So attached were they to their way of life that they did not realize that by backing the OAS they were hastening their own exodus. On April 20, Salan was captured, his hair dyed black, defiant to the end. By then, the *colons* were leaving by the thousands. Long lines waited for days at the harbor for ships and at Maison Blanche Airport, where a round-the-clock airlift was in place.

And so ended more than 130 years of French rule, with these forlorn families, the parents clutching a cardboard suitcase in one hand and a small child in the other, forced back to France to seek assistance from the state, though they had forced it upon themselves. By July 1, when 91% of the Algerian electorate voted for self-rule, there were 170,000 *colons* left out of a million. Algeria became an independent republic, and all its difficulties and travails were now its own. As for de Gaulle, he might have been a dissembler, but he realized that colonialism was part of the dustbin of history, and that the war was destroying France. In 1959, he was named president of the Fifth Republic under a new constitution, and he remained in that post until 1969. He died in 1970 at the age of 80.

Index